THE BEEHIVE.

Old Yellowstone Days

THE GREAT CANON OF THE YELLOWSTONE.

Old

COLORADO

ellowstone Days

John Burroughs ❖ *Theodore Roosevelt*
Frederic Remington ❖ *Owen Wister*
Rudyard Kipling ❖ *Mrs. George Cowan*
John Muir ❖ *Charles Dudley Warner*
William O. Owen ❖ *George Anderson*
Emerson Hough

Edited by Paul Schullery

Foreword By John Townsley
Superintendent, Yellowstone National Park

ASSOCIATED UNIVERSITY PRESS • BOULDER

Publication of this book was made possible in part by a generous grant from the Vanetta Rickards Betts Memorial Fund.

To Aubrey Haines

Contents

Foreword

Yellowstone National Park is a name that carries world-wide significance. Visitors have come here by the millions through the past 100 years to view its wonders. Some of these people are fortunate enough to have worked in Yellowstone part of their lives. In doing so, a special feeling for this great park often develops in the heart of that person. Paul Schullery is one of these individuals.

Paul worked in Yellowstone Park for six summers and part of several winters from 1972 - 1977 as a park historian and naturalist. During these years he became intimately acquainted with the history of Yellowstone National Park. In fact, he became so engrossed in the archival material on deposit here, that he completed a master's thesis on "The Yellowstone Archives: Past, Present, and Future" through the history department of Ohio University. Through this effort, Paul became thoroughly familiar with Yellowstone's archives and the history of the park. He also gained tremendous insight into the historical events that transpired during the park's one hundred year history. Largely through Paul's efforts, the Yellowstone archives were inventoried, catalogued, properly stored, and put on microfilm so they now provide a chronological reference for the serious researcher of Yellowstone history. Through this minute examination of the archives, Paul uncovered letters and documents from many famous people who visited Yellowstone National Park in its earlier days, and reacted with memorable thoughts and words. Some of the more outstanding ones are assembled in this book. Paul's contribution to Yellowstone's history program is monumental. Enjoying these vignettes of Yellowstone's history should be a delightful experience for the reader.

John A. Townsley

Acknowledgments

Alan Mebane, Chief Park Naturalist at Yellowstone, supported my proposal for this book, and guided me in locating a publisher. Mary Meagher, Supervisory Research Biologist of Yellowstone, read portions of the introductory material and made many useful suggestions. Ila Jane Bucknall, Yellowstone Park Reference Librarian, was an extraordinary help in my search for early accounts of Yellowstone.

Several of my colleagues, including Charles Brooks, Dale Greenley, Kenneth Keller, Chris Judson and Jeremy Schmidt, offered needed encouragement.

My work in Yellowstone as Historian/Archivist was an extension of the work of former Park Historian Aubrey Haines. All students of Yellowstone, whatever they are studying, are indebted to him, but I especially have benefited from his friendship as well as from his expertise. In gratitude for his unfailing generosity, and in honor of his magnificent contribution to Yellowstone's historical scholarship, I dedicate this book to him.

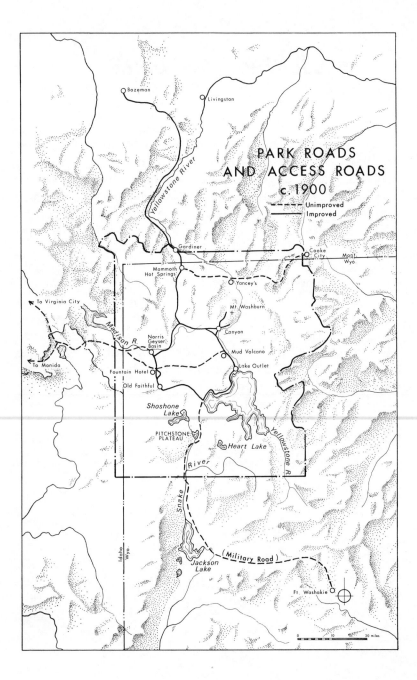

PARK ROADS
AND ACCESS ROADS
c. 1900

- - - - Unimproved
———— Improved

Bozeman

Livingston

Yellowstone River

Gardiner

Cooke City

Mont
Wyo

Mammoth
Hot Springs

Yancey's

To Virginia City

Mt. Washburn

Madison R.

Canyon

Norris
Geyser
Basin

Mud Volcano

To Monida

Lake Outlet

Fountain Hotel

Old Faithful

Shoshone Lake

PITCHSTONE
PLATEAU

Heart Lake

Yellowstone R.

River

Snake

Idaho
Wyo.

(Military Road)

Jackson
Lake

Ft. Washakie

0   10   20 miles

Introduction

he word "Yellowstone" is universally evocative of a few images: bears and geysers foremost, but underlying those first thoughts of the Park's wonders is a more fundamental recollection, or anticipation, of leisure—the American vacation. Yellowstone has long been a major vacation goal, a family pilgrimage planned for years and remembered for a lifetime. Depending on the success of the trip, the memories range from sublime to painful. If the weather, geysers, and wildlife cooperated, Yellowstone's reputation is secure in yet another household. If, on the other hand, the car broke down, the children were too young to appreciate the trip (is anyone *ever* too old?), or the hotels and campgrounds were all full, mention of Yellowstone may only result in a disgusted snarl.

A place must have a special magic to endure so successfully as a recreation mecca. After a century of entertaining, after fifty million guests, it is only the rarest of hosts who can draw more visitors each year than the year before. The Yellowstone experience has a timelessness beyond any popular fashion or commercial marketability, a worth much more profound than any artificial entertainment. Yellowstone was nicknamed "Wonderland" in its first years, and Wonderland it has remained, in spite of huge crowds, monolithic motor homes, and soaring travel costs. Old-timers and people returning to Yellowstone after many years frequently mourn the passing of the good old days, when the roads were unpaved, the trails empty, and the bears were entirely too visible for *anyone's* good, but wise managers realize that national parks must look forward, not back, if they are to survive in fit shape for ever-increasing crowds of visitors in the future.

The attractions of Yellowstone have not changed materially in all these years, though the way we enjoy them has been adjusted to the swift pace of the 1970s. The average visit, which once was five days long (with many people staying several weeks) has been reduced to less than forty-eight hours, yet it covers the same territory. In fact it covers more, for the road system is more extensive than it was in 1900. The canyons and mountains are as awesome as ever, a testament to their magnificence in the eyes of an audience jaded by the wonders of modern media. The hydrothermal features still inspire dark satanic thoughts. The wildlife, having been allowed the prerogatives entitled to any prior tenant, still roam at will across the land. The Park is in the unusual situation of being so close to its primeval state that visitors, programmed by our technologically controlled world, cannot resist the thought that there's something downright *unnatural* about this place!

So what are we to do about the good old days? We could simply push them aside, since that world is gone, presumably forever. Or we could take time to appreciate them, which is what this book intends. Through it we may enjoy the flavor of what Wister called the "Old Yellowstone Days," a whole different world of recreation, and some very good reading. The Americans who had the foresight to create Yellowstone Park gave us another gift—they gave us their experiences and their feelings here. Hundreds of books, articles, and journals appeared in Yellowstone's first half-century, and from that great body of material the following accounts have been drawn. Some are introspective, some are purely factual. They represent many different viewpoints, from stagecoach tourist to naturalist to administrator. No claim is made that they are the only ones worth reading, for you are cordially invited to pursue your tour of Old Yellowstone with the help of the bibliography at the end of the book. The readings are an opportunity to compare notes, as it were, with other Yellowstone enthusiasts.

As the first of all national parks, Yellowstone was viewed for a long time as a rather odd institution. Into the generally utilitarian domain of the federal bureaucracy there came this exception, a governmental responsibility (custodianship) devoted quite simply "to the benefit and enjoyment of the people." That so long ago there were visionaries who sensed the practical value of recreation to the health of a nation was not so remarkable as was the approval of the idea by Congress (that congressional approval, incidentally, is *another* story!). The rightness of that approval has since become manifest in the spread of the national park idea, both in the United States and around the world. The accounts in this book are examples of the enthusiasm and wonder which greeted the first of all national parks. By reading them we can enjoy Yellowstone, vicariously at least, in its stagecoach heyday; they add yet one more dimension to the "benefit and enjoyment" to be derived from the Grand Old Park.

Mrs. Cowan a few years after her trip through Yellowstone Park.
Yellowstone Park files

Mrs. George Cowan
1877

Indian attacks were of great concern to the early explorers of the Yellowstone; such fears on the part of tourists later in the century, however, were largely unfounded. Yet, an occasional encounter with unfriendly Indians did occur in the Park with unfortunate results for tourists.

The Nez Perce tribe had a record of cordial coexistence with white men until whites cast greedy eyes on their ancestral homeland in eastern Oregon and western Idaho. When pressured to move to a reservation, part of the tribe refused and began a long flight. Their travels were interrupted by several battles with United States Cavalry, who finally defeated and captured them in northern Montana.[1]

It was on this journey, in the summer of 1877, that the Nez Perce passed through Yellowstone. They encountered a few tourist groups, and small raiding parties left the main group, burned a bridge near the junction of the Lamar (then known as the East Fork of the Yellowstone) and Yellowstone rivers, and attacked other visitors.[2]

Mrs. George Cowan had come to Montana in 1864 at the age of ten. At that time, living in Virginia City, she first heard of the wonders of Yellowstone from an old trapper whose tales were generally disregarded. She did not forget the tales, though, and in 1873, the year after the Park was established, she made her first visit. Two years later she married Mr. Cowan, a Civil War veteran and lawyer. In 1877 they made their ill-fated trip to the Park.

Her suffering and her husband's near-death at the hands of the Nez Perce did not embitter her. Years later she expressed wonder that she was treated so well by a tribe that had been so abused:

> Yet, at this day, knowing something of the circumstances that led to the final outbreak and uprising of these Indians, I wonder that any of us were spared. Truly a quality of mercy was shown us during our captivity that a Christian might emulate, and at a time when they must have hated the very name of the white race.[3]

2

The summer of 1877 was exceedingly hot and dry. This, together with a grasshopper raid, which was not the least of the trials of the pioneer, made the necessity of closing up the house to keep out the pests almost unbearable. My brother Frank, visiting us from Helena, told us of his intention to visit the Park, and asked us to be of the party. It required but little effort on his part to enthuse us, and we soon began preparations for the trip. Several people from our town, Radersburg, talked also of going, but by the time we were ready, one acquaintance only, Mr. Charles Mann, joined our party from that town. I induced my mother to allow my young sister, a child of a little more than a dozen years, to accompany me, as I was to be the only woman of the party and she would be so much company for me.

The party consisted all told of the following persons: A.J. Arnold, J. A. Oldham and Mr. Dingee, all of Helena, Mr. Charles Mann, my brother, Frank Carpenter, Mr. Cowan, my sister, self and cook named Myers. We were nicely outfitted with an easy double-seated carriage, baggage wagon and four saddle horses, one of them my own pony, a birthday gift from my father years before, which I named Bird because she was trim and fleet. That I was fond of her goes without saying. We were well equipped in the way of provisions, tents, guns and last, but not least, musical instruments. With J.A. Oldham as violinist, my brother's guitar, and two or three fair voices, we anticipated no end of pleasure.

We left Radersburg the sixth of August, camping the first night at Three Forks. Our way lay up the Madison via Henry Lake, a road having been built to the Lower Geyser Basin from that direction. Although some parts of this would scarcely pass as a road, we traveled it without mishap. The second day's ride brought us to Sterling, a small town in Madison county, and it was a pleasant one. But as night approached, we were still some miles from town. Leaving our slower baggage wagon, we pushed on, reaching town after dark. As we could not camp until the wagon came, we went to the hotel for supper, and made camp later. Several of the townspeople joined us there, and we heard for the first time rumors of Indian trouble. Some advised us not to go farther, but we did

3

not think it more than an old-time Indian scare, and when morning came, bright and beautiful, we decided to go on our way. Often, with night, I would feel somewhat timid, but with the daylight my fears would be dispelled.

The next noon found us at Ennis, and twelve miles farther up the Madison for our night camp. At Ennis, my husband had been told we would find fine fishing at Henry Lake, also boats, spears, skeins and all sorts of tackle. The man to whom they belonged, however, was at one of the ranches cutting hay, but would give us the key to the boat house if we could find him. Inquiring at the ranch to which we had been directed, we found that he was gone to another, some five miles distant. My disappointment may be imagined, for my fancy had run riot and I fully expected to see the Old Man of the tales of my childhood. A horseback ride of a few miles obtained the keys but my curiosity was not satisfied then or afterward.

In the afternoon two days later, we left the Madison River, up which we had been traveling, and crossed a low divide, getting our first glimpse of the lake. The view from this point is exceedingly pretty. Some of the pleasantest days of our outing trip were spent here. Innumerable flock of wild fowl have their home in this isolated spot. Low, marshy land encircles the greater part of the lake, but where the houses are built the ground is much higher, giving a fine view of the lake and surrounding hills. An immense spring affords a sufficient stream of water to float boats through the marsh and out to the lake.

Torchlight fishing by night was a unique pastime. Great schools of fish, attracted by the glare of light from the blazing pine knots, gathered about the prow of the boat. Some fine ones were speared and delicious meals enjoyed. Nothing quite equals the fine salmon trout unless it may be a venison steak or the perfectly delicious grouse, the thought of which sets my heart longing for the breezy pine-capped hills and mountain stream.

One summer day Mr. Cowan and I mounted our horses in search of larger game, to-wit: the venison steak. But though we spent the entire day in the saddle, ranging over the hills and gulches, we found not a track. At sundown we returned

4

to camp, only to find it deserted. The others of the party had planned to cross the lake and explore Snake River, which has its source in Henry Lake. They had not yet returned and we could see nothing of them. The day, which had been lovely, changed with the setting of the sun. Great banks of clouds came scurrying across the sky. The soughing of wind through the pines brought the thought of storm, the darkness was coming rapidly and the day ending drearily. I was in a fever of anxiety, feeling sure some accident had befallen them. We made a great bonfire, and not long afterward there came a faint hello from across the water, a most welcome sound. A long half-hour elapsed then before they reached camp, tired but jolly. A strong head wind and a broken oar had made it all but impossible to land. A rousing fire, good supper, comparing notes, telling stories, singing songs, ended a long remembered day.

The following morn we broke camp and continued our travel. We passed to the southeast and crossed Targhee Pass, then through ten miles of pine barrens, and camped again on the Madison River at the mouth of the canyon. This point was used some years later by the soldiers who were stationed in the Park, and called Riverside station. It was finally abandoned because of the small amount of travel by way of Henry Lake. Some nineteen times we crossed the river in traveling through the canyon. Fortunately, the water was low, so we had no trouble on that score. The road was very dim, however, and the men rode in advance. As they passed out of the stream they would tie a white cloth to a bush or bough, thus indicating just where to ford. Some very picturesque scenery is found along this route. Flowers grew in profusion, many varieties I had not found elsewhere.

Our last camp before reaching the Lower Basin was at the junction of the Gibbon and Firehole rivers, these two forming the Madison. We caught some delicious speckled trout here, our last good fishing grounds. The appetite of the crowd by this time was something appalling, or so the cook seemed to think. At the present a strike would have been in order. As it was, he could only shirk. We all assisted with the work, which soon meant doing the greater part of it. However, we were good campers and not inclined to grumble. We were in fine

5

health and enjoying the outdoor life to the utmost. We seemed to be in a world of our own. Not a soul had we seen save our own party, and neither mail nor news of any sort had reached us since leaving the ranches on the Madison. Although we were having a pleasant time, it seemed months rather than days since we had left the haunts of man. With the Park teeming with life, as it is today, one can scarcely realize the intense solitude which then pervaded this land, fresh from the Maker's hand as it were.

Leaving the Gibbon Fork after dinner, we traveled several miles of low foothills and entered the Lower Geyser Basin. We had at last reached Wonderland. Mr. Cowan insisted always on making camp before doing anything else, putting up tents, gathering the fragrant pine boughs for our camp beds, getting things to rights in regular house-keeping order. But this day our first sight of the geysers with columns of steam rising from innumerable vents and the smell of the Inferno in the air from the numerous sulphur springs, made us simply wild with the eagerness of seeing all things at once. We left the teams, which, by the way, entered no protest, being worn out by the long travel, and we ran and shouted and called to each other to see this or that, so that we soon became separated and knew it not.

My small sister and I could scarcely keep pace with the men, but we found enough to interest us, turn where we would. I recalled and told to her many of the tales told me of this weird land in earlier years. How vividly they came to mind! As we wandered about we found some things that were curious, but not altogether pleasant. Among them was a deep depression, full of mud as thick as hasty pudding, that bubbled and spluttered and popped with a loud explosion. A stick thrown in was quickly sucked out of sight, and the fate of a human being falling in could easily be imagined. It gave one a somewhat creepy feeling. At length, as it was nearly sundown and some distance from where we had left the teams, we deemed it best to retrace our steps. We were hungry and tired, but altogether happy. We had realized our expectations. Our camp that night was not quite up to the standard, but no complaints were entered.

6

The next day we established a permanent camp near the Fountain Geyser, and made daily short excursions to the different points of interest. We explored every nook and cranny of the Lower Basin and were ready for pastures new. We had reached the terminus of the wagon road, but trails led in various directions, one to the Upper Geyser Basin, another to the Falls and Yellowstone Lake by way of Mary's Lake. As we could go no farther with the wagon we decided to leave our camp intact, only taking the few things necessary for a few days' stay in the Upper Basin, and go horseback. This we did, and pitched our tent that night in a point of timber, very close to the Castle Geyser, which by way of reception, gave a night eruption, covering us with spray and making a most unearthly noise. I was sure the earth would be rent asunder and we would be swallowed up. At night, with our heads pillowed on the breast of Mother Earth, one seemed in close proximity to Dante's Inferno. I think his spirit must have visited the Park in some remote age for inspiration.

At dawn we circled around the crater, too late to see more than great columns of steam. We saw this geyser in eruption several times while in the basin, but by daylight it did not seem so terrifying. The Giantess was not in eruption during our stay of five days. We enjoyed the Grand, considering it rightly named. In the meantime my brother, with some others of the party, had gone to the Falls and Yellowstone Lake. We remained five days in the Upper Basin and arranged to meet the others on the twenty-second in the Lower Basin.

Thursday, the twenty-third of August, found us all at the home camp, as we termed it, ready to retrace our steps towards civilization. We had had a delightful time, but were ready for home. This day we encountered the first and only party of tourists we had seen, General Sherman and party. They had come into the Park by way of the Mammoth Hot Springs. Of them we learned of the Nez Perce raid and the Big Hole fight. We also received the very unpleasant impression that we might meet the Indians before we reached home. No one seemed to know just where they were going. The scout who was with the General's party assured us we would be perfectly safe if we

7

would remain in the Basin, as the Indians would never come into the Park. I observed, however, that his party preferred being elsewhere, as they left the Basin that same night.

That afternoon another visitor called at camp, an old man by the name of Shively, who was traveling from the Black Hills and was camped half a mile down the valley. Home seemed a very desirable place just at this particular time, and we decided with one accord to break camp in the morning, with a view of reaching it as soon as possible. Naturally we felt somewhat depressed and worried over the news received. My brother Frank and Al Oldham, in order to enliven us somewhat, sang songs, told jokes, and finally dressed up as brigands, with pistols, knives and guns strapped on them. Al Oldham, with his swart complexion, wearing a broad sombrero, looked a typical one, showing off to good advantage before the glaring camp fire. They made the woods ring with their nonsense and merriment for some time.

We probably would not have been so serene, had we known that the larger part of the audience consisted of the Indians, who were lurking out in the darkness, watching and probably enjoying the fun. Such was really the fact, as they informed us later, designating Oldham as Big Chief. The advance party of Indians had come into the Basin early in the evening. Before morning the entire Indian encampment was within a mile of us, and we had not heard an unusual sound, though, I for one slept lightly.

I was already awake when the men began building the camp fire, and I heard the first guttural tones of the two or three Indians who suddenly stood by the fire. I peeped out through the flap of the tent, although I was sure they were Indians before I looked. I immediately aroused my husband, who was soon out. They pretended to be friendly, but talked little. After some consultation the men decided to break camp at once and attempt to move out as though nothing unusual was at hand. No one cared for breakfast save the Indians, who quickly devoured evetything that was prepared. By this time twenty or thirty Indians were about to camp, and more coming. The woods seemed full of them. A line of timber was between us and the main camp. Some little time was required to pull down

8

tents, load the wagons, harness and saddle the horses, and make ready for travel. While Mr. Cowan was engaged elsewhere one of the men—Mr. Arnold, I think— began dealing out sugar and flour to the Indians on their demand. My husband soon observed this and peremptorily ordered the Indians away, not very mildly either. Naturally they resented it, and I think this materially lessened his chances of escape.

So much ammunition had been used on the trip, especially at Henry Lake, that the supply was practically exhausted. Mr. Cowan had five cartridges only, about ten all told in the party. It was a fortunate thing probably that we had no more, for had the men been well armed, they would have attempted a defense, which could only have ended disastrously to us. Six men arrayed against several hundred Indians splendidly armed would not have survived long.

We drove out finally on the home trail, escorted by forty or fifty Indians. In fact, they all seemed to be going our way except the squaw camp, which we met and passed as they were traveling up the Firehole towards Mary's Lake. A mile or more was traveled in this way, when the Indians for some reason called a halt. We were then a few hundred yards from where the road enters the timber and ascends the hill-side. One of the Indians seated on a horse near Mr. Cowan, who was also on horseback, raised his hand and voice, apparently giving some commands, for immediately forty or fifty Indians came out of the line of timber, where they had evidently been in ambush for our benefit. Another Indian, addressing Mr. Cowan and pointing to the Indian who had given the command, said in good English, "Him Joseph." And this was our introduction to that chief. Every Indian carried splendid guns, with belts full of cartridges. As the morning sunshine glinted on the polished surface of the gun barrels a regiment of soldiers could not have looked more formidable. We were told to backtrack, which we did, not without some protest, realizing however the utter futility. The Indians pretended all this while to be our very good friends, saying that if they should let us go, bad Indians, as they termed them, would kill us.

Passing and leaving our morning camp to the right, we traversed the trail towards Mary's Lake for two miles. We could go no farther with the wagons on account of fallen timber. Here we unhitched, mounted the horses, taking from the wagon the few things in the way of wraps that we could carry conveniently, and moved on. It gave us no pleasure to see our wagons overhauled, ransacked and destroyed. Spokes were cut from the buggy wheels and used as whip handles. We did not appreciate the fact that the Indians seemed to enjoy the confiscated property. One young chap dashed past us with several yards of pink mosquito bar tied to his horse's tail. A fine strip of swansdown, a trophy from Henry Lake, which an ugly old Indian had wrapped around his head turban fashion, did not please me either.

Regardless of the fact that they had been harassed and hard pressed and expected battle any moment—not from Howard's command, whom they termed for some reason "squaw soldiers,"—but from the Bannock Indians, eighty of whom were the advance scouts for General Howard—the majority of the Nez Perces were light-hearted and seemed not to worry over the outcome of their campaign. Perhaps to worry is a prerogative of the white race. The Bannock scouts referred to were following closely at the heels of the Nez Perces and could have attacked them several times had they so desired, but for some reason they did not.

After traveling some ten miles, a noon camp was made, fires lighted and dinner prepared. Poker Joe (we did not learn the Indian name) acted as interpreter. He talked good English, as could all of them when they desired. Through him we were told that if we could give up our horses and saddles for others that would be good enough to take us home, they would release us and we would be allowed to return to the settlement without harm. Many of their horses were worn out from the long, hurried march. Under the circumstances we acquiesced, and an exchange began. I was seated on my pony, watching proceedings, when I observed that two or three Indians were gathering around me, apparently admiring my horse, also gently leading her away from the rest of my party. They evidently wanted the animal and I immediately slipped out of the saddle to the ground, knowing I should never see my pony again, and went over to where Mr. Cowan was being persuaded that an

10

old rackabone gray horse was a fair exchange for his fine mount. He was persuaded.

It occurs to me at this writing that the above mode of trading is a fair reflection of the lesson taught by the whites. For instance, a tribe of Indians are located on a reservation. Gold is discovered thereon by some prospector. A stampede follows. The strong arm of the government alone prevents the avaricious pale face from possessing himself of the land forthwith. Soon negotiations are pending with as little delay as a few yards of red tape will admit. A treaty is signed, the strip ceded to the government and opened to settlers, and "Lo, the poor Indian" finds himself on a tract a few degrees more arid, a little less desirable than his former home. The Indian has few rights the average white settler feels bound to respect.

In a measure I had gotten over my first fright. The Indians seemed friendly and the prospect of release probable. Poker Joe, mounted on my husband's horse, made the circle of the camp, shouting in a sonorous voice some commands relative to the march apparently, as the squaws soon began moving. He came to us finally and told us we could go. We lost no time in obeying the order. Two of our party, Dingee and Arnold, escaped into the timber at this time, though they were not missed by Mr. Cowan or me until later. All went well with us for half a mile or so. Then to our dismay we discovered Indians following us. They soon came up and said the chief wanted to see us again. Back we turned, passed the noon camp, now deserted, and up and on to higher timbered ground. My side saddle had been placed on a poor old horse and given to me, but the others were without saddles. We rode along the trail, my husband and I in advance, followed by my sister and brother and others of our party, Indians on every side, twenty or thirty of them. Their gaity of the morning was lacking, the silence seemed ominous. The pallor of my husband's face told me he thought our danger great. I hoped we would soon overtake the squaw camp, for I fancied we would be safer. They seemed the old dirty Indians familiar to all Western people.

Suddenly, without warning, shots rang out. Two Indians came dashing down the trail in front of us. My husband was

11

getting off his horse. I wondered for what reason. I soon knew, for he fell as soon as he reached the ground—fell headlong down the hill. Shots followed and Indian yells, and all was confusion. In less time that it takes me to tell it, I was off my horse and by my husband's side, where he lay against a fallen pine tree. I heard my sister's screams and called to her. She came and crouched by me, as I knelt by his side. I saw he was wounded in the leg above the knee, and by the way the blood spurted out I feared an artery had been severed. He asked for water, I dared not leave him to get it, even had it been near. I think we both glanced up the hill at the same moment, for he said, "Keep quiet. It won't last long." That thought had flashed through my mind also. Every gun of the whole party of Indians was leveled on us three. I shall never forget the picture, which left an impress that years cannot efface. The holes in those guns barrels looked as big as saucers.

I gave it only a glance, for my attention was drawn to something near at hand. A pressure on my shoulder was drawing me away from by husband. Looking back and up over my shoulder, I saw an Indian with an immense navy pistol trying to get a shot at my husband's head. Wrenching my arm from his grasp, I leaned over my husband, only to be roughly drawn aside. Another Indian stepped up, a pistol shot rang out, my husband's head fell back, and a red stream trickled down his face from beneath his hat. The warm sunshine, the smell of blood, the horror of it all, a faint remembrance of seeing rocks thrown at his head, my sister's screams, a sick faint feeling, and all was blank.

Of the others of the party, all had run for the brush, including my brother. An Indian followed him and was about to fire, when for a reason best known to himself, made the sign of the cross. The Indian immediately lowered his gun and told my brother to follow him. No other attempt was made on his life. He saw me ahead of him several times, fastened with a strap behind an Indian. He did not dare to make a point of getting near enough to speak. He was helping to drive the horses. We had overtaken the squaw camp. We afterwards learned that the chiefs, suspecting mischief from a few lawless Indians, had sent back Poker Joe to prevent further trouble.

12

After coming to my senses my first recollection was of a great variety of noises—hooting, yelling, neighing of horses—all jumbled together. For a while it seemed afar off. I became conscious finally that someone was calling my name, and I tried to answer. Presently my brother rode close beside me. He told me later that I looked years older and that I was ghostly white. He tried to comfort me and said the Indians had told him no further harm should befall us. It seemed to me the assurance had come too late. I could see nothing but my husband's dead face with the blood upon it. I remember Frank's telling me my sister was safe, but it seemed not to impress me much at the time.

The Indians soon learned that my brother was familiar with the trail, and he was sent forward. Over this mountain range, almost impassable because of the dense timber, several hundred head of loose horses, pack horses, camp accoutrements, and the five or six hundred Indians were trying to force a passage. A narrow trail had sufficed for tourists. It was a feat few white people could have accomplished without axe or implements of some sort to cut the way. It required constant watching to prevent the loose horses from straying away. As it was, many were lost and recovered by the Bannock Indians later. The pack horses also caused trouble, often getting wedged in between trees. An old squaw would pound them on the head until they backed out. And such yelling! Their lungs seemed in excellent condition.

The wearisome up-hill travel was at length accomplished. Beyond the summit the timber was less dense, with open glades and parks. Finally, at dusk we came to quite a valley, which had already begun to glow with campfires, though many were not lighted until some time later. The Indian who was leading my horse—for I had been allowed to ride alone after recovering consciousness, the Indian retaining a grip on the bridle—threaded his way past numerous campfires and finally stopped near one. As if by a pre-arranged plan someone came to the horse, enveloped in a blanket. Until he spoke I thought it to be an Indian, and I was clasped in the arms of my brother. Tears then, the first in all these dreary hours, came to my relief. He led me to the fire and spoke to an Indian seated there, who,

13

I was told, was Chief Joseph. He did not speak, but motioned me to sit down. Frank spread a blanket on the ground, and I sank down on it, thoroughly exhausted. A number of squaws about the fire were getting supper. My first question had been for my sister. I was told she was at Poker Joe's camp, some little distance away, together with the old man Shively, who was captured the evening before we were. I was told I could see her in the morning, and with this assurance I had to be satisfied. Food was offered me, but I could not eat.

My brother tried to converse with Chief Joseph, but without avail. The chief sat by the fire, sombre and silent, foreseeing in his gloomy meditations possibly the unhappy ending of his campaign. The "noble red man" we read of was more nearly impersonated in this Indian than in any I have ever met. Grave and dignified, he looked a chief.

A squaw sat down near me with a babe in her arms. My brother wishing to conciliate them, I suppose, lifted it up and placed it on my lap. I glanced at the chief and saw the glimmer of a smile on his face, showing that he had heart beneath the stony exterior. The squaw was all smiles, showing her white teeth. Seeing that I was crying, the squaw seemed troubled and said to my brother, "Why cry?" He told her my husband had been killed that day. She replied, "She heart-sick." I was indeed.

The Indians were without tepees, which had been abandoned in their flight from the Big Hole fight, but pieces of canvas were stretched over a pole or bush, thus affording some protection from the cold night air. My brother and I sat out a weary vigil by the dying embers of the campfire, sadly wondering what the coming day would bring forth. The Indian who had befriended him told him we should be liberated and sent home. But they had assured us a safe retreat the day previous and had not kept faith. Near morning, rain began falling. A squaw arose, replenished the fire, and then came and spread a piece of canvas over my shoulders to keep off the dampness.

At dawn, fires were lighted, and soon all was activity, and breakfast under way. I was surprised to see, as the morning sunshine gleamed on them, innumerable brand-new brass kettles. Later, we learned that the Indians at Camas Creek had made

14

a flank movement and captured some of General Howard's commissary supplies. The squaws evidently prized the kettles very highly, showing a true housewifely care in not allowing them to be used on the campfire, using them for water only. Some bread, yellow with soda, from the same source probably, and willow tea were offered me, but I was not yet hungry. Poker Joe came up and offered to take me to my sister. Frank was told to remain at the camp for the present, and I clasped his hand, not knowing if I should see him again.

Only a short distance away, which I would have walked gladly the night before, I found my sister. Such a forlorn looking child I trust I may never again see. She threw herself into my arms in a very paroxysm of joy. She seemed not to be quite certain that I was alive, even though she had been told. Mr. Shively, the old man before referred to, was at this camp, and I was as glad to see him as though I had known him always. He gave us much encouragement. The Indians had talked more freely with him and he had tried to impress upon them the wisdom of releasing us, telling them we had lived many years in the West and had many friends and that it would be to their advantage to let us go.

Poker Joe again made the circle of the camp, giving orders for the day's march. We were furnished with horses and my brother came up leading them. The four of us rode together that morning. We reached the crossing of the Yellowstone near the mud geysers at noon. The Indians plunged into the stream without paying much regard to the regular ford, and camped on the opposite shore. At this point a few days later, the Bannock Indians, scouting for Howard, came to this camp and found a poor old wounded Nez Perce squaw, who, too sick to travel, had been left here with bread and water within reach. They proceeded to kill and scalp her without delay, celebrating this great achievement with a war dance when the General's command arrived.

We watched the fording for some time, and finally crossed, finding the water deep enough near the farther bank to swim the horses, thus getting ourselves uncomfortably wet. Fortunately, one seldom takes cold in camp life, however great the exposure. During the forenoon the Indians had captured a soldier, a deserter evidently. He told them of the Helena tourists camped near the Falls, the number of the men and horses. In fording, we observed that five warriors were with the party. It was composed chiefly of the squaw camp, and we concluded the warriors had retraced their steps to attack the Helena party. Why they were not attacked until the next noon we could only conjecture.

At the squaw camp, dinner was being prepared. I had begun to feel faint from lack of food. I forced down a little bread, but nothing more. Fish was offered me, but I declined with thanks. I had watched the squaw prepare them something after this wise: From a great string of fish the largest were selected, cut in two, dumped into an immense camp-kettle filled with water, and boiled to a pulp. The formality of cleaning had not entered into the formula. While I admit that tastes differ, I prefer having them dressed.

A council was being held. We were seated in the shade of some trees watching proceedings. Six or seven Indians—the only ones who seemed to be in camp at the time—sat in a circle and passed the long pipe one to another. Each took a few whiffs of smoke, and then one by one they arose and spoke. Poker Joe interpreted for us. Presently he said the Indians had decided to let my sister and me go, together with the soldier who had been captured that morning, but would hold my brother and Shively for guides. I had not been favorably impressed with the soldier. Intuition told me he was not trustworthy, and I refused to go unless my brother was also released. This caused another discussion, but they agreed to it and preparations were made for our departure. A search was made for my side saddle, but without avail. It was found later by some of Howard's soldiers near where Mr. Cowan was shot.

Some of our own bedding, a waterproof wrap, a jacket for my sister, bread and matches, and two old worn out horses were brought, and we were ready. We clasped hands sadly with our good friend Shively, promising to deliver some messages to friends in Philipsburg should we escape. His eyes were dim with tears. In reality, I considered his chances of escape better than our own, and so told him. The Indians needed him for a guide. "We may be intercepted by the warriors out of camp,"

I said. "No," he replied, "Something tells me you will get out safely."

We crossed the river again, my brother riding behind Poker Joe, who went with us a half a mile or more, showing us presently a well defined trail down the river. He told us we must ride "all night, all day, no sleep," and we would reach Bozeman on second day. He reiterated again and again that we must ride all night. We shook hands and set out, not very rapidly. My brother walked and the horses we rode were played out. It seemed folly to think we could escape. Furthermore, we placed no confidence in the Indian. I regret to say that as soon as he was out of sight we left the river trail and skirted along in the timber.

After several miles of travel in this way, we came to a valley through which we must pass to reach the trail down by the Falls. We decided to wait on a timbered knoll over-looking the valley until the darkest part of the night, so that we might cross without being seen by the Indians. The moonlight was so bright that it was two o'clock or more before we attempted it. After crossing nearly half way, we came to a washout or cut, over which we could jump the horses. It seemed to me hours before we finally came to a place where we could cross, so that before we gained the shelter of the timber once more, it was broad daylight. We were on the lookout for both Indians and white men. We knew the Helena party must be in this vicinity unless they had been attacked. Near the Falls we heard a noise that sounded like someone chopping. We did not think it best to stop and investigate, but moved on as rapidly as possibly. The poor old horses needed constant urging to make them travel as fast as my brother walked.

We passed down the river, leaving to our left the mountain pass over which the Indians had brought us the day before. We dared not retrace that route, even though my husband lay dead there—dead and unburied, perhaps dragged and torn by wild beasts. My own peril seemed of little consequence, compared with the cruel agony of this thought. We passed the Falls. I was familiar with the route from this point. I was sure we should find friends nearer than Bozeman, as Poker Joe had said. We would find them at the Mammoth Hot Springs.

17

About noon the signs of some one ahead were apparent. In crossing streams, pony tracks in the wet sand were plainly seen, and the marks of a rope or lasso that had been dragged in the dust of the trail indicated Indians. They often drag the rope thus, I am told. We passed Tower Creek and stopped a very short time to rest the horses. A few hours later, in rounding a point of timber, we saw in a little meadow not far beyond a number of horses and men. At the first glance we thought them Indians. Frank drew our horses back into the timber and went forward to investigate. He returned in a very few minutes and declared them soldiers. Oh, such a feeling of relief!

Imagine their surprise when we rode into the camp and my brother told them we were fleeing from the Indians, the only survivors of our party, as he believed. The soldier we had left in the Nez Perce camp the day before was a deserter from this company. Retribution closely followed transgression in his case. Mr. Shively escaped after being with the Indians ten days, but the fate of the soldier we did not learn.

This company of soldiers was a detachment from Fort Ellis, with Lieutenant Schofield in command. They were sent out to ascertain the whereabouts of the Nez Perces, and were returning in the belief that the Indians were not in that vicinity. Of them we learned that General Howard was closely following the Indians. Many of their actions were thus accounted for. The soldiers kindly prepared supper for us. I remember being nearly famished. Camp had been made for the night but was quickly abandoned, and arrangements made for quick travel. We were mounted on good horses, and the poor old ones, that had done us good service, notwithstanding their condition, were turned out to graze to their hearts content.

As we were about to move off, a man came hurrying down the trail. He proved to be one of the Helena party and believed himself the only one alive of that party. He said they were attacked at noon. Frank and I concluded that Poker Joe knew what he was talking about when he told us to travel all night. A horse was provided for this man, hurry orders given, and we set out for the Springs some seventeen miles distant. This night, unlike the previous one, was dark and cloudy. We passed over some of the roughest mountain trails near Gardiner that

18

I ever remember traveling. Many of the soldiers walked and led their horses. Near midnight we reached the Mammoth Hot Springs, tired out and stiff from long riding, but truly thankful for our escape.

I found, as I anticipated, some acquaintances, and strangers as well as friends did everything possible for our comfort. During the night two more members of the Helena party came to the Springs. One man, Stewart, was badly wounded. Two Englishmen with their guides were about to make a tour of the Park. One of these gentlemen was a physician and kindly assisted in dressing the wounds. I am sure he never found a time when his services were more appreciated. A semi-weekly stage had been run to the Springs that season. We were told that if we desired we could rest till Wednesday and return to Bozeman on that stage. No one thought of danger from the Indians at the Springs. A number of men were there. Yet on Wednesday, Dietrich of the Helena party was killed by the Indians in the door of the house we then occupied.

On Monday, Mr. Calfee, a photographer, invited us to go to Bozeman with him. He said he had a pair of wild mules and a big wagon, but if we wished he would take us. We were anxious to get home and very glad of so good an opportunity. The Englishmen and their guide also decided to return to Bozeman. Wonderland had lost its attractions for the nonce.

A somewhat amusing incident occurred on the down trip. We had traveled only a few miles when the guide for the Englishmen declared he had sighted Indians through his field glass in the direction of the trail over which we had come the night previous. He was quite positive, although no one else could see them. Finally he made a detour in that direction. He was soon out of sight, but in a very few minutes we heard several shots fired in rapid succession. Presently the guide came dashing up to the wagon, declaring he had been fired upon by the Indians, and as evidence exhibiting a stirrup with a bullet hole straight through the bottom of it. The Englishmen, however, seemed skeptical. Finally they examined the stirrup and asked him to explain why the splinters all pointed down. It was apparent that the hole could have been made only by removing his foot and firing the shot himself. He subsided for the time, but he had created a sensation for a few minutes at any rate.

A long day's ride brought us to the Bottler ranch on the Yellowstone. Mr. Calfee decided to remain here a day or so. His photographic supplies were somewhat shaken, likewise his passengers. We found excitement rife at this point. Chief Joseph and his band were expected to raid every section of Montana at the same moment apparently. The Crow Indians, whose reservation is just across the Yellowstone River, extending miles up and down, took advantage of this fact, and numerous horse stealing raids occurred, for which the Nez Perces received the credit.

In the afternoon of the next day a friend drove out for us from Bozeman, and we made twelve of the forty-mile drive that evening, remaining at the Ferril home on Trail Creek all night. They received us kindly, and though their own family was large, they made room for us. A sitting room was converted into a bed-room, with camp beds made down for several children. During the evening we gave them the details of our encounter with the Indians. To them, Indian scares were common. Living so close to the Crow reservation they were always on the alert and never felt quite safe. The children listened with great interest, telling us afterward what they would do, should they be captured. They knew where to dig for camas root, and they would escape to the brush and live on that.

We had only gotten settled for the night when a neighbor came tapping at the door, telling us to get up quickly and dress, as Indians were about. Such scrambling for clothes in the dark. A light was not to be thought of. A regular mix-up of children and clothes occurred, which the mother alone could straighten out. The little folks seemed rather to enjoy the excitement. Several shots were exchanged, but the Indians, who were undoubtedly Crows on a horse stealing raid, as soon as they found themselves discovered, disappeared. We retired again, but did not sleep much.

We drove to Bozeman next day. A few miles from the town we met seventy or eighty Crows, escorted by Lieutenant Doane on their way to intercept the Nez Perces. They looked rather

20

more dangerous than any we had yet met. After reaching Bozeman, my brother eventually went with this party nearly to the Mammoth Hot Springs in his endeavor to reach the point where Mr. Cowan was shot, but was compelled to return again to Bozeman without accomplishing that result.

In the meantime I had reached my father's home. Kind friends and neighbors had kept the news of our capture from my people until the day we reached home, then prepared them for our coming, thus sparing them much of the suspense. I reached there worn out with excitement and sorrow. Years seemed to have passed over my head since I had left my home a month previous.

From the time I learned of the close proximity of General Howard's command to the Nez Perces at the time Mr. Cowan was shot, I could not but entertain a faint hope that the soldiers might have found my husband alive. Yet, in reviewing all of the circumstances, I could find little to base such a hope upon. Still as one after another of the party were accounted for, all living, the thought would come. I believed I should know to a certainty when my brother returned from his quest.

I had been at home a week, when one afternoon two acquaintances drove to the house. My father not being in, I went to the door. They would not come in, but talked a few minutes on ordinary subjects. Then one of them handed me a paper and said news had been received of Mr. Cowan, that he was alive.

Some way the doorstep seemed conveniently near as a resting place just at that particular time. Presently they told me the particulars. He was badly wounded, but would live; was with Howard's command, and would either be sent back to Virginia City or brought the other way to Bozeman. For the time being, this news was all sufficient. A day or two passed. I learned nothing more. My brother Frank came, but had the same news only that had been given me. The hours began to drag. I decided to go to Helena with my brother, as from that point telegraphed news could reach me much sooner. After arriving at Helena however, a whole week passed before a telegram came to me, stating that my husband would be in Bozeman the following day.

21

I lost no time in going. At Bozeman, however, I found he had given out at the Bottler ranch on the Yellowstone. A double-seated carriage was procured for the trip, and once again I found myself traversing the familiar and oft traveled road. But this day the sun shone. My husband had notice of my coming and was expecting me. I found him much better than I dared anticipate, and insistant on setting out for home without delay.

We arranged robes and blankets in the bed of the carriage. With his back propped up against the back seat, he was made quite comfortable.

I occupied the back seat, Mr. Arnold and the driver the front. Mr. Arnold, whose escape is elsewhere noted, reached the Howard command and was among the first to aid Mr. Cowan when that command found him, and he had remained with and cared for him like a brother ever since.

We stopped for a hand shake and congratulation at the Ferril home on Trail Creek. We had rather a spirited team and made fair progress. Late in the afternoon we were at a point seven miles from Bozeman in Rocky Canyon. The road bed was graded around a steep hillside for some distance.

We could look down and see the tops of trees that grew on the stream far below. Presently we experienced the novel and very peculiar sensation of seeing our carriage resting on those self-same trees, wheels uppermost, ourselves a huddled mass on the roadside. Merely a broken pole strap, a lunge forward of the horses as the carriage ran up against them. The buggy tongue caught, snapped and threw the carriage completely over. Fortunately the seats were not fastened, and we were left, a bundle of seats, robes, blanket and people on the hillside, shaken but not much hurt. The carriage, from which the horses had freed themselves, made one or more revolution as it went over and landed as described. We were thankful to have left it at the first tip.

Mr. Cowan was lifted to a more comfortable position by the road-side. Not long after, a horseman leading a pack animal came along. Our driver borrowed the horse, making the trip to Fort Ellis and back in the shortest possible time and returning with an ambulance. The seven miles seemed long ones, and before we reached Bozeman Mr. Cowan was almost exhausted, his wounds bleeding and needing attention. He was carried by careful hands to a room in the hotel as soon as the crowd had thinned somewhat. Mr. Arnold arranged to dress the wounds, and in order to do so seated himself on the side of the bed, when lo, the additional weight caused the whole inside of the bed to drop out and down on the floor. This sudden and unexpected fall, in his enfeebled state, nearly finished him. A collapse followed, from which he did not rally for some time.

A week passed before we were able to travel further. I think the anxiety for my husband alone sustained me during this trying time. As it was, my nerves were all awry. Had I been morbidly inclined, I might have conceived the idea that some avenging Nemesis was following in his foot-steps, which nothing but the forfeit of his life would satisfy.

By the time we reached home Mr. Cowan was able to hobble about on crutches. The winter passed however before he was entirely well. A severe gunshot wound through the hip, a bullet hole in the thigh, a ball flattened on the forehead, and the head badly cut with rocks—few, indeed, are the men who could have survived so severe an ordeal. Our month of out-door life and a fine constitution, coupled with a strong will power, worked a miracle almost.

After receiving the pistol shot in the head, some time must have passed before he regained consciousness as the sun was just tipping the treetops, proving that the afternoon was far advanced. At the time of receiving the shot in the thigh he supposed the bone broken, as he was unable to stand. By this time, however, the numbness was gone, the blood had begun to circulate, and he could move his foot.

The intolerable thirst that follows gunshot wounds impelled him to try to reach water. Absolute quiet reigned. Yet, as he raised himself by the branch of a fallen tree, an Indian who had evidently been waiting for other Indians observed the movements and immediately fired at him.

The ball passed through the point of the left hip, and he fell, fully expecting the Indian to come up and complete the work. Presently several Indians passed along the trail, and again all was silence.

Some time passed before he again began the quest for water, crawling on hands and knees, as he could not now stand. He would go until exhausted and then rest in the branchesof some fallen pine tree. Not before noon of the next day did he finally reach a stream of water, he had crawled parallel with it some miles without being aware of the fact on account of the timber and dense undergrowth. He fairly lay in the water, quenching his thirst. Then with hands and teeth he tore his underwear into bandages and dressed his wounds as best he could.

Even though the month was August the nights were cold in this altitude, so that this was added to his other discomforts. He continued crawling, getting up on the hillside that he might better watch the trail.

Several times he heard and saw Indians passing, and one night nearly came upon two who were sleeping.

His idea was to reach the home camp in the Lower Basin, believing he might be found more readily in that vicinity, also that he would possibly find food and matches there. He was four days and nights crawling the ten miles. Tuesday he reached the camp and found a few matches, but nothing to eat. A double handful of coffee was picked up, which he contrived to pound up in a cloth, and an empty syrup can answered very well to boil it in. Nearly half was lost by the can's falling into the fire. Still, enough remained to strengthen him considerably.

In the afternoon of the next day two of Howard's scouts found him and gave him food and blankets, placing him where Howard's command would find him. The scouts were taking rations to the Bannock Indians, who, with Fisher, were scouting for Howard. They had passed Mr. Cowan the day before and been seen by him, but of course he supposed them Nez Perces. The scouts left him after building a fire which came near being his undoing. A heavy wind in the night caused it to get beyond his control, and a timber fire resulted from which he had great difficulty in escaping. As it was, hands and knees were burned in trying to crawl away.

Thursday brought to him Howard's command, also Arnold and Oldham, of our party, the latter slightly wounded in the face, and he was assured of the safety of his wife, her brother

24

and sister. His wounds were dressed, the bullet that had flattened on his skull removed, and he was made as comfortable as circumstances would permit.

And then began the hard wearisome travel. Over rough new-made roads he was carried by the command where oftentimes the wagon was let down the mountain side with ropes. Over stumps and rocks and fallen timber they made their way. From fever and the sloughing of the wounds, he had become so emaciated that Arnold, though himself a small man, could easily lift him out of the wagon. The trip was indeed a hard one. It would seem that the determination to live, come what would, alone brought him out alive, where others with less will power would have succumbed.

Many years have passed since the events herein narrated occurred, yet retrospection is all that is needed to bring them to mind clear and distinct as events of yesterday—many years, since which life has glided on and on, with scarce a ripple beyond the everyday sunshine and shadow that falls to the lot of each and all of God's people.

William O. Owen back on his "ordinary" in 1933, fifty years after his ride through Yellowstone. Courtesy of the Western History Research Center, University of Wyoming

William O. Owen
1883

William O. Owen was a prominent Wyoming citizen for many years, serving as state auditor in the late 1890s. Bicycling around Yellowstone Park was not the only "first" he claimed, for in August of 1898 he was a member of a successful expedition to the top of Grand Teton, in present Grand Teton National Park. After his climb Owen launched a campaign to discredit the only previous successful climb, claimed by Nathaniel Langford and James Stevenson in 1872. The battle between the supporters of both parties continued in the popular press long after all the climbers were dead. Even an official Declaration by the Wyoming State Legislature, awarding the honor of the first successful ascent to the Owen party, did not really settle the matter, though Owen reaped the most visible fruits of victory: in 1927 a plaque was placed on the summit of Grand Teton in recognition of his ascent, and two years later a neighboring peak was named for him.[1]

Bicycles as practical touring vehicles were new to the Montana-Wyoming area in the 1880s. They were a far cry from today's sophisticated lightweight racing machines—these were the "ordinaries," with a huge front wheel (three to five feet in diameter) and a tiny rear one. Even after the advent of tubular framing such an outfit might weigh upwards of fifty pounds.

The Owen party tour did not open a door for multitudes of other "wheelmen," but it did demonstrate an interesting possibility, one that today is being discovered by many cycling enthusiasts. Scenery passes much more slowly when biking, allowing (or requiring) a more leisurely enjoyment of the Park.

Yellowstone's road system has never lent itself to a compatible bicycle-automobile relationship, but bike trails have been created recently and more are envisioned. Today's visitor may even be treated to the sight of a national park service ranger, pedaling from one duty to another, on a bicycle whose rear license plate bears the legend, "This Vehicle is Smog Free."

o three members of the Laramie Bicycle Club—C.S. Greenbaum, W.K. Sinclair and W.O. Owen—belongs the honor
of having made the first wheel tour of the Yellowstone
National Park, and, having been appointed historian on this
memorable trip, it falls to my lot to set down the incidents
of the journey for the readers of *Outing*. There are two routes
open to residents of Wyoming; one lies by way of Bozeman,
Mont., the other via Beaver Canon, Idaho.

The feasibility of making this tour by wheel had been the
subject of much discussion among the members of our club,
and it was the opinion of a large majority that it could not be
successfully made. Three of us, however, decided to attempt
it, choosing the Beaver Canon route as preferable in many ways
for our purpose. We went via Ogden by rail, and after a visit to
Salt Lake City and a pleasant meeting with the wheelmen of
that burg, we finally reached Beaver Canon.

Here a team, wagon, complete camp outfit and a good guide,
to act also as teamster, were secured, and we set out eastward
over an excellent road having a general upgrade and hard
as adamant.

Thirteen miles out we obtained our first view of the Three
Tetons, lofty peaks, the culmination of a mighty mountain
range of the same name. They stood out sharp in the pure,
strong blue with faultless definition. The altitude of the Grand
Teton, loftiest of the three, is 11,000 feet, and a nobler peak
lifts not its head among the Rocky Mountains, it seeming
almost to meet the sky, where a coronet of fleecy white cloud
trimmed it gracefully. Clinging to its lofty brow is a mighty
glacier, which on near approach reflects the solar rays in
myriads of diamond flashes.

Leaving thirty miles of open plain behind we rode out of
the dazzling light of the prairie into a region of dense woodland, our road winding through avenues of pines so tall that the
afternoon light came down to us only in scattered rays. Under
the deep shade of these trees we found an air pure and grate-
fully cool. Passing from the glare of the open country into the
dusky forest we seemed to ride into a vast covered hall, roofed
and inclosed. One never tires of gazing down the long vistas,
where, in stately groups, stand tall shafts of pine. Columns
they are, each with its own characteristic tinting and finish,

29

yet all standing together with an air of relationship and harmony. Feathery branches trimmed with living green waved through the upper air, opening broken glimpses of the far blue, and catching on their polished surfaces reflections of the sun. All that is dark and cool and grave in color, the beauty of distant blue, all the sudden brilliance of strong local lights tinted upon green boughs, surrounded us in ever-changing combination as we wheeled along.

Nearly fifty miles out we reached Henry's Fork of Snake River, a stream whose great width and depth compelled us to await the coming of our wagon, which an hour later carried us to the opposite bank. Here a steep ascent begins, and we started up the slope just as the sun was sinking behind a distant wall of purple mountains, whose rugged profile made sharp silhouettes on the western sky. We continued through dense pine timber, and as night approached absolute quiet came with it. The summit of the hill at length was reached and we began a gentle descent over the smoothest of roads. My Columbia carried me ahead of my companions, and I was alone save for my thoughts to bear me company.

I looked in vain for an opening in this wall of timber and asked myself if it had no bounds.

Ere thought could frame an answer a rush of wheels brought my companions up with me and a moment later we emerged into a beautiful open park, grass carpeted and hemmed about with trembling aspen trees. Once more we saw the sky, and but a short distance to the north the placid, lake-like surface of Snake River. As we drew near it a flock of geese arose from its surface, and with majestic wheel of wing and the familiar honk lost themselves in the leaden shades of night now settling down upon us.

Pursuing our way close to the river we soon crossed it, and after a mile's run arrived at the mountain home of George W. Rea, a name familiar to every tourist entering the Park by the Beaver Canon route.

This gentlemen claims to be the discoverer of the geysers in the National Park, and says he first saw them in 1865. Subsequently he visited Virginia City, Mont., where his story was told, but not believed, the people treating the whole matter with contempt.

Some time in the following year, however, Mr. Rea organized a party to explore the then unknown region. Of course his narrative was verified and much added to it. From that date to the present time discoveries have followed in rapid succession, and to-day the United States has in the Yellowstone Park a greater number of natural curiosities than can be found in an equal area on any other known portion of the globe.

We remained all night at Rea's and set out early next morning over a fair road through heavy pine timber.

Soon after starting we could see the chain of mountains which forms the boundary between Idaho and Montana and could almost fix the locus of the west line of the Park. This fact was no sooner mentioned than we all set out at the top of our speed, each one determined to reach this wonderland first.

For two miles we rode neck and neck and it seemed as if all were to share the honor equally, when suddenly Sinclair took a stunning header and left but two of us to finish. A dead heat was the result, for we crossed the line together. Soon after we were joined by Sinclair, who was looking very well, everything considered, and the ascent of the Continental Divide was commenced.

By severe pedaling the top was reached, when, throwing legs over handles, we began our first coast and flew down the mountain with the speed of the wind. Some distance ahead we observed a large, moving body square in the road, coming our way, but with all our eyes we could not satisfy our minds as to what it might be. At the speed we were going, however, the distance was soon sufficiently shortened to explain the matter, and we ascertained that it was a number of Indians traveling west. Here was a predicament indeed, and how to extricate ourselves was the next problem demanding speedy solution. We had no means of knowing whether these Americans were peaceable or on the warpath, and, fearing it might be the latter, it was deemed best to make a rush and frighten them before they could realize what was in the wind.

31

Accordingly we released our wheels from the brake and gave them entire freedom down this slope, which certainly has a fall of 400 feet to the mile. At this moment we were about a quarter of a mile from the Indians and perhaps a mile from the foot of the mountain. In my heart I believe that no men ever moved with greater velocity on a wheel than did we on this occasion. We dashed into their midst at a speed which I dare not even conjecture, and, with the most unearthly yells that ever reached human ears, squaws, chiefs, horses and innumerable dogs scattered in as many directions as there are points to the mariner's compass. It was a desperate charge, but entirely successful, and, passing the Indians, we reached the foot of the hill in safety.

Crossing the Madison River we encountered a slope so steep as to render wheeling impossible, and we were obliged to push our machines three miles to the mountain top. From this point eastward lofty pines obstructed the view, but looking to the west a bewitching landscape unfolded itself. Skirting the mountain's base, the Madison River, with majestic curve, marked out a path of deepest blue through the green and yellow forest. Along its course, at irregular intervals, stood little groves of trembling aspens, whose once green foliage had turned golden yellow; for the mellow hand of autumn had touched them daintily, and with alchemic power transmuted the baser color to a golden hue.

Numberless mountain peaks, seeming to mount up forever, carved their huge forms on the western heaven, whose blue was palpitating with light and seemed to rise with infinite perspective. The hazy quiet of a September evening was upon us, and we seemed lost in the depths of the forest. Without a word to break the stillness we mounted our wheels and were soon rolling down the mountain side. A coast of twelve miles brought us to the Firehole or Lower Geyser Basin, where we obtained accommodations at Marshall's Hotel, and after supper set about deciding on a route through the Park. This was soon arranged, and it was settled that we should start the next morning.

Before proceeding it may be well to say that from Firehole Basin roads diverge in all directions to the principal points of

interest, and in visiting the geyser basins, falls, lake, etc., one is
obliged to return to this point many times, for heavy timber
and rugged mountains preclude "cutting across lots." Through
the basin runs the Firehole River, one of the sources of the
Missouri and the outlet for all waters erupted by the geysers
in the upper, middle and lower basins. Its water is exceedingly
disagreeable to the palate, being highly impregnated with soda
and silica, and this is true of by far the greater part of the water
throughout the Park. It is difficult indeed to obtain a glass of
the liquid fit to drink, save in a few favored localities.

Retaining our team, camp outfit and guide, and providing
ourselves liberally with commissary supplies, we set out early
in the morning for the Upper Geyser Basin, where the giant
geysers of this whole region are situated.

A short distance from Firehole we left the main road and
wheeled for half a mile over a bed of silicate deposited by the
Fountain geyser, a magnificent eruption of which we witnessed
a short time later. All around this geyser, on the silicate formation, are written scores of names, indelibly retained there by
the subsequent overflow of water, which contains large
quantities of mineral in solution and which forms a perfect
coating over the writing. To the many autographs already in-
scribed here we added this modest legend: "C.S. Greenbaum,
W.K. Sinclair and W.O. Owen, first bicycle tourists in Yellowstone Park."

Continuing our journey over the silicate bed a mile farther
we reached the road and moved southward. All around us were
seething, boiling springs whose vapors filled the air and at times
obscured the sun. Arriving at the upper basin we pitched our
tent on the east side of Firehole River in the very midst of the
geysers, at a point commanding an excellent view of the valley.
The scene presented recalled most forcibly to mind Doré's
illustration of a certain portion of the infernal regions
described in Dante's divine comedy in Canto XIX. From a
thousand pits arose clouds of vapor, burdening the air with
such sulphurous odors that at times it was rendered almost
unfit for respiration. We spent two days in this basin, and
during that time we were unusually favored in witnessing the
eruption of nearly all the largest geysers. And here another

33

popular fallacy was exploded. The prevailing opinion is that all the geysers run on schedule time, i.e., that they have regular periods of activity and quiescence. With a single exception this is erroneous, for the eruptive periods can no more be predicted with anything like precision than one's fortune can be foretold. In order to see them all during activity the tourist must bide his time and watch both day and night. The one exception is "Old Faithful," and the regularity of this noble geyser is quite as remarkable as the irregularity of the others. It never varies many minutes from its predicted period, playing once an hour, frequently to the very minute.

The vast quantity of water erupted by the largest of the geysers and the height to which it is thrown are almost beyond belief, and beside them those of Iceland and New Zealand are dwarfed to comparative insignificance.

In the latter countries if a geyser project its water 75 feet upward it is considered a remarkable display, while our National Park contains not less than five that erupt columns of boiling liquid of from 20 to 150 feet in diameter 200 feet and more in the air.

The hissings and rumblings attending an eruption of these large geysers are almost unbearable, and the very earth trembles beneath your feet. Hell's Half Acre, known also as the Excelsior geyser, is the largest in the Park and has traits peculiar to itself. For several years it remained inactive and it was generally supposed to have lost its eruptive powers; but it has lately resumed operations. During this geyser's activity not only water but immense rocks and vast quantities of mud are belched forth from this giant's throat to a height of 300 feet, seemingly with the ease of feathers. The water discharged in a single eruption is sufficient to raise the Firehole River fifteen inches, and this stream is 100 feet wide.

Nearby are many deep pools of beautifully colored water, the most prominent one being known as Crystal Lake. Its surface, although the water is hot, is unruffled by ebullition, affording an excellent opportunity of examining the delicate tint of the liquid and the exquisite tracery on the walls. So perfectly transparent is this pool that the most microscopic fretting deep down is plainly visible. The crystal clearness of all these ponds and their matchless delicacy and variety of tint cannot be described—they must be seen to be appreciated.

Returning to our camp a hasty dinner was prepared, connected with which is a little incident too good to go unsung. A brilliant idea seized me that a cup of tea made from boiling geyser water would be something to boast of at home. Accordingly the teapot was filled with geyser liquid, a handful of tea thrown in and in a few minutes the mixture was declared ready for use. The idea was so romantic and unusual that nothing short of three cups of this delightful beverage would appease me, although my companions were prudent enough to be satisfied with a much less quantity. In less than an hour I was visited with an attack of seasickness that even now makes me shudder to recall. The most violent retching and blinding headache, accompanied with vertigo, were the prevailing symptoms; and for a short time it seemed that one-third of the bicycle party would find a resting place in the Upper Geyser Basin.

The following morning we set out for the Yellowstone Falls over a most excellent road, on which good time was made. Many points of interest were passed, but space forbids dwelling on them, and we will carry our readers to our camp on the Yellowstone River near the upper fall, which after dinner we proceeded to visit. It is a picture in itself, this plunging fall, so full of life and activity and possessed of a beauty peculiarly its own. Foaming, plunging and tossing about, the water works itself into a creamy foam, and dashing over the brink drops sheer down 115 feet into its basin below. Confined as it is by vertical walls of rock, and secluded by sombre forests of pine, it forms a picture than cannot be described in words and which the most skillful artists could not hope to reproduce.

Early on the following morning, leaving our wheels at camp, we stole down the rugged mountain over a winding path and reached the Grand Fall of the Yellowstone.

From this point we could see only the foamy rush of a vast volume of water as it plunged over the brink, the face of the fall being hidden from view, but proceeding a short half mile down stream we reached Lookout Point and turned our eyes westward on the grandest cañon of all those that pierce the Rocky

Mountains. The awful heights and yawning depths bewildered us. All around are castellated peaks, thousands of pinnacles and endless rocky spires rearing their craggy heads aloft in infinity of form, height and opulence of color. The graceful front of rocky walls stands out sharp and terrible, sweeping down in broken crag and cliff to the mighty river, which distance reduces to a foamy ribbon, upon the lip of which the depth has laid its silent finger. But the picture is not yet complete. Over the whole is thrown a rich mantle of golden tint, enveloping crag and cliff in a dreamy cloud of color, and softening the Gothic outline of giant spires, which stand like sentinels, on the brink of the gorge.

But how can the gorgeous coloring of this golden-walled cañon be described! Words have not the wealth to make it known. The impression steals upon you that a firmament of rainbows has been thrown into this mighty gorge, and catching on the thousands of pinnacles have suspended themselves across the canon. Up the river is the silver face of the Grand Fall. The curb of rock over which it leaps is level. On the very margin of the bench the river seems to pause, and then in an unbroken, shining volume falls majestically 300 feet to its stony bed, below whence it rebounds in a wealth of spray that flashes like a cloud of diamond dust in the bright morning sunlight. You can see the momentous rush and tumultuous leaping of the water, but no sound reaches your ears, for the distance and profound depth of the cañon swallow it up, and the rays of light are the only messengers to bring tidings of its activity. Leaving this glorious spectacle we returned to camp, and retracing our road a few miles turned southward to visit the Yellowstone Lake, wheeling over a road that could not be improved.

The lake is a picturesque sheet of water twenty by fifteen miles in extent and at an altitude of 7,800 feet. It is situated in the midst of snow-capped peaks, whose lofty summits are from ten to twelve thousand feet above the sea, and is the largest body of fresh water in the world at this altitude. Its area is 300 square miles.

Myriads of waterfowl are found here and excellent fishing on every hand. Returning to Firehole Basin we set out next morning northward for the Mammoth Hot Springs, wheeling and walking over the vilest roads bicycler ever set eyes on. Two days were consumed in making this trip, owing to sandy roads; and although there are many objects along the route to interest the tourist a description of them cannot be attempted.

Having arrived at the springs we visited the superintendent of the Park and were courteously received.

A peculiar property of the water in these springs is worthy of mention. It contains large quantities of silica in solution, and if any article, such as a bottle, piece of wood, an old shoe or the like be inserted therein and allowed to remain from twenty-four to forty-eight hours, it will receive a hard, white coating that is not easily removed.

Horseshoes, bottles and picture frames are the articles most frequently placed in the springs by tourists, and after withdrawing them they are suspended on a rack to dry.

Leaving the springs we reached the Firehole Basin the same day, after twelve hours of as difficult wheeling and walking as ever fell to our lot. On the following morning we headed westward and in two days' run reached Beaver Canon, whence we were carried by rail to Laramie, our home.

Of the two days consumed in returning from the Park the first was all that could be desired, being fair and sunny. The second was made miserable by a heavy rainfall.

And so ended the first wheel tour of the Yellowstone Park, and we felt what I trust is a pardonable pride in having taken the first bicycles through the northern wonderland and also in having been the first to cross the Continental Divide awheel.

It would be difficult to arrange a trip of equal interest, and I trust many others will be persuaded to take it.

Some toil and hardship, to be sure, must accompany the undertaking, but what figure do they cut? The shadowy forms of obstacles that were met and turned on this journey arise before me; but all the toil and hardship endured pale and grow dim when compared with the pleasure and the friendship of those whose welcome made our home where night o'ertook us, and left a green spot in our memory that time cannot efface.

John Muir at his home in California at about the time of his trip to Yellowstone Park. Courtesy of the Holt-Atherton Pacific Center for Western Historical Studies

John Muir
1885

John Muir's reputation as one of the great defenders of wilderness is secure, and is based mostly on the work he did on behalf of his beloved Yosemite and its sister parks in California. Perhaps this relation of Muir to the Sierra has been overstated, for now many people are surprised to learn how widely he travelled and how extensive his non-California writings were.

He visited Yellowstone in 1885. His week in the Park was marred by a serious personal illness and lesser misfortunes: he was thrown from a horse at one point and drenched by rain at another.[1] These circumstances did not prevent him from responding to the "exciting wonders" he saw, however, and his appreciation of the region was manifest in the following account.[2]

Though it was written more as an introduction to Yellowstone than as a journal of his own experiences, Muir's article still contained much personal reflection. His writings were testaments of his own faith, no matter what the subject, and in Yellowstone he found an ideal topic. It was Yellowstone, in fact, that inspired what was probably his most enduring exhortation to lovers of nature:

Climb the mountains and get their good tidings. Nature's peace will flow into you as sunshine flows into trees. The winds will blow their own freshness into you and the storms their energy, while cares will drop off like autumn leaves.[3]

An 1871 Thomas Moran woodcut of Giant geyser. "Geysers are the main objects (of the Park)," Muir wrote, "and as soon as they come in sight other wonders are forgotten."

f the four national parks of the West, the Yellowstone is far the largest. It is a big, wholesome wilderness on the broad summit of the Rocky Mountains, favored with abundance of rain and snow,—a place of fountains where the greatest of the American rivers take their rise. The central portion is a densely forested and comparatively level volcanic plateau with an average elevation of about eight thousand feet above the sea, surrounded by an imposing host of mountains belonging to the subordinate Gallatin, Wind River, Teton, Absaroka, and snowy ranges. Unnumbered lakes shine in it, united by a famous band of streams that rush up out of hot lava beds, or fall from the frosty peaks in channels rocky and bare, mossy and bosky, to the main rivers, singing cheerily on through every difficulty, cunningly dividing and finding their way east and west to the two far-off seas.

Glacier meadows and beaver meadows are outspread with charming effect along the banks of the streams, parklike expanses in the woods, and innumerable small gardens in rocky recesses of the mountains, some of them containing more petals than leaves, while the whole wilderness is enlivened with happy animals.

Beside the treasures common to most mountain regions that are wild and blessed with a kind climate, the Park is full of exciting wonders. The wildest geysers in the world, in bright, triumphant bands, are dancing and singing in it amid thousands of boiling springs, beautiful and awful, their basins arrayed in georgeous colors like gigantic flowers; and hot paint-pots, mud springs, mud volcanoes, mush and broth caldrons whose contents are of every color and consistency, plash and heave and roar in bewildering abundance. In the adjacent mountains, beneath the living trees the edges of petrified forests are exposed to view, like specimens on the shelves of a museum, standing on ledges tier above tier where they grew, solemnly silent in rigid crystalline beauty after swaying in the winds thousands of centuries ago, opening marvelous views back into the years and climates and life of the past. Here, too, are hills of sparkling crystals, hills of sulphur, hills of glass, hills of cinders and ashes, mountains of every style of architecture, icy or forested, mountains covered with honey-bloom sweet as Hymettus, mountains boiled soft like potatoes and colored

41

like a sunset sky. A' that and a' that, and twice as muckle 's a' that, Nature has on show in the Yellowstone Park. Therefore it is called Wonderland, and thousands of tourists and travelers stream into it every summer, and wander about in it enchanted.

Fortunately, almost as soon as it was discovered it was dedicated and set apart for the benefit of the people, a piece of legislation that shines benignly amid the common dust-and-ashes history of the public domain, for which the world must thank Professor Hayden above all others; for he led the first scientific exploring party into it, described it, and with admirable enthusiasm urged Congress to preserve it. As delineated in the year 1872, the Park contained about 3,344 square miles. On March 30, 1891, it was to all intents and purposes enlarged by the Yellowstone National Park Timber Reserve, and in December, 1897, by the Teton Forest Reserve; thus nearly doubling its original area, and extending the southern boundary far enough to take in the sublime Teton range and the famous pasture lands of the big Rocky Mountain game animals. The withdrawal of this large tract from the public domain did no harm to any one; for its height, six thousand to over thirteen thousand feet above the sea, and its thick mantle of volcanic rocks, prevent its ever being available for agriculture or mining, while on the other hand its geographical position, reviving climate, and wonderful scenery combine to make it a grand health, pleasure, and study resort,—a gathering-place for travelers from all the world.

The national parks are not only withdrawn from sale and entry like the forest reservations, but are efficiently managed and guarded by small troops of United States cavalry, directed by the Secretary of the Interior. Under this care the forests are flourishing, protected from both axe and fire; and so, of course, are the shaggy beds of underbrush and the herbaceous vegetation. The so-called curiosities, also, are preserved, and the furred and feathered tribes, many of which, in danger of extinction a short time ago, are now increasing in numbers,— a refreshing thing to see amid the blind, ruthless destruction that is going on in the adjacent regions. In pleasing contrast to the noisy, ever-changing management, or mismanagement,

42

of blundering, plundering, money-making vote-sellers who receive their places from boss politicians as purchased goods, the soldiers do their duty so quietly that the traveler is scarce aware of their presence.

However orderly your excursions or aimless, again and again amid the calmest, stillest scenery you will be brought to a stand-still hushed and awe-stricken before phenomena wholly new to you. Boiling springs and huge deep pools of purest green and azure water, thousands of them, are plashing and heaving in these high, cool mountains as if a fierce furnace fire were burning beneath each one of them; and a hundred geysers, white torrents of boiling water and steam, like inverted waterfalls, are ever and anon rushing up out of the hot, black under-world. Some of these ponderous geyser columns are as large as sequoias,—five to sixty feet in diameter, one hundred and fifty to three hundred feet high,—and are sustained at this great height with tremendous energy for a few minutes, or perhaps nearly an hour, standing rigid and erect, hissing, throbbing, booming, as if thunderstorms were raging beneath their roots, their sides roughened or fluted like the furrowed boles of trees, their tops dissolving in feathery branches, while the irised spray, like misty bloom is at times blown aside, revealing the massive shafts shining against a background of pine-covered hills. Some of them lean more or less, as if storm-bent, and instead of being round are flat or fan-shaped, issuing from irregular slits in silex pavements with radiate structure, the sunbeams shifting through them in ravishing splendor. Some are broad and round-headed like oaks; others are low and bunchy, branching near the ground like bushes; and a few are hollow in the centre like big daisies or water-lilies. No frost cools them, snow never covers them nor lodges in their branches; winter and summer they welcome alike; all of them, of whatever form or size, faithfully rising and sinking in fairy rhythmic dance night and day, in all sorts of weather, at varying periods of minutes, hours, or weeks, growing up rapidly, uncontrollable as fate, tossing their pearly branches in the wind, bursting into bloom and vanishing like the frailest flowers,—plants of which Nature raises hundreds or thousands of crops a year with no apparent exhaustion of the fiery soil.

43

The so-called geyser basins, in which this rare sort of vegetation is growing, are mostly open valleys on the central plateau that were eroded by glaciers after the greater volcanic fires had ceased to burn. Looking down over the forests as you approach them from the surrounding heights, you see a multitude of white columns, broad, reeking masses, and irregular jets and puffs of misty vapor ascending from the bottom of the valley, or entangled like smoke among the neighboring trees, suggesting the factories of some busy town or the camp-fires of an army. These mark the position of each mush-pot, paint-pot, hot spring, and geyser, or gusher, as the Icelandic words mean. And when you saunter into the midst of them over the bright sinter pavements, and see how pure and white and pearly gray they are in the shade of the mountains, and how radiant in the sunshine, you are fairly enchanted. So numerous they are and varied, Nature seems to have gathered them from all the world as specimens of her rarest fountains, to show in one place what she can do. Over four thousand hot springs have been counted in the Park, and a hundred geysers; how many more there are nobody knows.

These valleys at the heads of the great rivers may be regarded as laboratories and kitchens, in which, amid a thousand retorts and pots, we may see Nature at work as chemist or cook, cunningly compounding an infinite variety of mineral messes; cooking whole mountains; boiling and steaming flinty rocks to smooth paste and mush,—yellow, brown, red, pink, lavender, gray, and creamy white,—making the most beautiful mud in the world; and distilling the most ethereal essences. Many of these pots and caldrons have been boiling thousands of years. Pots of sulphurous mush, stringy and lumpy, and pots of broth as black as ink, are tossed and stirred with constant care, and thin transparent essences, too pure and fine to be called water, are kept simmering gently in beautiful sinter cups and bowls that grow ever more beautiful the longer they are used. In some of the spring basins, the waters, though still warm, are perfectly calm, and shine blandly in a sod of overleaning grass and flowers, as if they were thoroughly cooked at last, and set aside to settle and cool. Others are wildly boiling over as if running to waste, thousands of tons of the precious liquids

44

being thrown into the air to fall in scalding floods on the clean coral floor of the establishment, keeping onlookers at a distance. Instead of holding limpid pale green or azure water, other pots and craters are filled with scalding mud, which is tossed up from three or four feet to thirty feet, in sticky, rank-smelling masses, with gasping, belching, thudding sounds, plastering the branches of neighboring trees; every flask, retort, hot spring, and geyser has something special in it, no two being the same in temperature, color, or composition.

In these natural laboratories one needs stout faith to feel at ease. The ground sounds hollow underfoot, and the awful subterranean thunder shakes one's mind as the ground is shaken, especially at night in the pale moonlight, or when the sky is overcast with storm-clouds. In the solemn gloom, the geysers, dimly visible, look like monstrous dancing ghosts, and their wild songs and the earthquake thunder replying to the storms overhead seem doubly terrible, as if divine government were at an end. But the trembling hills keep their places. The sky clears, the rosy dawn is reassuring, and up comes the sun like a god, pouring his faithful beams across the mountains and forest, lighting each peak and tree and ghastly geyser alike, and shining into the eyes of the reeking springs, clothing them with rainbow light, and dissolving the seeming chaos of darkness into varied forms of harmony. The ordinary work of the world goes on. Gladly we see the flies dancing in the sunbeams, birds feeding their young, squirrels gathering nuts, and hear the blessed ouzel singing confidingly in the shallows of the river,— most faithful evangel, calming every fear, reducing everything to love.

The variously tinted sinter and travertine formations, outspread like pavements over large areas of the geyser valleys, lining the spring basins and throats of the craters, and forming beautiful coral-like rims and curbs about them, always excite admiring attention; so also does the play of the waters from which they are deposited. The various minerals in them are rich in colors, and these are greatly heightened by a smooth, silky growth of brilliantly colored confervae which lines many of the pools and channels and terraces. No bed of flower-bloom is more exquisite than these myriads of minute plants, visible only in mass, growing in the hot waters. Most of the spring borders are low and daintily scalloped, crenelated, and beaded with sinter pearls. Some of the geyser craters are massive and picturesque, like ruined castles or old burned-out sequoia stumps, and are adorned on a grand scale with outbulging, cauliflower-like formations. From these as centers the silex pavements slope gently away in thin, crusty, overlapping layers, slightly interrupted in some places by low terraces. Or, as in the case of the Mammoth Hot Springs, at the north end of the Park, where the building waters issue from the side of a steep hill, the deposits form a succession of higher and broader terraces of white travertine tinged with purple, like the famous Pink Terrace at Rotomahana, New Zealand, draped in front with clustering stalactites, each terrace having a pool of indescribably beautiful water upon it in a basin with a raised rim that glistens with confervae,—the whole, when viewed at a distance of a mile or two, looking like a broad, massive cascade pouring over shelving rocks in snowy purpled foam.

The stones of this divine masonry, invisible particles of lime or silex, mined in quarries no eye has seen, go to their appointed places in gentle, tinkling, transparent currents or through the dashing turmoil of floods, as surely guided as the sap of plants streaming into bole and branch, leaf and flower. And thus from century to century this beauty-work has gone on and is going on.

Passing through many a mile of pine and spruce woods, toward the center of the Park you come to the famous Yellowstone Lake. It is about twenty miles long and fifteen wide, and lies at a height of nearly eight thousand feet above the level of the sea, amid dense black forests and snowy mountains. Around its winding, wavering shores, closely forested and picturesquely varied with promontories and bays, the distance is more than one hundred miles. It is not very deep, only from two hundred to three hundred feet, and contains less water than the celebrated Lake Tahoe of the California Sierra, which is nearly the same size, lies at a height of sixty-four hundred feet, and is over sixteen hundred feet deep. But no other lake in North America of equal area lies so high as the Yellowstone, or gives birth to so noble a river. The terraces around

46

its shores show that at the close of the glacial period its surface was about one hundred and sixty feet higher than it is now, and its area nearly twice as great.

It is full of trout, and a vast multitude of birds—swans, pelicans, geese, ducks, cranes, herons, curlews, plovers, snipe—feed in it and upon its shores; and many forest animals come out of the woods, and wade a little way in shallow, sandy places to drink and look about them, and cool themselves in the free flowing breezes.

In calm weather it is a magnificent mirror for the woods and mountains and sky, now pattered with hail and rain, now roughened with sudden storms that send waves to fringe the shores and wash its border of gravel and sand. The Absaroka Mountains and the Wind River Plateau on the east and south pour their gathered waters into it, and the river issues from the north side in a broad, smooth, stately current, silently gliding with such serene majesty that one fancies it knows the vast journey of four thousand miles that lies before it, and the work it has to do. For the first twenty miles its course is in a level, sunny valley lightly fringed with trees, through which it flows in silvery reaches stirred into spangles here and there by ducks and leaping trout, making no sound save a low whispering among the pebbles and the dipping willows and sedges of its banks. Then suddenly, as if preparing for hard work, it rushes eagerly, impetuously forward rejoicing in its strength, breaks into foam-bloom, and goes thundering down into the Grand Cañon in two magnificent falls, one hundred and three hundred feet high.

The cañon is so tremendously wild and impressive that even these great falls cannot hold your attention. It is about twenty miles long and a thousand feet deep,—a weird, unearthly-looking gorge of jagged, fantastic architecture, and most brilliantly colored. Here the Washburn range, forming the northern rim of the Yellowstone basin, made up mostly of beds of rhyolite decomposed by the action of thermal waters, has been cut through and laid open to view by the river; and a famous section it has made. It is not the depth or the shape of the cañon, nor the waterfall, nor the green and gray river chanting its brave song as it goes foaming on its way, that most impresses the observer, but the colors of the decomposed volcanic rocks. With few exceptions, the traveler in strange lands finds that, however much the scenery and vegetation in different countries may change, Mother Earth is ever familiar and the same. But here the very ground is changed, as if belonging to some other world. The walls of the cañon from top to bottom burn in a perfect glory of color, confounding and dazzling when the sun is shining,—white, yellow, green, blue, vermilion, and various other shades of red indefinitely blending. All the earth hereabouts seems to be paint. Millions of tons of it lie in sight, exposed to wind and weather as if of no account, yet marvelously fresh and bright, fast colors not to be washed out or bleached out by either sunshine or storms. The effect is so novel and awful, we imagine that even a river might be afraid to enter such a place. But the rich and gentle beauty of the vegetation is reassuring. The lovely *Linnaea borealis* hangs her twin bells over the brink of the cliffs, forests and gardens extend their treasures in smiling confidence on either side, nuts and berries ripen well whatever may be going on below; blind fears vanish, and the grand gorge seems a kindly, beautiful part of the general harmony, full of peace and joy and good will.

The Park is easy of access. Locomotives drag you to its northern boundary at Cinnabar, and horses and guides do the rest. From Cinnabar you will be whirled in coaches along the foaming Gardner River to Mammoth Hot Springs; thence through woods and meadows, gulches and ravines along branches of the Upper Gallatin, Madison, and Firehole rivers to the main geyser basins; thence over the Continental Divide and back again, up and down through dense pine, spruce, and fir woods to the magnificent Yellowstone Lake, along its northern shore to the outlet, down the river to the falls and Grand Cañon, and thence back through the woods to Mammoth Hot Springs and Cinnabar; stopping here and there at the so-called points of interest among the geysers, springs, paint-pots, mud volcanoes, etc., where you will be allowed a few minutes or hours to saunter over the sinter pavements, watch the play of a few of the geysers, and peer into some of the most beautiful and terrible of the craters and pools. These wonders you

48

will enjoy, and also the views of the mountains, especially the
Gallatin and Absaroka ranges, the long, willowy glacier and
beaver meadows, the beds of violets, gentians, phloxes, asters,
phacelias, goldenrods, eriogonums, and many other flowers,
some species giving color to whole meadows and hillsides. And
you will enjoy your short views of the great lake and river and
cañon. No scalping Indians will you see. The Blackfeet and
Bannocks that once roamed here are gone; so are the old
beaver-catchers, the Coulters and Bridgers, with all their
attractive buckskin and romance. There are several bands of
buffaloes in the Park, but you will not thus cheaply in tourist
fashion see them nor many of the other large animals hidden
in the wilderness. The song-birds, too, keep mostly out of
sight of the rushing tourist, though off the roads thrushes,
warblers, orioles, grosbeaks, etc., keep the air sweet and merry.
Perhaps in passing rapids and falls you may catch glimpses of
the water-ouzel, but in the whirling noise you will not hear
his song. Fortunately, no road noise frightens the Douglas
squirrel, and his merry play and gossip will amuse you all
through the woods. Here and there a deer may be seen crossing
the road, or a bear. Most likely, however, the only bears you
will see are the half tame ones that go to the hotels every night
for dinner-table scraps,—yeast-powder biscuit, Chicago canned
stuff, mixed pickles, and beefsteaks that have proved too tough
for the tourists.

Among the gains of a coach trip are the acquaintances made
and the fresh views into human nature; for the wilderness
is a shrewd touchstone, even thus lightly approached, and brings
many a curious trait to view. Setting out, the driver cracks
his whip and the four horses go off at half gallop, half trot,
in trained, showy style, until out of sight of the hotel. The
coach is crowded, old and young side by side, blooming and
fading, full of hope and fun and care. Some look at the scenery
or the horses, and all ask questions, an odd mixed lot of them:
"Where is the umbrella? What is the name of that blue flower
over there? Are you sure the little bag is aboard? Is that hollow
yonder a crater? How is your throat this morning? How high
did you say the geysers spout? How does the elevation affect
your head? Is that a geyser reeking over there in the rocks,

49

or only a hot spring?" A long ascent is made, the solemn mountains come to view, small cares are quenched, and all become natural and silent, save perhaps some unfortunate expounder who has been reading guidebook geology, and rumbles forth foggy subsidences and upheavals until he is in danger of being heaved overboard. The driver will give you the names of the peaks and meadows and streams as you come to them, call attention to the glass road, tell how hard it was to build,—how the obsidian cliffs naturally pushed the surveyor's lines to the right, and the industrious beavers, by flooding the valley in front of the cliff, pushed them to the left.

Geysers, however, are the main objects, and as soon as they come in sight other wonders are forgotten. All gather around the crater of the one that is expected to play first. During the eruptions of the smaller geysers, such as the Beehive and Old Faithful, though a little frightened at first, all welcome the glorious show with enthusiasm, and shout, "Oh, how wonderful, beautiful, splendid, majestic!" Some venture near enough to stroke the column with a stick, as if it were a stone pillar or a tree, so firm and substantial and permanent it seems. While tourists wait around a large geyser, such as the Castle or the Giant, there is a chatter of small talk in anything but solemn mood; and during the intervals between the preliminary splashes and upheavals some adventurer occasionally looks down the throat of the crater, admiring the silex formations and wondering whether Hades is as beautiful. But when, with awful uproar as if avalanches were falling and storms thundering in the depths, the tremendous outburst begins, all run away to a safe distance, and look on, awe-stricken and silent, in devout, worshiping wonder.

The largest and one of the most wonderfully beautiful of the springs is the Prismatic, which the guide will be sure to show you. With a circumference of three hundred yards, it is more like a lake than a spring. The water is pure deep blue in the center, fading to green on the edges, and its basin and the slightly terraced pavement about it are astonishingly bright and varied in color. This one of the multitude of Yellowstone fountains is of itself object enough for a trip across the continent. No wonder that so many fine myths have originated in springs; that so many fountains were held sacred in the youth of the world, and had miraculous virtues ascribed to them. Even in these cold, doubting, questioning, scientific times many of the Yellowstone fountains seem able to work miracles. Near the Prismatic Spring is the great Excelsior Geyser, which is said to throw a column of boiling water sixty to seventy feet in diameter to a height of from fifty to three hundred feet, at irregular periods. This is the greatest of all the geysers yet discovered anywhere. The Firehole River, which sweeps past it, is, at ordinary stages, a stream about one hundred yards wide and three feet deep; but when the geyser is in eruption, so great is the quantity of water discharged that the volume of the river is doubled, and it is rendered too hot and rapid to be forded.

Geysers are found in many other volcanic regions,—in Iceland, New Zealand, Japan, the Himalayas, the Eastern Archipelago, South America, the Azores, and elsewhere; but only in Iceland, New Zealand, and this Rocky Mountain park do they display their grandest forms, and of these three famous regions the Yellowstone is easily first, both in the number and in the size of its geysers. The greatest height of the column of the Great Geyser of Iceland actually measured was two hundred and twelve feet, and of the Strokhr one hundred and sixty-two feet.

In New Zealand, the Te Pueia at Lake Taupo, the Waikite at Rotorna, and two others are said to lift their waters occasionally to a height of one hundred feet, while the celebrated Te Tarata at Rotomahana sometimes lifts a boiling column twenty feet in diameter to a height of sixty feet. But all these are far surpassed by the Excelsior. Few tourists, however, will see the Excelsior in action, or a thousand other interesting features of the Park that lie beyond the wagon-roads and the hotels. The regular trips—from three to five days—are too short. Nothing can be done well at a speed of forty miles a day. The multitude of mixed, novel impressions rapidly piled on one another make only a dreamy, bewildering, swirling blur, most of which is unrememberable. Far more time should be taken. Walk away quietly in any direction and taste the freedom of the mountaineer. Camp out among the grass and gentians of glacier meadows, in craggy garden nooks full of Nature's darlings. Climb the mountains and get their good tidings. Nature's peace will flow into you as sunshine flows into trees. The winds will blow their own freshness into you, and the storms their energy, while cares will drop off like autumn leaves. As age comes on, one source of enjoyment after another is closed, but Nature's sources never fail. Like a generous host, she offers here brimming cups in endless variety, served in a grand hall, the sky its ceiling, the mountains its walls, decorated with glorious paintings and enlivened with bands of music ever playing. The petty discomforts that beset the awkward guest, the unskilled camper, are quickly forgotten, while all that is precious remains. Fears vanish as soon as one is fairly free in the wilderness.

Most of the dangers that haunt the unseasoned citizen are imaginary; the real ones are perhaps too few rather than too many for his good. The bears that always seem to spring up thick as trees, in fighting, devouring attitudes before the frightened tourist whenever a camping trip is proposed, are gentle now, finding they are no longer likely to be shot; and rattlesnakes, the other big irrational dread of over-civilized people, are scarce here, for most of the Park lies above the snake-line. Poor creatures, loved only by their Maker, they are timid and bashful, as mountaineers know; and though perhaps not possessed of much of that charity that suffers long and is kind, seldom, either by mistake or by mishaps, do harm to any one. Certainly they cause not the hundredth part of the pain and death that follow the footsteps of the admired Rocky Mountain trapper. Nevertheless, again and again, in season and out of season, the question comes up, "What are rattlesnakes good for?" As if nothing that does not obviously make for the benefit of man had any right to exist; as if our ways were God's ways. Long ago, an Indian to whom a French traveler put this old question replied that their tails were good for toothache, and their heads for fever. Anyhow, they are all, head and tail, good for themselves, and we need not begrudge them their share of life.

Fear nothing. No town park you have been accustomed to saunter in is so free from danger as the Yellowstone. It is a hard place to leave. Even its names in your guidebook are attractive, and should draw you far from wagon-roads,—all save the early ones, derived from the infernal regions: Hell Roaring River, Hell Broth Springs, The Devil's Caldron, etc. Indeed, the whole region was at first called Colter's Hell, from the fiery brimstone stories told by trapper Colter, who left the Lewis and Clark expedition and wandered through the Park, in the year 1807, with a band of Bannock Indians. The later names, many of which we owe to Mr. Arnold Hague of the U.S. Geological Survey, are so telling and exhilarating that they set our pulses dancing and make us begin to enjoy the pleasures of excursions ere they are commenced. Three River Peak, Two Ocean Pass, Continental Divide, are capital geographical descriptions, suggesting thousands of miles of rejoicing streams and all that belongs to them. Big Horn Pass, Bison Peak, Big Game Ridge, bring brave mountain animals to mind. Birch Hills, Garnet Hills, Amethyst Mountain, Storm Peak, Electric Peak, Roaring Mountain, are bright, bracing names. Wapiti, Beaver, Tern, and Swan lakes conjure up fine pictures, and so also do Osprey and Ouzel falls. Antelope Creek, Otter, Mink, and Grayling creeks, Geode, Jasper, Opal, Carnelian, and Chalcedony creeks, are lively and sparkling names that help the streams to shine; and Azalea, Stellaria, Arnica, Aster, and Phlox creeks, what pictures these bring up! Violet, Morning Mist, Hygeia, Beryl, Vermilion, and Indigo springs, and many beside, give us visions of fountains more beautifully arrayed than Solomon in all his purple and golden glory. All these and a host of others call you to camp. You may be a little cold some nights on mountain tops above the timber-line, but you will see the stars, and by and by you can sleep enough in your town bed, or at least in your grave. Keep awake while you may in mountain mansions so rare.

If you are not very strong, try to climb Electric Peak when a big bossy, well-charged thunder-cloud is on it, to breathe the ozone set free, and get yourself kindly shaken and shocked. You are sure to be lost in wonder and praise, and every hair of your head will stand up and hum and sing like an enthusiastic congregation.

After this reviving experience, you should take a look into a few of the tertiary volumes of the grand geological library of the Park, and see how God writes history. No technical knowledge is required; only a calm day and a calm mind. Perhaps nowhere else in the Rocky Mountains have the volcanic forces been so busy. More than ten thousand square miles hereabouts have been covered to a depth of at least five thousand feet with material spouted from chasms and craters during the tertiary period, forming broad sheets of basalt, andesite, rhyolite, etc., and marvelous masses of ashes, sand, cinders, and stones now consolidated into conglomerates, charged with the remains of plants and animals that lived in the calm, genial periods that separated the volcanic outbursts.

Perhaps the most interesting and telling of these rocks, to the hasty tourist, are those that make up the mass of Amethyst Mountain. On its north side it presents a section two thousand feet high of roughly stratified beds of sand, ashes, and conglomerates coarse and fine, forming the untrimmed edges of a wonderful set of volumes lying on their sides,—books a million years old, well bound, miles in size, with full-page illustrations. On the ledges of this one section we see trunks and stumps of fifteen or twenty ancient forests ranged one above another, standing where they grew, or prostrate and broken like the pillars of ruined temples in desert sands,—a forest fifteen or twenty stories high, the roots of each spread above the tops of the next beneath it, telling wonderful tales of the bygone centuries, with their winters and summers, growth and death, fire, ice, and flood.

There were giants in those days. The largest of the standing opal and agate stumps and prostrate sections of the trunks are from two or three to fifty feet in height or length, and from five to ten feet in diameter; and so perfect is the petrifaction that the annual rings and ducts are clearer and more easily counted than those of living trees, centuries of burial having brightened the records instead of blurring them. They show that the winters of the tertiary period gave as decided a check to vegetable growth as do those of the present time. Some trees favorably located grew rapidly, increasing twenty inches in diameter in as many years, while others of the same species, on poorer soil or overshadowed, increased only two or three inches in the same time.

Among the roots and stumps on the old forest floors we find the remains of ferns and bushes, and the seeds and leaves of trees like those now growing on the southern Alleghanies,—such as magnolia, sassafras, laurel, linden, persimmon, ash, alder, dogwood. Studying the lowest of these forests, the soil it grew on and the deposits it is buried in, we see that it was rich in species, and flourished in a genial, sunny climate. When its stately trees were in their glory, volcanic fires broke forth from chasms and craters, like larger geysers, spouting ashes, cinders, stones, and mud, which fell on the doomed forest like hail and snow; sifting, hurtling through the leaves and branches, choking the streams, covering the ground, crushing bushes and ferns, rapidly deepening, packing around the trees and breaking them, rising higher until the top-most boughs of the giants were buried, leaving not a leaf or twig in sight, so complete was the desolation. At last the vocanic storm began to abate, the fiery soil settled; mud floods and boulder floods passed over it, enriching it, cooling it; rains fell and mellow sunshine, and it became fertile and ready for another crop. Birds, and the winds, and roaming animals brought seeds from more fortunate woods, and a new forest grew up on the top of the buried one. Centuries of genial growing seasons passed. The seedling trees became giants, and with strong outreaching branches spread a leafy canopy over the gray land.

The sleeping subterranean fires again awake and shake the mountains, and every leaf trembles. The old craters, with perhaps new ones, are opened, and immense quantities of ashes, pumice, and cinders are again thrown into the sky. The sun, shorn of his beams, glows like a dull red ball, until hidden in sulphurous clouds. Volcanic snow, hail, and floods fall on the new forest, burying it alive, like the one beneath its roots. Then come another noisy band of mud floods and boulder floods, mixing, settling, enriching the new ground, more seeds, quickening sunshine and showers; and a third noble magnolia forest is carefully raised on the top of the second. And so on. Forest was planted above forest and destroyed, as if Nature were ever repenting, undoing the work she had so industriously done, and burying it.

Of course this destruction was creation, progress in the march of beauty through death. How quickly these old monuments excite and hold the imagination! We see the old stone stumps budding and blossoming and waving in the wind as magnificent trees, standing shoulder to shoulder, branches interlacing in grand varied round-headed forests; see the sunshine of morning and evening gilding their mossy trunks, and at high noon spangling on the thick glossy leaves of the magnolia, filtering through translucent canopies of linden and ash, and falling in mellow patches on the ferny floor; see the shining after rain, breathe the exhaling fragrance, and hear the winds and birds and the murmur of brooks and insects. We watch them from season to season; see the swelling buds when the sap begins to flow in the spring, the opening leaves and blossoms, the ripening of summer fruits, the colors of autumn, and the maze of leafless branches and sprays in winter; and we see the sudden oncome of the storms that overwhelmed them.

One calm morning at sunrise I saw the oaks and pines in Yosemite Valley shaken by an earthquake, their tops swishing back and forth, and every branch and needle shuddering as if in distress like the frightened screaming birds. One may imagine the trembling, rocking, tumultuous waving of those ancient Yellowstone woods, and the terror of their inhabitants when the first foreboding shocks were felt, the sky grew dark, and rock-laden floods began to roar. But though they were close pressed and buried, cut off from sun and wind, all their happy leaf-fluttering and waving done, other currents coursed through them, fondling and thrilling every fibre, and beautiful wood was replaced by beautiful stone. Now their rocky sepulchres are partly open, and show forth the natural beauty of death.

After the forest times and fire times had passed away, and the volcanic furnaces were banked and held in abeyance, another great change occurred. The glacial winter came on. The sky was again darkened, not with dust and ashes, but with snow which fell in glorious abundance, piling deeper, deeper, slipping from the overladen heights in booming avalanches, compacting into glaciers, that flowed over all the landscape, wiping off forests, grinding, sculpturing, fashioning the comparatively featureless lava beds into the beautiful rhythm of hill and dale and ranges of mountains we behold to-day; forming basins for lakes, channels for streams, new soils for forests, gardens, and meadows. While this ice-work was going on, the slumbering volcanic fires were boiling the subterranean waters, and with curious chemistry decomposing the rocks, making beauty in the darkness; these forces, seemingly antagonistic, working harmoniously together. How wild their meetings on the surface were we may imagine. When the glacier period began, geysers and hot springs were playing in grander volume, it may be, than those of to-day. The glaciers flowed over them while they spouted and thundered, carrying away their fine sinter and travertine structures, and shortening their mysterious channels.

The soils made in the down-grinding required to bring the present features of the landscape into relief are possibly no better than were some of the old volcanic soils that were carried away, and which, as we have seen, nourished magnificent forests, but the glacial landscapes are incomparably more beautiful than the old volcanic ones were. The glacial winter has passed away, like the ancient summers and fire periods, though in the chronology of the geologist all these times are recent. Only small residual glaciers on the cool northern slopes of the highest mountains are left of the vast all-embracing ice-mantle, as solfataras and geysers are all that are left of the ancient volcanoes.

Now the post-glacial agents are at work on the grand old palimpsest of the park region, inscribing new characters; but still in its main telling features it remains distinctly glacial. The moraine soils are being leveled, sorted, refined, re-formed, and covered with vegetation; the polished pavements and scoring and other superficial glacial inscriptions on the crumbling lavas are being rapidly obliterated; gorges are being cut in the decomposed rhyolites and loose conglomerates, and turrets and pinnacles seem to be springing up like growing trees; while the geysers are depositing miles of sinter and travertine. Nevertheless, the ice-work is scarce blurred as yet. These later effects are only spots and wrinkles on the grand glacial countenance of the Park.

Perhaps you have already said that you have seen enough for a lifetime. But before you go away you should spend at least one day and a night on a mountain top, for a last general, calming, settling view. Mount Washburn is a good one for the purpose, because it stands in the middle of the Park, is un-encumbered with other peaks, and is so easy of access that the climb to its summit is only a saunter. First your eye goes roving around the mountain rim amid the hundreds of peaks: some with plain flowing skirts, others abruptly precipitous and defended by sheer battlemented escarpments; flat-topped or round; heaving like sea-waves or spired and turreted like Gothic cathedrals; streaked with snow in the ravines, and darkened with files of adventurous trees climbing the ridges. The nearer peaks are perchance clad in sapphire blue, others far off in creamy white. In the broad glare of noon they seem to shrink and crouch to less than half their real stature, and grow dull and uncommunicative,—mere dead, draggled heaps of waste ashes and stone, giving no hint of the multitude of animals enjoying life in their fastnesses, or of the bright bloom-bordered streams and lakes. But when storms blow they awake and arise, wearing robes of cloud and mist in majestic speaking attitudes like gods. In the color glory of morning and evening they become still more impressive; steeped in the divine light of the alpenglow their earthiness disappears, and, blending with the heavens, they seem neither high nor low.

Over all the central plateau, which from here seems level, and over the foothills and lower slopes of the mountains, the forest extends like a black uniform bed of weeds, interrupted only by lakes and meadows and small burned spots called parks,—all of them, except the Yellowstone Lake, being mere dots and spangles in general views, made conspicuous by their color and brightness. About eighty-five per cent of the entire area of the Park is covered with trees, mostly the indomitable lodge-pole pine (*Pinus contorta,* var. *Murrayana*), with a few patches and sprinklings of Douglas spruce, Engelmann spruce, silver fir (*Abies lasiocarpa*), *Pinus flexilis,* and a few alders, aspens, and birches. The Douglas spruce is found only on the lowest portions, the silver fir on the highest, and the Engel-mann spruce on the dampest places, best defended from fire. Some fine specimens of the flexilis pine are growing on the margins of openings,—wide-branching, sturdy trees, as broad as high, with trunks five feet in diameter, leafy and shady, laden with purple cones and rose-colored flowers. The

58

Engelmann spruce and sub-alpine silver fir are beautiful and notable trees,—tall, spiry, hardy, frost and snow defying, and widely distributed over the West, wherever there is a mountain to climb or a cold moraine slope to cover. But neither of these is a good fire-fighter. With rather thin bark, and scattering their seeds every year as soon as they are ripe, they are quickly driven out of fire-swept regions. When the glaciers were melting, these hardy mountaineering trees were probably among the first to arrive on the new moraine soil beds; but as the plateau became drier and fires began to run, they were driven up the mountains, and into the wet spots and islands where we now find them, leaving nearly all the Park to the lodge-pole pine, which though as thin-skinned as they and as easily killed by fire, takes pains to store up its seeds in firmly closed cones, and holds them from three to nine years, so that, let the fire come when it may, it is ready to die and ready to live again in a new generation. For when the killing fires have devoured the leaves and thin resinous bark, many of the cones, only scorched, open as soon as the smoke clears away; the hoarded store of seeds is sown broadcast on the cleared ground, and a new growth immediately springs up triumphant out of the ashes. Therefore, this tree not only holds its ground, but extends its conquests farther after every fire. Thus the evenness and closeness of its growth are accounted for. In one part of the forest that I examined, the growth was about as close as a cane-brake. The trees were from four to eight inches in diameter, one hundred feet high, and one hundred and seventy-five years old. The lower limbs die young and drop off for want of light. Life with these close-planted trees is a race for light, more light, and so they push straight for the sky. Mowing off ten feet from the top of the forest would make it look like a crowded mass of telegraph-poles; for only the sunny tops are leafy. A sapling ten years old, growing in the sunshine, has as many leaves as a crowded tree one or two hundred years old. As fires are multiplied and the mountains become drier, this wonderful lodge-pole pine bids fair to obtain possession of nearly all the forest ground in the West.

How still the woods seem from here, yet how lively a stir the hidden animals are making; digging, gnawing, biting, eyes shining, at work and play, getting food, rearing young, roving through the underbrush, climbing the rocks, wading solitary marshes, tracing the banks of the lakes and streams! Insect swarms are dancing in the sunbeams, burrowing in the ground, diving, swimming,—a cloud of witnesses telling Nature's joy. The plants are as busy as the animals, every cell in a swirl of enjoyment, humming like a hive, singing the old new song of creation. A few columns and puffs of steam are seen rising above the tree-tops, some near, but most of them far off, indicating geysers and hot springs, gentle-looking and noiseless as downy clouds, softly hinting the reaction going on between the surface and the hot interior. From here you see them better than when you are standing beside them, frightened and confused, regarding them as lawless cataclysms. The shocks and outbursts of earthquakes, volcanoes, geysers, storms, the pounding of waves, the uprush of sap in plants, each and all tell the orderly love-beats of Nature's heart.

Turning to the eastward, you have the Grand Cañon and reaches of the river in full view; and yonder to the southward lies the great lake, the largest and most important of all the high fountains of the Missouri-Mississippi, and the last to be discovered.

In the year 1541, when De Soto, with a romantic band of adventurers, was seeking gold and glory and the fountain of youth, he found the Mississippi a few hundred miles above its mouth, and made his grave beneath its floods. La Salle, in 1682, after discovering the Ohio, one of the largest and most beautiful branches of the Mississippi, traced the latter to the sea from the mouth of the Illinois, through adventures and privations not easily realized now. About the same time Joliet and Father Marquette reached the "Father of Waters" by way of the Wisconsin, but more than a century passed ere its highest sources in these mountains were seen. The advancing stream of civilization has ever followed its guidance toward the west, but none of the thousand tribes of Indians living on its banks could tell the explorer whence it came. From those romantic De Soto and La Salle days to these times of locomotives and tourists, how much has the great river seen and done! Great as it now is, and still growing longer through the ground of its

60

delta and the basins of receding glaciers at its head, it was immensely broader toward the close of the glacial period, when the ice-mantle of the mountains was melting: then with its three hundred thousand miles of branches outspread over the plains and valleys of the continent, laden with fertile mud, it made the biggest and most generous bed of soil in the world.

Think of this mighty stream springing in the first place in vapor from the sea, flying on the wind, alighting on the mountains in hail and snow and rain, lingering in many a fountain feeding the trees and grass; then gathering its scattered waters, gliding from its noble lake, and going back home to the sea, singing all the way! On it sweeps, through the gates of the mountains, across the vast prairies and plains, through many a wild, gloomy forest, cane-brake, and sunny savanna; from glaciers and snowbanks and pine woods to warm groves of magnolia and palm; geysers dancing at its head keeping time with the sea-waves at its mouth; roaring and gray in rapids, booming in broad, bossy falls, murmuring, gleaming in long, silvery reaches, swaying now hither, now thither, whirling, bending in huge doubling, eddying folds, serene, majestic, ungovernable, overflowing all its metes and bounds, frightening the dwellers upon its banks; building, wasting, uprooting, planting; engulfing old islands and making new ones, taking away fields and towns as if in sport, carrying canoes and ships of commerce in the midst of its spoils and drift, fertilizing the continent as one vast farm. Then, its work done, it gladly vanishes in its ocean home, welcomed by the waiting waves.

Thus naturally, standing here in the midst of its fountains, we trace the fortunes of the great river. And how much more comes to mind as we overlook this wonderful wilderness! Fountains of the Columbia and Colorado lie before us, interlaced with those of the Yellowstone and Missouri, and fine it would be to go with them to the Pacific; but the sun is already in the west, and soon our day will be done.

Yonder is Amethyst Mountain, and other mountains hardly less rich in old forests, which now seem to spring up again in their glory; and you see the storms that buried them— the ashes and torrents laden with boulders and mud, the centuries of sunshine, and the dark, lurid nights. You see again the vast

61

floods of lava, red-hot and white-hot, pouring out from gigantic geysers, usurping the basins of lakes and streams, absorbing or driving away their hissing, screaming waters, flowing around hills and ridges, submerging every subordinate feature. Then you see the snow and glaciers taking possession of the land, making new landscapes. How admirable it is that, after passing through so many vicissitudes of frost and fire and flood, the physiognomy and even the complexion of the landscape should still be so divinely fine!

Thus reviewing the eventful past, we see Nature working with enthusiasm like a man, blowing her volcanic forges like a blacksmith blowing his smithy fires, shoving glaciers over the landscapes like a carpenter shoving his planes, clearing, ploughing, harrowing, irrigating, planting, and sowing broadcast like a farmer and gardener, doing rough work and fine work, planting sequoias and pines, roses-bushes and daisies; working in gems, filling every crack and hollow with them; distilling fine essences; painting plants and shells, clouds, mountains, all the earth and heavens, like an artist,—ever working toward beauty higher and higher. Where may the mind find more stimulating, quickening pasturage? A thousand Yellowstone wonders are calling, "Look up and down and round about you!" And a multitude of still, small voices may be heard directing you to look through all this transient, shifting show of things called "substantial" into the truly substantial spiritual world whose forms flesh and wood, rock and water, air and sunshine, only veil and conceal, and to learn that here is heaven and the dwelling-place of the angels.

The sun is setting; long, violet shadows are growing out over the woods from the mountains along the western rim of the Park; the Absaroka range is baptized in the divine light of the alpenglow, and its rocks and trees are transfigured. Next to the light of the dawn on high mountain tops, the alpenglow is the most impressive of all the terrestrial manifestations of God.

Now comes the gloaming. The alpenglow is fading into earthy, murky gloom, but do not let your town habits draw you away to the hotel. Stay on this good fire-mountain and spend the night among the stars. Watch · their glorious bloom until the dawn, and get one more baptism of light. Then, with fresh heart, go down to your work, and whatever your fate, under whatever ignorance or knowledge you may afterward chance to suffer, you will remember these fine, wild views, and look back with joy to your wanderings in the blessed old Yellowstone Wonderland.

Owen Wister in Yellowstone Park. Courtesy of the Western History
Research Center, University of Wyoming

Owen Wister
1887

Owen Wister visited Yellowstone Park several times in the late 1880s and early 1890s. At the time of the visit recounted here he was several years from beginning his career as a western writer. His first western story, "Hank's Woman," was published in 1892. *The Virginian,* his best-remembered book, did not appear until 1902. By 1887, however, he had already recognized that the West held something special for him, and he was keeping a diary of his experiences. "I don't know why I wrote it all down so carefully. I had no purpose in doing so, or any suspicion that it was driving Wyoming into my blood and marrow, and fixing it there."[1] It was from these early journals that he was later to reconstruct the details of his visit.

Originally sent west for his health, Wister returned year after year, making eight visits by 1894. Yellowstone never ceased to draw him, and he called the Lower Falls in the Grand Canyon of the Yellowstone "the most beautiful thing I have ever seen."[2]

Wister's story, told in retrospect, includes incidents from several of his later visits, and these provide insight into how Wister saw the Park adjusting to increased visitation. In his remarks about the bears, the hotels and the local characters, Wister opined that his experiences of the 1880s were different, better even, than later visitors could know. This is a provocative thought—that even in the "Old Yellowstone Days," when the Park hosted only a few thousand visitors a year, some had already begun to lament the passing of the good old days. The price for accessibility and popularity was a loss of certain earlier charms. Wister had mixed emotions about that loss.

A Yellowstone Park stagecoach loaded with the kind of "dusty tourists" that Wister's party "haughtily ignored." Yellowstone Park files

n the American we speak now they would have called us a bum bunch of guys. But this was 1887. I don't know what words those dusty tourists in the stagecoaches (whom we haughtily ignored) applied to us when we met them on the road; but we heard their sight-seeing screams, we saw them stare and crane their tame citified necks after us. Had we been bears or bandits (I am sure some of them took us for the latter) they couldn't have broken into more excitement. The bears in 1887 mostly kept themselves out of sight; they had a justifiable distrust of human nature, at least the black bears and silver-tips had; they had not yet learned that shooting in the Park was forbidden. But bandits you might see—possibly; there have been hold-ups in the Park. And there is no doubt that the Park with its violent phenomena could throw some visitors into a very special state of mind; they became ready to expect anything, they were credulous to the point of distortion.

We were merely five white men and one Indian, on six horses, with eight packs, in single file, riding at a walk, perfectly harmless, and as new to the Park as were the tourists who leaped from the stagecoaches to snapshot us. Variously scattered among these United States, our cavalcade may still be enshrined in albums of photographic souvenirs. Of course we were not the sort of spectacle you are likely to see unless the circus or rodeo comes to town. At the cañon, a well-to-do youth whose acquaintance I had made the year before at Jackson in the White Mountains, recognized me, came up, shook my hand with solicitude, and said that if a hundred dollars would help . . . And they put us all safe and far at a side table at the Mammoth Springs, so as not to alarm the tourists. I find in my diary that my spurs jingled so boisterously upon the wooden floors in that hotel that I removed them, blushing the while.

My diary reveals to me that I had forgotten more than I recollected of that first camping trip; so novel, so vivid, so charged with adventure and delight and lusty vigor and laughter, that to think of it makes me homesick for the past—and the past comes to be the mental home of those who can look back a long way. Weeks before we had excited the tourists, or washed our underwear in a geyser, other experiences had marked that summer as a high spot among holidays. George and I had swum naked in the quiet edge of the whirlpool below Niagara Falls; we had ridden on the cowcatcher all through the mountain scenery of the Canadian Pacific (You couldn't do that now, the cowcatcher is shrunk to a mere shadow of its former self, but it's the best seat in the train for a view). We had seen Seattle as a ragged village of one lumpy street and frame houses, reached by steamers alone; a short railroad with a long title—Seattle Lake Shore and Eastern—carried lumber only, and soon terminated at a place called by humorists (I must suppose) Stuck Junction. The University, into which I wandered through a wooden gate swung shut by a chain weighted by a tin can filled with stones, matched its large name as imperfectly as the railroad. In an upper room I found a blackboard and a stuffed owl; and in this company sat a lone young woman reading *Les Miserables.* She asked me what the word in queer letters on a front page meant; and I could tell her, because Greek was required when I entered Harvard. Presently followed seven glorious days and nights in San Francisco, the High Jinks of the Bohemian Club among the great redwoods—but I am meandering; I must get back to the one red man and the five whites and the Park.

The red man was Tighee, a full-blooded Shoshone, speaking English incompletely, and seldom speaking at all. He was our huntsman. Two of the whites were cook, packer and horse wrangler; we were the other three; and in my pocket I carried a letter from General Sheridan, recommending me to all officers of the Army. Thirty-six hours in the stage from Rawlins on the railroad to Fort Washakie on the Shoshone Indian reservation brought us to our point for outfitting. Once outfitted, we started northwestward, and reached Wind River the second day. And here goes my diary:

"This afternoon George saw about six wild geese waddling about in a stream. He was desirous to test his horse's taste for shooting, so he fired from the saddle, thereby adding one to the number of geese. Nobody hurt." I had forgotten this.

It was the Sheridan Trail we followed up Wind River. Four years before us, General Sheridan, with President Arthur and a large escort, had taken this same route. It was nothing but a trail; solitary, wild, the Divide to our left, buttes and sagebrush to our right, and the streaming river beside us. Up the river 90 miles or so, and over a low part of the Continental Divide a bit south of Two-gwo-tee Pass, and down the Gros Ventre into Jackson's Hole, after lingering and killing bear and elk on the Divide. (It was curious to ride by, in 1893, the site of that camp two miles down the Pacific side from the summit of the Divide, that place which had been our headquarters for ten days, and find the stakes we had stretched our bear hides on in 1887 still in the ground, not one missing.)

Again my diary: "Sunday, Aug. 21. Camp 10. Head of Jackson's Lake, 7 p.m. Got here last night after 32 or 33 more miles . . . . The Tetons across the lake magnificent. I hunted all day for elk with Tighee—9 till 4—in cross timber. Awful. Tracks everywhere. Only 2 elk—which I missed like a fool. Our friend the horse thief joined us yesterday. He turned out a harmless shepherd with a nice dog, who eats your supper when we are not looking."

Of course I had forgotten about missing the elk; any thoughtful man would. But why forget the dog?

And here let me pause to lay my ineffectual but heartfelt curse upon the commercial vandals who desecrated the outlet of Jackson's Lake with an ugly dam to irrigate some desert land away off in Idaho. As that lake used to be, it narrowed in a long bend by degrees, until placidly and imperceptibly it became once more the Snake River sliding out of it below as the Snake River had flowed into it above. Serenity and solitude everywhere; antelope in herds like cattle in the open spread of sagebrush between Snake and the Tetons; these rising from the dusky blur of pines to steeps of grass, slants of rock, streaks of snow like linen drying away up, and at last the far peaks. At sunset they turned lilac, and all their angles swam together in a misty blue. Just below the outlet among scattered pines near the river, an old cabin, gaping to the weather, roof going, each year a little less of a shelter, made the silence seem more silent, the past more distant, the wilderness more present. And

69

there among the brush was a tattered legend in print: "This very fine old rum is widely known." This relic of man crashed into the quiet spell of nature not nearly so harshly as does that disgusting dam. There is more beauty in Jackson's Hole than even such a beastly thing could kill; but it has destroyed the august serenity of the lake's outlet forever; and it has defaced and degraded the shores of the lake where once the pines grew green and dark. They stand now white skeletons, drowned by the rising level of the water.

The Sheridan Trail left the lake and the river and crossed three miles of level, turned up into timber, ran through a valley of young symmetric spruce like a nursery; cold air came up to us from a stream flowing invisible in the depths of a little cañon; and by and by we descended to a flat of thick willows that brushed your knees as the trail sneaked through them till you came out on Snake again, forded it, and met discipline and law at the sergeant's cabin. Our packs were proud with trophies, heads and pelts; lucky that we needed no more of these to justify our wild and predatory aspect and prove our competence with the rifle; for here we crossed the sacred line, the southern boundary (as it was then) of the Park, and all shooting must cease; we had entered the sanctuary. The sergeant sealed our rifles. We took our way into the haunted land, the domain possessed of devils, shunned by the Indians of old.

II

Strange how readily the American mind swallows whole the promises in a political platform, and believes so little in any other statements, unless it is those of quack medicines! Vesuvius and Aetna had been heard of in the United States, long before John Colter of the Lewis and Clark expedition came back from his wild explorations and told the people of St. Louis about the hissing and rumbling and boiling phenomena he had beheld during his wanderings in the region of the upper Yellowstone. They set him down for a liar, and as a liar he passed for a matter of fifty years. During these, James Bridger got the same reputation. There's not a doubt that other white men saw the wonders of that weird country during those fifty years. Their traces have been found. But they were Hudson

70

Bay fur trappers, and because of the fur they kept the secret. Not until gold-seekers rushed into Montana and parties of them (in 1863) actually saw much more of the wonders than even Colter had, were his words substantiated—or they might have been had gold not so utterly obsessed the minds of these prospectors that they hardly noticed the geysers. It was in 1870, through the official reports of a special expedition, that the whole country knew and believed for the first time that the hissing and boiling, with many other strange things, were no myth—realized this too soon for vandal exploiters, like the builders of the Jackson Lake dam, to grab and spoil; for the Government took charge of the place and by law set it aside for the recreation of the people.

As we rode into it from the sergeant's cabin through jack pines and fallen timber, at a walk, "haunted" did not seem a far-fetched expression. Mud spots of odd hue and consistency were passed; one's horse went down into them deep and suddenly; once through the trees we saw a little pond steaming; stealthy, unusual smells prowled among the pines; after skirting Lewis Lake, the trail diverged from where the present road runs north across the Divide to the Thumb, and after going northwest along Shoshone Lake, went over the Divide at a rockier place, and so down the Fire Hole River through the trees toward the geysers; and my diary says:

"The Basin came in sight over the tree-tops below us—merely a litter of steam-jets. It might have been Lowell." Yes; the prospect suggested to my modern mind a manufacturing center in full swing. No wonder those shooting columns of steam scared the Indians of old.

The hotel at the Upper Geyser Basin was chiefly of canvas, walls and roof; and to sleep there must have made you intimately acquainted with how your neighbors were passing the night. We didn't sleep there, we camped within the trees a short ride away; but we rejoiced in the blackberry brandy we bought from the hotel clerk; it was provided to check disturbances which drinking queer water from highly chemical brooks often raised in human interiors. And we also rejoiced in a bath the soldiers had constructed in a cabin by the river. The cool river flowed into the wooden trough one way, and

71

through another spout, which you let loose with a wooden peg, astonishingly hot water poured from a little boiling hole in the formation above the cabin, and brought your bath to the temperature you desired. Both brandy and bath were a source of rejoicing; and after emerging clean and new from the latter, the spectacle of a little gray bird, like a fat catbird, skimming along the river like a bullet and suddenly dropping below the surface where it was shallow, and walking along the bottom with its tail sticking out in the air, filled me with such elation that I forgot the geysers and watched him. Where it was deeper he would plunge wholly out of sight, run along submerged, reach a shallow place, with his tail again sticking out. Then he would take it into his head to float on top and swim. I came to know him well. In 1896 I took his photograph high among the Teton range. I was washing at the creek before breakfast. He was sitting on a stone covered with snow in the middle of the creek, singing blithely: the water ouzel.

But I do not think that anybody there rejoiced quite as utterly as a boy employed in the hotel. He must have been somewhere in his 'teens; he was like the true love in "Twelfth Night" that could sing both high and low. In calm moments he would answer you in a deep bass. In excitement, into which he periodically fell, the bass cracked to a wild treble. He would be called a bell-hop to-day; in that day no bell was there, but the boy hopped a good deal. We would be sitting tilted back, reading our mail, the tourists would have ceased talking and be lounging drowsily, the boy would be at the door, motionless as a set steel trap. Suddenly the trap would spring, the boy would catapult into the door, and in his piping treble scream out:

"Beehive's a-goin' off!"

at which every tourist instantly started from his chair, and a leaping crowd gushed out of the hotel and sprinted down over the formation to catch the Beehive at it. Beehive finally quiescent, they returned slowly, sank into chairs and exhausted silence; you could have heard a mosquito. But the steel trap was again set, sprang soon, and again the silence was pierced:

"There goes Old Faithful!"

Up and out they flew once more, watched Old Faithful, and

came back to their chairs and to silence more exhausted.

Was the boy exhausted? Never. It might be the Castle, it might be the Grotto—whatever it might be, that pre-Ritz-Carlton bell-hop routed those torpid tourists from their repose to set them trooping across the formation to gape at some geyser in action, and again seek their chairs, feebler each time. Has he in his mature years ever known more joy? I doubt it.

An Englishman, who sat with me (it may have been that year or a later one) on the hotel's narrow porch, had evidently had his credulity so distorted by the freaks of nature he had seen that everything amazed him. Had I seen any gray geese? Yes, I had. But large flocks? Well, I didn't know.

"There are large flocks of them, sir. Gray geese. Large flocks. God bless my soul! I saw them yesterday."

And just about then, Old Faithful played.

"How high do you take that column of water to be?"

I told him the number of feet I had been told.

"Dear me, no. You must be wrong. I understand that ridge over there is the Continental Divide?"

I believed it was.

"Well, sir, are you aware that the Continental Divide is some six thousand-and-odd feet high, and that geyser is rising into the sky clear above that ridge?"

My diary: "Friday, August 26. Washing clothes at a small geyser. . . .We steep the garment in a quiet blue pool, deep, and shaped exactly like a great calla lily, filled to the brim and some ten feet across. Then we soap and then with a pole poke it down a spluttering crevice that foams all over it until it is ready to take out and dry."

Have you ever soaped a geyser? Then you know it is true. If you have not you may think I am taking advantage of your credulity. Science explains the matter; I need not. But to soap a geyser is very bad for it; disturbs its rhythm, dislocates its circulation, makes it play when it isn't due to play, has killed one important geyser, I have heard. Before 1887, and before the effect of soap on geysers was widely known, a Chinaman had set up a laundry above an unemployed and inconspicuous vent in the formation at the Upper Geyser Basin. Hot water boiled in the vent, steam rose from it day and night, and the

Chinaman was happy in the thought of needing neither fire nor stove nor pots, since he had taken Mother Nature into partnership, and she would wash his linen with her own hands. A few seconds after the first bundle of soaped clothes was stirred into the vent out jumped the geyser, hissing and spitting, and away blew the roof. The Chinaman escaped. That is the story; and early in my western adventures, when what they were telling me grew very remarkable, I always said, "Let me assure you that I make it a rule to believe everything I hear." But when they told me of a hole into which you could toss your soiled handkerchief and have it disappear and in a minute be thrown out washed, ironed, folded, and with a laundry mark, I drew the line. That Chinaman in 1887 had an establishment behind the hotel, where I saw the huge unnatural cucumbers he had raised with the help of hot moisture from the bowels of the earth; but his laundry was now beside, not above, Mother Nature's boiling water. By the time I had camped several times through the Park the uncertain temper of these bubbling holes had been more generally rumored. Not far from the Mud Geyser one day, I was passing a little girl who was poking one of them about the size of a soup plate with a stick, when a loud voice, which I presume was her mother's, shouted behind me:

"Louisa, quit fooling with that thing or it'll bust!"

Why will people scrawl their silly names on the scenery? Why thus disclose to thousands who will read this evidence that you are a thoughtless ass? All very well if you wrote your name, your address, and the date on the North Pole; but why do it in some wholly accessible spot where your presence represents no daring, no endurance, nothing but the necessary cash to go there? Around the base of Old Faithful (for example) are little scoops in the formation, little shallow white saucers into which the hot water has flowed and remained. Well, beneath the water on the bottom of these saucers the names of asses were to be seen, written in pencil. I doubt if this often happens nowadays; it doesn't pay. It was a deep satisfaction to talk of the vandals with Major Harris, or Captain Boutelle, or George Anderson, or Jack Pitcher, military commandants of the Park before it was turned over to the Department of the

Interior. The opinions they variously expressed about those
who defaced nature were to the point. And they devised punishment for the offenders before punishment was provided by law.
The soldiers patrolled the places where vandalism was likely
to occur. If they caught a tourist writing on the formation or
breaking it off they stopped him, compelled him to efface the
writing and give up the specimen. If they found a name after
its writer had gone on they rode after him and brought him
back to rub it out. It has happened that a man, having completed the round of the Park, has been about to take the train
when his name, discovered on the formation by a soldier and
telephoned to the Mammoth Springs, has led to its being duly
and fittingly effaced by himself, escorted back clean across
the Park. Captain Edwards (not a commandant, but on duty
there in 1891) told me this:

A soldier at the Upper Basin had reported a clergyman
as having broken off a bagful of formation. Edwards found him
seated in the stage, about to depart from the Fountain.

"You have taken no specimens of course?"

"No."

"You give me your word as a preacher of the Gospel that
you have nothing of the sort in that bag?"

"I do."

Edwards let him go.

"But why?" I asked.

"I couldn't humiliate a minister in front of the crowd."

Boutelle had a hard time to stop a commercial clique from
installing an elevator at the Lower Falls. Politics was behind
it, as usual. To put a lot of machinery by those Falls at the head
of that cañon, where the sublime merges with the exquisite,
and which alone is worth crossing the continent to see, would
have been an outrage more abominable than the dam at Jackson Lake.

"But why should your refined taste," objected a lover of the
multitude to whom I told this, "interfere with the enjoyment
of the plain people?"

"Have the plain people told you or anybody that the one
thing they lie sleepless craving for is an elevator to go up and
down by those falls the way they do in hotels?"

"They would like it if it was there."

"Of course they would. Is that a reason to vulgarize a supreme piece of wild natural beauty for all time? How are the plain people to learn better things than they know if you lower to their level everything above it?"

But who could convince a female philanthropist?

The would-be exploiter of the Park never dies. It may be a railroad, a light and power company—anything. It is a ceaseless menace, invariably supported by plausible argument and political influence. Had the language of the original act setting the Park aside in 1872 for the benefit and enjoyment of the people been so phrased as to bar exploiters as it was phrased to protect the game and fish from capture or destruction "for the purposes of merchandise and profit," safety from the despoiler would be better assured. Boutelle staved off the exploitation during his term as commandant. But George Anderson related many tales of poachers and attempted exploitation. None of them was quite so evil as the way the army canteen was abolished; but as that concerns not the Park, but the enlisted man, and a clique of distillers, and the Federated Spinsters of Uplift, it does not belong here; I doubt if it is ever told.

My diary: "Monday, August 29. West, George Norman, and I are having a hell of a time trying to get down to the bottom of the cañon with ropes. . . . I am at present sitting about nowhere, halfway . . . George is above, undecided whether he'll untie the rope from the last tree, or not."

As I read this over—it was written forty-nine years ago— West's remarks at various stages of our descent come back to me: (1) that he would give ten dollars not to have started, (2) that he would give fifty, (3) that he hadn't enough cash in the world to give what he'd like to. We got all the way down and back without hurt. It was somewhere between Inspiration Point and the Falls. Farther down there's no trouble, there's a trail to the water, where you can catch trout.

III

When we returned to the Park in 1896 many changes had occurred in it since our first sight of it in 1887. The stage road now went from the Upper Basin to the Thumb, no longer (as we had gone then) from the Lower Basin up Nez Perce Creek and over the Divide by Mary's Mountain along Trout Creek in the Hayden Valley to the Yellowstone River between the Mud Geyser and the Sulphur Mountain. There you met the road between the Cañon and the Thumb; and the hotel at the Cañon could easily have been dropped whole into the great reception room of the present hotel there. Its site was not at all the same—it was about at the junction of the road to Norris; it had but one storey, and its shape reminded you of a bowling alley or a shooting gallery.

We didn't go to the Lake in 1887. I have often seen it since, and once camped and fished at the outlet for a number of days. Not much to record of that, except the occasional wormy trout—you know them by their feeble fight, their unwholesome color, and their emaciation (I believe their state is due to a parasite peculiar to the waters of the Yellowstone Lake, I never caught any elsewhere than in the Lake or the river below it) and the reprehensible conduct of the sea gulls one day: that is unforgettable. I was catching many fish and cleaning them, and the cleanings attracted some dozen gulls. They hovered in the air, swooped on the guts I cut out of each trout, gobbled them and were ready for more. There was a young gull among them, and he was never quick enough for his parents, or his uncles, or his aunts. They always got there first, sometimes only a second ahead of him, snapped it from under his callow beak, and left him sadder and sadder. At length in pity I threw a large meal close to him; he got it, made off along the shore by himself a little way, and had it partially swallowed, when an adult relative spied it, dashed down, dragged it out of his poor little throat, and it was gone. He acted precisely like a child of three in a parlor car. He threw his head up to the sky, beat his wings, shut his eyes, opened his beak, and bawled and bawled.

Long before 1896 the hotels were larger, and the education of the bears had begun. They were now aware that man did not shoot them and they had discovered that campers carried good things to eat. One night in 1891 our sleep was murdered by sudden loud rattling and clashing of our tin plates and other hardware. We rushed out of the tent into silence and darkness.

In the morning our sugar sack lay wounded, but still with us. Macbeth while dragging at it had tumbled the hardware about him. He was not educated enough to stand that and had taken to the woods. Another bear took to a tree that week. As dusk was descending, campers found him in suspicious proximity to their provender and raised a shout. The shouting brought us and others not to the rescue, but to the highly entertaining spectacle of a tree surrounded by fascinated people waving their arms, and a bear sitting philosophically above their din. Night came on, the campers went to bed, and the bear went away. Many years have now gone since the bears discovered the treasures that are concealed in the garbage piles behind the hotels. I walked out once in the early evening at the Lake Hotel and counted twenty-one bears feasting. I saw a bear march up to a tourist and accept candy from his hand, while his wife stood at a safe distance, protesting vainly, but I think rightly. I saw the twenty-one bears suddenly cease feasting and withdraw to a short distance. Out of the trees came a true grizzly, long-snouted and ugly; and while he selected his dinner with ostentatious care and began to enjoy it, a cinnamon bear stole discreetly, as if on tip-toe, toward the meal he had left behind him. He got pretty near it, when the grizzly paused in eating and merely swung his head at him—no more than that; in a flash the cinnamon had galloped humpty-dumptily off and sat down watching. He came back presently; and the scene was re-enacted three times before I had enough of it and left; each time when the cinnamon had reached a certain point the grizzly swung his head, and this invariably sufficed. It is my notion that the cinnamon was a bit of a wag.

As our outfit rode into the Mammoth Springs, Tighee at sight of the hotel made (I think) his first remark that day:

"All same one big mountain."

What would he have said to the present hotel? It dwarfs the old one, which is where the stage-drivers and various employees live—or did on my last visit there in 1916. What would he have said about the Old Faithful Inn, which has long replaced that primitive canvas affair where the blackberry brandy and the bell-hop once flourished, and the Englishman had been amazed at the gigantic height of Old Faithful in action, and the flocks of gray geese? These birds have amazed me, but not in the same way. Dawn after dawn in camp above Crawford's shack by Jackson Lake, two of us left warm beds for the freezing air, and crawled like turtles towards a flat where the geese were feeding. We sneaked along, so close to the cold earth that the brush hid the geese from us. Every day the flock saw us first, flapped up far out of range, and departed. I am certain that they had a sentinel posted and enjoyed us as the cinnamon did the grizzly.

"To call these birds geese," I said to my companion, "is an outrage."

"Or rather," he corrected me, "the term is misapplied to foolish persons."

What do you think of that?

Upon another occasion, while at breakfast, I contemplated a pot of preserves made in Dundee, and remarked:

"Who could have expected orange marmalade to come from Scotland?"

And he explained: "They import the oranges, you know."

Eight weeks of that. It came near to aging me.

Something worse—no, almost as bad—happened during those same eight weeks. I cannot tell if Tighee would have treated us so had we taken him away from the beaten track. We never did, in the Park or out of it; for though we had hunted and fished in a virtually untenanted wilderness, the Sheridan Trail ran through it, familiar ground to Tighee; and in the Park we followed the conventional route and visited none except the regulation sights. But with Dick Washakie (our hunter on this later excursion, another full-blooded Shoshone, who spoke a little more English, having once been at the Carlisle school) we struck off the beaten trail. I was anxious to get mountain sheep after visiting the geysers and Cañon; so I turned our backs on the known and our faces to the unknown, using maps, and no longer consulting Dick Washakie about where we should go next. I wished if it were possible to get into the high country eastward, where three ranges of mountains may be said to collide and produce steep and complicated results, far from tourists, far from everybody. The third morning—we were nowhere near the high country yet—West came and told me

Dick Washakie was leaving us. So I went to him. His horse was packed. Nothing availed. Not our predicament, not the wages he would lose, nothing. He gave so many reasons—his father was old—he must cut his hay—I forget the rest—that I knew he never gave the real one.

A previous experience with another Indian, Paul La Rose, made me certain that West had guessed right: they distrusted country where they had never been. With Paul La Rose we had forded Snake below the outlet. He objected to fording it at all. At every step we took on the far side he objected more. I kept on. From the Sheridan Trail on the east side of Snake. I had stared too many days across the spread of land at the Tetons: I intended to get close to them. We should find no water, said Paul. Look at the snow up there, I said; that must melt and feed some creek at the base of those big mountains. We'd better turn back, said Paul. We'll go on, Paul. Well, you'll have dry camp to-night. Paul, we'll go on. You take the lead then. He dropped sulkily away from the head of our procession, I took his place, and in about an hour we heard the quiet sound of a waterfall and came to an opening in the narrow belt of pines to which I headed, and found the stream that flows between Leigh's and Jenny's Lake. At that camp we fished and hunted for a week in solitude unbroken. That was 1888. Since then the dude ranch has been established in that country, Snake is bridged.

But Dick Washakie's desertion changed our plans; we needed a hunter. We renounced that high country where the mountain ranges collide and journeyed back into the known; and so began my acquaintance with Yancey. Yancey was of that frontier type which is no more to be seen; the goat-bearded, shrewd-eyed, lank Uncle Sam type. He and his cabins had been there a long while. The legend ran that he was once a Confederate soldier, and had struck out from the land of the Lost Cause quite unreconstructed, and would never wear blue jeans because blue reminded him of the Union army. He was known as Uncle John by that whole country. One of his cabins was a rough wayside inn for miners traveling between Cinnabar and Cooke City at the northeastern edge of the Park. Yancey did not talk much to mere people; and I should have been mere people to him, but that I knew Boies Penrose (later Senator from Pennsylvania), who had camped more than once on Hell Roaring Creek nearby, and for whose good shooting, fishing, and horsemanship the old timer had warm respect. He unbent at the name of Penrose. What could he do for me? I told him of our hunterless plight. James Woody was due to-morrow. He would guide us to a sheep country. And then Uncle John led me across the road to—not his wine, but his whisky cellar. Handsome barrels. I came to know it well. He had some sort of fermented stuff made from oranges, which he obtained from California. Mingled properly with whisky, the like of it I have never elsewhere tasted. Woody didn't want to go. He was waiting to join Theodore Roosevelt; but on Yancey's persuasion he would go with us, leave us where sheep were to be expected, and send Donohue in his stead. I had no money for wages here; it was in a safe at Fort Washakie, where I had expected to pay Dick off. I wrote East and, just like a play, an old Cinnabar acquaintance of 1887 turned up and was glad to convey the letter to the mail. Joe Keeney was his name, and we became acquainted thus:

My diary, Sept. 1: "A lucky chance made us cared for at Cinnabar. When we were some 500 yards from it (it is merely a railroad depot, one saloon, a hotel, and some sheds) a little child passed us full tilt. As there was a ranch behind us we did not stop her, but supposed she was going there. Then far ahead we saw a man beckoning violently. When we came to him he said, 'Damn it, I signalled to head her off.' 'Well, I didn't see you. Get on my horse and go after her.' Which he did, catching her and bringing her back in his arms. It appeared he had sent her with a message to some men in a buggy who were stopping at the ranch but started away before she could get to them. 'And she'd have run till she ran them down in the mountains,' her parent added. He turned out to be the landlord, Joe Keeney, who became our friend, gave us drinks, and turned his family out of their room and made us sleep in it."

Joe Keeney rode off from Yancey's with my letter under his hat, so as not to forget it; James Woody guided us to the Hoodoos (which are pillared erosions of sandstone, and look like a church organ that has met with a railroad accident);

Donohue arrived in his place and took us to Saddle Mountain; I got a black tail, but never a sheep, nothing of interest save petrified fragments of wood and seashells lying over a region at present six or seven thousand feet above sea level; we returned to Yancey's where a letter was put in my hand. It was muddy. It was my own. Joe Keeney must have scratched his head all the way to Gardiner (to which the railroad had now been extended from Cinnabar). I was penniless. As I lay in camp in the meadows toward Baronet's bridge next morning, Yancey came by.

"What can I do for you?"

"Whisky and that orange shrub. And lend me a hundred dollars."

He did.

Back home, I sent him a flask engraved "John Yancey, from the Dead Beat," with the date.

He was at Livingston the next autumn when I stopped off with the skins of white goat I had shot in the mountains of Washington territory. Those skins increased his respect for me; we went to a show that evening, and through the night I was introduced, I think, to the whole town, male and female.

In these days, the Park bear has almost completed his education. His children for generations have known the way to the garbage pile. And all have learned the hour when the train of stages passes along the road through the various woods. Along the road they wait, begging; and the tourists place chocolate and other dainties in their paws and maws. They have gone on the dole. The one step remaining is for them to take charge of the hotels and expel the management.

Yancey is gone, Beaver Dick is gone; awake at night sometimes, the tide of streamline thought sets West, and I recall that porcupine tastes like roast pig it was a hornet's nest in that tree across the trail the pack horse trod into and the dutch oven fell off first and he bounced down through the timber with the tin plates rolling every which way the roll of bedding stuck in a bush but you get tired of trout we caught little minnows thick as mosquitoes in a net in that camp above Jenny's Lake for white bait I shouldn't want to see Brook's

Lake now any fool can go along the road in a car and find his way there just below was where we clubbed those young geese they couldn't fly yet swimming Wild River was just a creek very good tender eating so was the sand hill crane Copley Amory shot but not like the young geese the white columbine at that camp larger than the garden sort and there was a white swan out on the lake gosh how good it used to be to swab up the melted lard off your tin plate with a lump of bread and swallow it was it wild carrots or parsnips that would poison gosh those miles of flowers in the big meadow below the scoop in the rocks where Grant La Farge found we could get out and cross the Divide . . . and so on, and so on.

Rudyard Kipling, from a pencil drawing by William Strang (1859-1921).
Courtesy National Portrait Gallery, London

Rudyard Kipling
1889

Rudyard Kipling was not yet twenty-five years old when he visited Yellowstone; his literary career had barely begun. He was traveling, at a leisurely pace, from India to England and was enjoying his first look at America. He was in turn appalled and delighted by what he saw, at one moment charmed, then exasperated, by the people he encountered. Kipling had a gift for finding worth and lesson in the mundane routine of American life: "Why does the Westerner spit? It can't amuse him, and it does not interest his neighbor," or, "Late in the night we ran over a skunk—ran over it in the dark. Everything that has been said about the skunk is true. It is an Awesome Stink."[1]

In Kipling's Yellowstone the scenery, as much as it impressed him, was only a backdrop for his real subject, the people. Kipling's portrayals, whether of tourists, soldiers, or park employees, are timeless. They may seem like caricatures, but they are not, any more than the personalities he gives the geysers are inappropriate or overdrawn. A modern ranger would recognize any of Kipling's characters, for their grandchildren are the same; he would have even *more* personal acquaintances among the geysers. And, like Kipling, that ranger's tales of Yellowstone would usually involve people—for all their love of yarns about geysers, blizzards, and bears, rangers would probably all agree that there is nothing to match a good "tourist story."

Tourists on the Mammoth Hot Springs terraces, ca. 1910. Yellowstone tourists were frequently the target of Kipling's devastating wit. Yellowstone Park files

I

To-day I am in the Yellowstone Park, and I wish I were dead. The train halted at Cinnabar station, and we were decanted, a howling crowd of us, into stages, variously horsed, for the eight-mile drive to the first spectacle of the Park—a place called the Mammoth Hot Springs. "What means this eager, anxious throng?" I asked the driver. "You've struck one of Rayment's excursion parties—that's all—a crowd of Creator-condemned fools mostly. Aren't you one of 'em?" "No," I said. "May I sit up here with you, great chief and man with a golden tongue? I do not know Mister Rayment. I belong to T. Cook and Son." The other person, from the quality of the material he handles, must be the son of a sea-cook. He collects masses of Down-Easters from the New England States and elsewhere and hurls them across the Continent and into the Yellowstone Park on tour. A brake-load of Cook's Continental tourists trapezing through Paris (I've seen 'em) are angels of light compared to the Rayment trippers. It is not the ghastly vulgarity, the oozing, rampant Bessemer-steel self-sufficiency and ignorance of the men that revolts me, so much as the display of these same qualities in the women-folk. I saw a new type in the coach, and all my dreams of a better and more perfect East died away. "Are these—um—persons here any sort of persons in their own places?" I asked a shepherd who appeared to be herding them.

"Why, certainly. They include very many prominent and representative citizens from seven States of the Union, and most of them are wealthy. Yes, *sir*. Representative and prominent."

We ran across bare hills on an unmetalled road under a burning sun in front of a volley of playful repartee from the prominent citizens inside. It was the 4th of July. The horses had American flags in their head-stalls, some of the women wore flags and coloured handkerchiefs in their belts, and a young German on the box-seat with me was bewailing the loss of a box of crackers. He said he had been sent to the Continent to get his schooling and so had lost his American accent; but no Continental schooling writes German...all over a man's face and nose. He was a rabid American citizen—one of a very difficult class to deal with. As a general rule, praise unsparingly, and without discrimination. That keeps most men quiet: but some, if you fail to keep up a continuous stream of praise, proceed to revile the Old Country—Germans and Irish who are more Americans than the Americans are the chief offenders. This young American began to attack the English army. He had seen some of it on parade and he pitied the men in bearskins as "slaves." The citizen, by the way, has a contempt for his own army which exceeds anything you meet among the most illiberal classes in England. I admitted that our army was very poor, had done nothing, and had been nowhere. This exasperated him, for he expected an argument, and he trampled on the British Lion generally. Failing to move me, he vowed that I had no patriotism like his own. I said I had not, and further ventured that very few Englishmen had; which, when you come to think of it, is quite true. By the time he had proved conclusively that before the Prince of Wales came to the throne we should be a blethering republic, we struck a road that overhung a river, and my interest in "politics" was lost in admiration of the driver's skill as he sent his four big horses along that winding road. There was no room for any sort of accident—a shy or a swerve would have dropped us sixty feet into the roaring Gardner River. Some of the persons in the coach remarked that the scenery was "elegant." Wherefore, even at the risk of my own life, I did urgently desire an accident and the massacre of some of the more prominent citizens. What "elegance" lies in a thousand-foot pile of honey-coloured rock, riven into peak and battlement, the highest peak defiantly crowned by an eagle's nest, the eaglet peering into the gulf and screaming for his food, I could not for the life of me understand. But they speak a strange tongue.

En route we passed other carriages full of trippers, who had done their appointed fives days in the Park, and yelped at us fraternally as they disappeared in clouds of red dust. When we struck the Mammoth Hot Springs Hotel—a huge yellow barn— a sign-board informed us that the altitude was six thousand two hundred feet. The Park is just a howling wilderness of three thousand square miles, full of all imaginable freaks of a fiery nature. An hotel company, assisted by the Secretary of State for the Interior, appears to control it; there are hotels at all the points of interest, guide-books, stalls for the sale of minerals, and so forth, after the model of Swiss summer places.

The tourists—may their master die an evil death at the hand of a mad locomotive!—poured into that place with a joyful whoop, and, scarce washing the dust from themselves, began to celebrate the 4th of July. They called it "patriotic exercises"; elected a clergyman of their own faith as president, and, sitting on the landing of the first floor, began to make speeches and read the Declaration of Independence. The clergyman rose up and told them they were the greatest, freest, sublimest, most chivalrous, and richest people on the face of the earth, and they all said Amen. Another clergyman asserted in the words of the Declaration that all men were created equal, and equally entitled to Life, Liberty, and the pursuit of Happiness. I should like to know whether the wild and woolly West recognises this first right as freely as the grantors intended. The clergyman than bade the world note that the tourists included represen- tatives of seven of the New England States; whereat I felt deep- ly sorry for the New England States in their latter days. He opined that this running to and fro upon the earth, under the auspices of the excellent Rayment, would draw America more closely together, especially when the Westerners remembered the perils that they of the East had surmounted by rail and river. At duly appointed intervals the congregation sang "My country, 'tis of thee" to the tune of "God save the Queen" (here they did not stand up) and the "Star-Spangled Banner" (here they did), winding up the exercise with some doggrel of their own composition to the tune of "John Brown's Body," movingly setting forth the perils before alluded to. They then adjourned to the verandahs and watched fire-crackers of the feeblest, exploding one by one, for several hours.

What amazed me was the calm with which these folks gathered together and commenced to belaud their noble selves, their country, and their "institootions" and everything else that was theirs. The language was, to these bewildered ears, wild advertisement, gas, bunkum, blow, anything you please beyond the bounds of common sense. An archangel, selling town-lots on the Glassy Sea, would have blushed to the tips of his wings to describe his property in similar terms. Then they gathered round the pastor and told him his little sermon was "perfectly glorious," really grand, sublime, and so forth, and he bridled ecclesiastically. At the end a perfectly unknown man attacked me and asked me what I thought of American patriotism. I said there was nothing like it in the Old Country. By the way, always tell an American this. It soothes him.

Then said he: "Are you going to get out your letters—your letters of naturalisation?"

"Why?" I asked.

"I presoom you do business in this country, and make money out of it—and it seems to me that it would be your dooty."

"Sir," said I, sweetly, "there is a forgotten little island across the seas called England. It is not much bigger than the Yellowstone Park. In that island a man of your country could work, marry, make his fortune or twenty fortunes, and die. Throughout his career not one soul would ask him whether he were a British subject or a child of the Devil. Do you understand?"

I think he did, because he said something about "Britishers" which wasn't complimentary.

II

Shows how I entered Mazanderan of the Persians and saw Devils of every Colour, and some Troopers. Hell and the Old Lady from Chicago. The Captain and the Lieutenant.

> "That desolate land and lone
> Where the Big Horn and Yellowstone
> Roar down their mountain path."

Twice have I written this letter from end to end. Twice have I torn it up, fearing lest those across the water should say that I had gone mad on a sudden. Now we will begin for the third time quite solemnly and soberly. I have been through the Yellowstone National Park in a buggy, in the company of an adventurous old lady from Chicago and her husband, who disapproved of scenery as being "ungodly." I fancy it scared them.

We began, as you know, with the Mammoth Hot Springs. They are only a gigantic edition of those pink and white terraces not long ago destroyed by earthquake in New Zealand. At one end of the little valley in which the hotel stands the lime-laden springs that break from the pine-covered hillsides have formed a frozen cataract of white, lemon, and palest pink formation, through and over and in which water of the warmest bubbles and drips and trickles from pale-green lagoon to exquisitely fretted basin. The ground rings hollow as a kerosene-tin, and some day the Mammoth Hotel, guests and all, will sink into the caverns below and be turned into a stalactite. When I set foot on the first of the terraces, a tourist-trampled ramp of scabby grey stuff, I met a stream of iron-red hot water which ducked into a hole like a rabbit. Followed a gentle chuckle of laughter, and then a deep, exhausted sigh from nowhere in particular. Fifty feet above my head a jet of steam rose up and died out in the blue. It was worse than the boiling mountain at Myanoshita. The dirty white deposit gave place to lime whiter than snow; and I found a basin which some learned hotel-keeper has christened Cleopatra's pitcher, or Mark Antony's whisky-jug, or something equally poetical. It was made of frosted silver; it was filled with water as clear as the sky. I do not know the depth of that wonder. The eye looked down beyond grottoes and caves of beryl into an abyss that communicated directly with the central fires of earth. And the pool was in pain, so that it could not refrain from talking about it; muttering and chattering and moaning. From the lips of the lime-ledges, forty feet under water, spurts of silver bubbles would fly up and break the peace of the crystal atop. Then the whole pool would shake and grow dim, and there were noises. I removed myself only to find other pools all equally unhappy, rifts in the ground, full of running, red-hot water, slippery sheets of deposit overlaid with greenish grey hot water, and here and there pit-holes dry as a rifled tomb in India, dusty and waterless. Elsewhere the infernal waters had first boiled dead and then embalmed the pines and underwood, or the forest trees had taken heart and smothered up a blind formation with greenery, so that it was only by scraping the earth you could tell what fires had raged beneath. Yet the pines will win the battle in years to come, because Nature, who first forges all her work in her great smithies, has nearly finished this job, and is ready to temper it in the soft brown earth. The fires are dying down; the hotel is built where terraces have overflowed into flat wastes of deposit; the pines have taken possession of the high ground whence the terraces first started. Only the actual curve of the cataract stands clear, and it is guarded by soldiers who patrol it with loaded six-shooters, in order that the tourist may not bring up fence-rails and sink them in a pool, or chip the fretted tracery of the formations with a geological hammer, or, walking where the crust is too thin, foolishly cook himself.

I manoeuvred round those soldiers. They were cavalry in a very slovenly uniform, dark-blue blouse, and light-blue trousers unstrapped, cut spoon-shape over the boot; cartridge belt, revolver, peaked cap, and worsted gloves—black buttons! By the mercy of Allah I opened conversation with a spectacled Scot. He had served the Queen in the Marines and a Line regiment, and the "go-fever" being in his bones, had drifted to America, there to serve Uncle Sam. We sat on the edge of an extinct little pool, that under happier circumstances would have grown into a geyser, and began to discuss things generally. To us appeared yet another soldier. No need to ask his nationality or to be told that the troop called him "The Henglishman." A cockney was he, who had seen something of warfare in Egypt, and had taken his discharge from a Fusilier regiment not unknown to you.

"And how do things go?"

"Very much as you please," said they. "There's not half the discipline here that there is in the Queen's service—not half—nor the work either, but what there is, is rough work. Why, there's a sergeant now with a black eye that one of our men gave him.

92

They won't say anything about that, of course. Our punishments? Fines mostly, and then if you carry on too much you go to the cooler—that's the clink. Yes, sir. Horses? Oh, they're devils, these Montana horses. Bronchos mostly. We don't slick 'em up for parade—not much. And the amount of schooling that you put into one English troop-horse would be enough for a whole squadron of these creatures. You'll meet more troopers further up the Park. Go and look at their horses and their turnouts. I fancy it'll startle you. I'm wearing a made tie and a breast-pin under my blouse? Of course I am! I can wear anything I darn please. We aren't particular here. I shouldn't dare come on parade—no, nor yet fatigue duty—in this condition in the Old Country; but it don't matter here. But don't you forget, sir, that it's taught me how to trust to myself, and my shooting irons. I don't want fifty orders to move me across the Park, and catch a poacher. Yes, they poach here. Men come in with an outfit and ponies, smuggle in a gun or two, and shoot the bison. If you interfere, they shoot at you. Then you confiscate all their outfit and their ponies. We have a pound full of them now down below. There's our Captain over yonder. Speak to him if you want to know anything special. This service isn't a patch on the Old Country's service; but you look, if it was worked up it would be just a Hell of a service. But these citizens despise us, and they put us on to road-mending, and such like. 'Nough to ruin any army."

To the Captain I addressed myself after my friends had gone. They told me that a good many American officers dressed by the French army. The Captain certainly might have been mistaken for a French officer of light cavalry, and he had more than the courtesy of a Frenchman. Yes, he had read a good deal about our Indian border warfare, and had been much struck with the likeness it bore to Red Indian warfare. I had better, when I reached the next cavalry post, scattered between two big geyser basins, introduce myself to a Captain and Lieutenant. They could show me things. He himself was devoting all his time to conserving the terraces, and surreptitiously running hot water into dried-up basins that fresh pools might form. "I get very interested in that sort of thing. It's not duty, but it's what I'm put here for." And then he began to talk of his troop as I have heard his brethren in India talk. Such a troop! Built up carefully, and watched lovingly; "not a man that I'd wish to exchange, and, what's more, I believe not a man that would wish to leave on his own account. We're different, I believe, from the English. Your officers value the horses; we set store on the men. We train them more than we do the horses."

Of the American trooper I will tell you more hereafter. He is not a gentleman to be trifled with.

Next dawning, entering a buggy of fragile construction, with the old people from Chicago, I embarked on my perilous career. We ran straight up a mountain till we could see, sixty miles away, the white houses of Cook City on another mountain, and the whiplash-like trail leading thereto. The live air made me drunk. If Tom, the driver, had proposed to send the mares in a bee-line to the city, I should have assented, and so would the old lady, who chewed gum and talked about her symptoms. The tub-ended rock-dog, which is but the translated prairie-dog, broke across the road under our horses' feet, the rabbit and the chipmunk danced with fright; we heard the roar of the river, and the road went round a corner. On one side piled rock and shale, that enjoined silence for fear of a general slide-down; on the other a sheer drop, and a fool of noisy river below. Then, apparently in the middle of the road, lest any should find driving too easy, a post of rock. Nothing beyond that save the flank of a cliff. Then my stomach departed from me, as it does when you swing, for we left the dirt, which was at least some guarantee of safety, and sailed out round the curve, and up a steep incline, on a plank-road built out from the cliff. The planks were nailed at the outer edge, and did not shift or creak very much—but enough, quite enough. That was the Golden Gate. I got my stomach back again when we trotted out on to a vast upland adorned with a lake and hills. Have you ever seen an untouched land—the face of virgin Nature? It is rather a curious sight, because the hills are choked with timber that has never known an axe, and the storm has rent a way through this timber, so that a hundred thousand trees lie matted together in swathes; and, since each tree lies where it falls, you may behold trunk and branch returning to the earth

94

whence they sprang—exactly as the body of man returns—each limb making its own little grave, the grass climbing above the bark, till at last there remains only the outline of a tree upon the rank undergrowth.

Then we drove under a cliff of obsidian, which is black glass, some two hundred feet high; and the road at its foot was made of black glass that crackled. This was no great matter, because half an hour before Tom had pulled up in the woods that we might sufficiently admire a mountain who stood all by himself, shaking with laughter or rage.

The glass cliff overlooks a lake where the beavers built a dam about a mile and a half long in a zigzag line, as their necessities prompted. Then came the Government and strictly preserved them, and, as you shall learn later on, they be damn impudent beasts. The old lady had hardly explained the natural history of beavers before we climbed some hills—it really didn't matter in that climate, because we could have scaled the stars—and (this mattered very much indeed) shot down a desperate, dusty slope, brakes shrieking on the wheels, the mares clicking among unseen rocks, the dust dense as a fog, and a wall of trees on either side. "How do the heavy four-horse coaches take it, Tom?" I asked, remembering that some twenty-three souls had gone that way half an hour before. "Take it at the run!" said Tom, spitting out the dust. Of course there was a sharp curve, and a bridge at the bottom, but luckily nothing met us, and we came to a wooden shanty called an hotel, in time for a crazy tiffin served by very gorgeous hand-maids with very pink cheeks. When health fails in other and more exciting pursuits, a season as "help" in one of the Yellow-stone hotels will restore the frailest constitution.

Then by companies after tiffin we walked chattering to the uplands of Hell. They call it the Norris Geyser Basin on Earth. It was as though the tide of desolation had gone out, but would presently return, across innumerable acres of dazzling white geyser formation. There were no terraces here, but all other horrors. Not ten yards from the road a blast of steam shot up roaring every few seconds, a mud volcano spat filth to Hea streams of hot water rumbled under foot, plunged thr dead pines in steaming cataracts and died on a v

95

where green-grey, black-yellow, and pink pools roared, shouted, bubbled, or hissed as their wicked fancies prompted. By the look of the eye the place should have been frozen over. By the feel of the feet it was warm. I ventured out among the pools, carefully following tracks, but one unwary foot began to sink, a squirt of water followed, and having no desire to descend quick into Tophet I returned to the shore where the mud and the sulphur and the nameless fat ooze-vegetation of Lethe lay. But the very road rang as though built over a gulf; and besides, how was I to tell when the raving blast of steam would find its vent insufficient and blow the whole affair into Nirvana? There was a potent stench of stale eggs everywhere, and crystals of sulphur crumbled under the foot, and the glare of the sun on the white stuff was blinding. Sitting under a bank, to me appeared a young trooper—ex-Cape Mounted Rifles, this man: the real American seems to object to his army— mounted on a horse half-maddened by the noise and steam and smell. He carried only the six-shooter and cartridge-belt. On service the Springfield carbine (which is clumsy) and a cart- ridge-belt slung diagonally complete equipment. The sword is no earthly use for Border warfare and, except at state parades, is never worn. The saddle is the McClellan tree over a four-folded blanket. Sweat-leathers you must pay for your- self. And the beauty of the tree is that it necessitates first very careful girthing and a thorough knowledge of tricks with the blanket to suit the varying conditions of the horse—a broncho will bloat in a night if he can get at a bellyful—and, secondly, even more careful riding to prevent galling. Crupper and breast-band do not seem to be used—but they are casual about their accoutrements—and the bit is the single, jaw- breaking curb which American war-pictures show us. That young man was very handsome, and the grey service hat—most like the under half of a seedy terai—shaded his strong face admirably as his horse backed and shivered and sidled and plunged all over the road, and he lectured from his saddle, one foot out of the heavy-hooded stirrup, one hand on the sweating neck. "He's not used to the Park, this brute, and he's a confirmed bolter on parade; but we understand each other." *Whoosh!* went the steam-blast down the road with a dry roar. Round spun the troop-horse prepared to bolt, and, his momentum being suddenly checked, reared till I thought he would fall back on his rider. "Oh no; we've settled that little matter when I was breaking him," said Centaur. "He used to try to fall back on me. Isn't he a devil? I think you'd laugh to see the way our regiments are horsed. Sometimes a big Montana beast like mine has a thirteen-two broncho pony for neighbour, and it's annoying if you're used to better things. And oh, how you have to ride your mount! It's necessary; but I can tell you at the end of a long day's march, when you'd give all the world to ride like a sack, it isn't sweet to get extra drill for slouching. When we're turned out, we're turned out for *anything*—not a fifteen-mile trot, but for the use and behoof of all the Northern States. I've been in Arizona. A trooper there who had been in India told me that Arizona was like Afghanistan. There's nothing under Heaven there except horned toads and rattlesnakes—and Indians. Our trouble is that we only deal with Indians and they don't teach us much, and of course the citizens look down on us and all that. As a matter of fact, I suppose we're really only mounted infantry; but remember we're the best mounted infantry in the world." And the horse danced a fandango in proof.

"My faith!" said I, looking at the dusty blouse, grey hat, soiled leather accoutrements, and whalebone poise of the wearer. "If they are all like you, you are."

"Thanks, whoever you may be. Of course if we were turned into a lawn-tennis court and told to resist, say, your heavy cavalry, we'd be ridden off the face of the earth if we couldn't get away. We have neither the weight nor the drill for a charge. My horse, for instance, by English standards, is half-broken, and like all the others, he bolts when we're in line. But cavalry charge against cavalry charge doesn't happen often, and if it did, well—all our men know that up to a hundred yards they are absolutely safe behind this old thing." He patted his revolver pouch. "Absolutely safe from any shooting of yours. What man do you think would dare to use a pistol at even thirty yards, if his life depended on it? Not one of *your* men. They can't shoot. We can. You'll hear about that down the Park—further up."

97

Then he added, courteously: "Just now it seems that the English supply all the men to the American Army. That's what makes them so good perhaps." And with mutual expressions of good-will we parted—he to an outlying patrol fifteen miles away, I to my buggy and the old lady, who, regarding the horrors of the fire-holes, could only say, "Good Lord!" at thirty-second intervals. Her husband talked about "dreffel waste of steam-power," and we went on in the clear, crisp afternoon, speculating as to the formation of geysers.

"What I say," shrieked the old lady *apropos* of matters theological, "and what I say more, after having seen all that, is that the Lord has ordained a Hell for such as disbelieve his gracious works."

Nota bene.—Tom had profanely cursed the near mare for stumbling. He looked straight in front of him and said no word, but the left corner of his left eye flickered in my direction.

"And if," continued the old lady, "if we find a thing so dreffel as all that steam and sulphur allowed on the face of the earth, mustn't we believe that there is something ten-thousand times more terrible below prepared un*toe* our destruction?"

Some people have a wonderful knack of extracting comfort from things. I am ashamed to say I agreed ostentatiously with the old lady. She developed the personal view of the matter.

"*Now* I shall be able to say something to Anna Fincher about her way of living. Sha'n't I, Blake?" This to her husband.

"Yes," said he, speaking slowly after a heavy tiffin. "But the girl's a good girl;" and they fell to arguing as to whether the luckless Anna Fincher really stood in need of lectures edged with Hell fire (she went to dances, I believe), while I got out and walked in the dust alongside of Tom.

"I drive blame cur'ous kinder folk through this place," said he. "Blame cur'ous. 'Seems a pity that they should ha' come so far just to liken Norris Basin to Hell. 'Guess Chicago would ha' served 'em, speaking in comparison, jest as good."

We curved the hill and entered a forest of spruce, the path serpentining between the tree-boles, the wheels running silent on immemorial mould. There was nothing alive in the forest save ourselves. Only a river was speaking angrily somewhere to the right. For miles we drove till Tom bade us alight and look

98

at certain falls. Wherefore we stepped out of that forest and nearly fell down a cliff which guarded a tumbled river and returned demanding fresh miracles. If the water had run up-hill, we should perhaps have taken more notice of it; but 'twas only a waterfall, and I really forget whether the water was warm or cold. There is a stream here called Firehole River. It is fed by the overflow from the various geysers and basins—a warm and deadly river wherein no fish breed. I think we crossed it a few dozen times in the course of a day.

Then the sun began to sink, and there was a taste of frost about, and we went swiftly from the forest into the open, dashed across a branch of the Firehole River and found a wood shanty, even rougher than the last, at which, after a forty-mile drive, we were to dine and sleep. Half a mile from this place stood, on the banks of the Firehole River, a "beaver-lodge," and there were rumours of bears and other cheerful monsters in the woods on the hill at the back of the building.

In the cool, crisp quiet of the evening I sought that river, and found a pile of newly gnawed sticks and twigs. The beaver works with the cold-chisel, and a few clean strokes suffice to level a four-inch bole. Across the water on the far bank glimmered, with the ghastly white of peeled dead timber, the beaver-lodge—a mass of dishevelled branches. The inhabitants had dammed the stream lower down and spread it into a nice little lake. The question was would they come out for their walk before it got too dark to see. They came—blessings on their blunt muzzles, they came—as shadows come, drifting down the stream, stirring neither foot nor tail. There were three of them. One went down to investigate the state of the dam; the other two began to look for supper. There is only one thing more startling than the noiselessness of a tiger in the jungle, and that is the noiselessness of a beaver in the water. The straining ear could catch no sound whatever till they began to eat the thick green river-scudge that they call beaver-grass. I, bowed among the logs, held my breath and stared with all my eyes. They were not ten yards from me, and they would have eaten their dinner in peace so long as I had kept abso-lutely still. They were dear and desirable beasts, and I was just preparing to creep a step nearer when that wicked old

99

lady from Chicago clattered down the bank, an umbrella in her hand, shrieking: "Beavers, beavers! Young man, whurr are those beavers? Good Lord! What was that now?"

The solitary watcher might have heard a pistol shot ring through the air. I wish it had killed the old lady, but it was only the beaver giving warning of danger with the slap of his tail on the water. It was exactly like the "phink" of a pistol fired with damp powder. Then there were no more beavers— not a whisker-end. The lodge, however, was there, and a beast lower than any beaver began to throw stones at it because the old lady from Chicago said: "P'raps, if you rattle them up they'll come out. I do so want to see a beaver."

Yet it cheers me to think I have seen the beaver in his wilds. Never will I go to the Zoo. That even, after supper—'twere flattery to call it dinner—a Captain and a Subaltern of the cavalry post appeared at the hotel. These were the officers of whom the Mammoth Springs Captain had spoken. The Lieutenant had read everything that he could lay hands on about the Indian army, especially our cavalry arrangements, and was very full of a scheme for raising the riding Red Indians—it is not every noble savage that will make a trooper— into frontier levies—a sort of Khyber guard. "Only," as he said ruefully, "there is no frontier these days, and all our Indian wars are nearly over. Those beautiful beasts will die out, and nobody will ever know what splendid cavalry they can make."

The Captain told stories of Border warfare—of ambush, firing on the rear-guard, heat that split the skull better than any tomahawk, cold that wrinkled the very liver, night-stampedes of baggage-mules, raiding of cattle, and hopeless stern-chases into inhospitable hills, when the cavalry knew that they were not only being outpaced but outspied. Then he spoke of one fair charge when a tribe gave battle in the open and the troopers rode in swordless, firing right and left with their revolvers and—it was excessively uncomfy for that tribe. And I spoke of what men had told me of huntings in Burma, of hill-climbing in the Black Mountain affair, and so forth.

"Exactly!" said the Captain. "Nobody knows and nobody cares. What does it matter to the Down-Easter who Wrap-up-his-Tail was?"

"And what does the fat Briton know or care about Boh Hla-Oo?" said I. Then both together: "Depend upon it, my dear sir, the army in both Anglo-Saxon countries is a mischievously underestimated institution, and it's a pleasure to meet a man who," etc., etc. And we nodded triangularly in all good will, and swore eternal friendship. The Lieutenant made a statement which rather amazed me. He said that, on account of the scarcity of business, many American officers were to be found getting practical instruction from little troubles among the South American Republics. When the need broke out they would return. "There is so little for us to do, and the Republic has a trick of making us hedge and ditch for our pay. A little road-making on service is not a bad thing, but continuous navvying is enough to knock the heart out of any army."

I agreed, and we sat up till two in the morning swapping lies of East and West. As that glorious chief Man-afraid-of-Pink-Rats once said to the Agent on the Reservation: "'Melican officer good man. Heap good man. Drink me. Drink he. Drink me. Drink he. Drink *he.* Me blind. *Heap* good man!'"

III

Ends with the Cañon of the Yellowstone. The Maiden from New Hampshire—Larry—"Wrap-up-his-Tail"—Tom—The Old Lady from Chicago—and a few Natural Phenomena—including one Briton.

"What man would read and read the selfsame faces
And like the marbles which the windmill grinds,
Rub smooth forever with the same smooth minds,
This year retracing last year's, every year's, dull traces,
When there are woods and unmanstifled places?"
—Lowell.

Once upon a time there was a carter who brought his team and a friend into the Yellowstone Park without due thought. Presently they came upon a few of the natural beauties of the place, and that carter turned his team into his friend's team, howling: "Get back o' this, Jim. All Hell's alight under our noses." And they call the place Hell's Half-acre to this day. We, too, the old lady from Chicago, her husband, Tom, and the good little mares came to Hell's Half-acre, which is about sixty acres, and when Tom said: "Would you like to drive over it?" we said: "Certainly no, and if you do, we shall report you to the authorities." There was a plain, blistered and peeled and abominable, and it was given over to the sportings and spoutings of devils who threw mud and steam and dirt at each other with whoops and halloos and bellowing curses. The place smelt of the refuse of the Pit, and that odour mixed with the clean, wholesome aroma of the pines in our nostrils throughout the day. Be it known that the Park is laid out, like Ollendorf, in exercises of progressive difficulty. Hell's Half-acre was a prelude to ten or twelve miles of geyser formation. We passed hot streams boiling in the forest; saw whiffs of steam beyond these, and yet other whiffs breaking through the misty green hills in the far distance; we trampled on sulphur, and sniffed things much worse than any sulphur which is known to the upper world; and so came upon a park-like place where Tom suggested we should get out and play with the geysers.

Imagine mighty green fields splattered with lime beds: all the flowers of the summer growing up to the very edge of the lime. That was the first glimpse of the geyser basins. The buggy had pulled up close to a rough, broken, blistered cone of stuff between ten and twenty feet high. There was trouble in that place—moaning, splashing, gurgling, and the clank of machinery. A spurt of boiling water jumped into the air and a wash of water followed. I removed swiftly. The old lady from Chicago shrieked. "What a wicked waste!" said her husband.

102

I think they call it the Riverside Geyser. Its spout was torn and ragged like the mouth of a gun when a shell has burst there. It grumbled madly for a moment or two and then was still. I crept over the steaming lime—it was the burning marl on which Satan lay—and looked fearfully down its mouth. You should never look a gift geyser in the mouth. I beheld a horrible slippery, slimy funnel with water rising and falling ten feet at a time. Then the water rose to lip level with a rush and an infernal bubbling troubled this Devil's Bethesda before the sullen heave of the crest of a wave lapped over the edge and made me run. Mark the nature of the human soul! I had begun with awe, not to say terror. I stepped back from the flanks of the Riverside Geyser saying: "Pooh! Is that all it can do?" Yet for aught I knew the whole thing might have blown up at a minute's notice; she, he, or it being an arrangement of uncertain temper.

We drifted on up that miraculous valley. On either side of us were hills from a thousand to fifteen feet high and wooded from heel to crest. As far as the eye could range forward were columns of steam in the air, misshapen lumps of lime, most like preadamite monsters, still pools of turquoise blue, stretches of blue corn-flowers, a river that coiled on itself twenty times, boulders of strange colours, and ridges of glaring, staring white.

The old lady from Chicago poked with her parasol at the pools as though they had been alive. On one particularly innocent-looking little puddle she turned her back for a moment, and there rose behind her a twenty-foot column of water and steam. Then she shrieked and protested that "she never thought it would ha' done it," and the old man chewed his tobacco steadily, and mourned for steam-power wasted. I embraced the whitened stump of a middle-sized pine that had grown all too close to a hot pool's lip, and the whole thing turned over under my hand as a tree would do in a nightmare. From right and left came the trumpetings of elephants at play. I stepped into a pool of old dried blood rimmed with the nodding corn-flowers; the blood changed to ink even as I trod; and ink and blood were washed away in a spurt of boiling sulphurous water spat out from the lee of a bank of flowers. This sounds mad, doesn't it?

A moon-faced trooper of German extraction—never was Park so carefully controlled—came up to inform us that as yet we had not seen any of the real geysers, that they were all a mile or so up the valley, tastefully scattered round the hotel in which we would rest for the night. America is a free country, but the citizens look down on the soldier. *I* had to entertain that trooper. The old lady from Chicago would have none of him; so we loafed along together, now across half-rotten pine logs sunk in swampy ground, anon over the ringing geyser formation, then knee-deep through long grass.

"And why did you 'list?" said I.

The moon-faced one's face began to work. I thought he would have a fit, but he told me a story instead—such a nice tale of a naughty little girl who wrote love letters to two men at once. She was a simple village wife, but a wicked "Family Novelette" countess couldn't have accomplished her ends better. She drove one man nearly wild with her pretty little treachery; and the other man abandoned her and came West to forget. Moonface was that man. We rounded a low spur of hill, and came out upon a field of aching snowy lime, rolled in sheets, twisted into knots, riven with rents and diamonds and stars, stretching for more than half a mile in every direction. In this place of despair lay most of the big geysers who know when there is trouble in Krakatoa, who tell the pines when there is a cyclone on the Atlantic seaboard, and who—are exhibited to visitors under pretty and fanciful names. The first mound that I encountered belonged to a goblin splashing in his tub. I heard him kick, pull a shower-bath on his shoulders, gasp, crack his joints, and rub himself down with a towel; then he let the water out of the bath, as a thoughtful man should, and it all sank down out of sight till another goblin arrived. Yet they called this place the Lioness and the Cubs. It lies not very far from the Lion, which is a sullen, roaring beast, and they say that when it is very active the other geysers presently follow suit. After the Krakatoa eruption all the geysers went mad together, spouting, spurting, and bellowing till men feared that they would rip up the whole field. Mysterious sympathies exist among them, and when the Giantess speaks (of her more anon) they all hold their peace.

I was watching a solitary spring, when, far across the fields, stood up a plume of spun glass, iridescent and superb, against the sky. "That," said the trooper, "is Old Faithful. He goes off every sixty-five minutes to the minute, plays for five minutes, and sends up a column of water a hundred and fifty feet high. By the time you have looked at all the other geysers he will be ready to play."

So we looked and we wondered at the Beehive, whose mouth is built up exactly like a hive; at the Turban (which is not in the least like a turban); and at many, many other geysers, hot holes, and springs. Some of them rumbled, some hissed, some went off spasmodically, and others lay still in sheets of sapphire and beryl.

Would you believe that even these terrible creatures have to be guarded by the troopers to prevent the irreverent American from chipping the cones to pieces, or worse still, making the geysers sick? If you take of soft-soap a small barrelful and drop it down a geyser's mouth, that geyser will presently be forced to lay all before you and for days afterwards will be of an irritated and inconsistent stomach. When they told me the tale I was filled with sympathy. Now I wish that I had stolen soap and tried the experiment on some lonely little beast of a geyser in the woods. It sounds so probable—and so human.

Yet he would be a bold man who would administer emetics to the Giantess. She is flat-lipped, having no mouth, she looks like a pool, fifty feet long and thirty wide, and there is no ornamentation about her. At irregular intervals she speaks, and sends up a column of water over two hundred feet high to begin with; then she is angry for a day and a half—sometimes for two days. Owing to her peculiarity of going mad in the night, not many people have seen the Giantess at her finest; but the clamour of her unrest, men say, shakes the wooden hotel, and echoes like thunder among the hills. When I saw her trouble was brewing. The pool bubbled seriously, and at five-minute intervals, sank a foot or two, then rose, washed over the rim, and huge steam bubbles broke on the top. Just before an eruption the water entirely disappears from view. Whenever you see the water die down in a geyser-mouth get away as fast as you can. I saw a tiny little geyser suck in its breath in this way, and instinct made me retire while it hooted after me.

Leaving the Giantess to swear, and spit, and thresh about, we went over to Old Faithful, who by reason of his faithfulness has benches close to him whence you may comfortably watch. At the appointed hour we heard the water flying up and down the mouth with the sob of waves in a cave. Then came the preliminary gouts, then a roar and a rush, and that glittering column of diamonds rose, quivered, stood still for a minute. Then it broke, and the rest was a confused snarl of water not thirty feet high. All the young ladies—not more than twenty—in the tourist band remarked that it was "elegant," and betook themselves to writing their names in the bottoms of shallow pools. Nature fixes the insult indelibly, and the after-years will learn that "Hattie," "Sadie," "Mamie," "Sophie," and so forth, have taken out their hairpins and scrawled in the face of Old Faithful.

The congregation returned to the hotel to put down their impressions in diaries and note-books which they wrote up ostentatiously in the verandahs. It was a sweltering hot day, albeit we stood somewhat higher than the summit of Jakko, and I left that raw pine-creaking caravanserai for the cool shade of a clump of pines between whose trunks glimmered tents. A batch of troopers came down the road, and flung themselves across country into their rough lines. Verily the 'Melican cavalry-man *can* ride, though he keeps his accoutrements pig- and his horse cow-fashion.

I was free of that camp in five minutes—free to play with the heavy lumpy carbines, to have the saddles stripped, and punch the horses knowingly in the ribs. One of the men had been in the fight with "Wrap-up-his-Tail" before alluded to, and he told me how that great chief, his horse's tail tied up in red calico, swaggered in front of the United States cavalry, challenging all to single combat. But he was slain, and a few of his tribe with him. "There's no use in an Indian, anyway," concluded my friend.

A couple of cowboys—real cowboys, not the Buffalo Bill article—jingled through the camp amid a shower of mild chaff. They were on their way to Cook City, I fancy, and I know that they never washed. But they were picturesque ruffians with long spurs, hooded stirrups, slouch hats, fur weather-cloths over their knees, and pistol-butts easy to hand.

"The cowboy's goin' under before long," said my friend. "Soon as the country's settled up he'll have to go. But he's mighty useful now. What should we do without the cowboy?"

"As how?" said I, and the camp laughed.

"He has the money. We have the know-how. He comes in in winter to play poker at the military posts. *We* play poker— a few. When he's lost his money we make him drunk and let him go. Sometimes we get the wrong man." And he told a tale of an innocent cowboy who turned up, cleaned out, at a post, and played poker for thirty-six hours. But it was the post that was cleaned out when that long-haired Caucasian Ah Sin removed himself, heavy with everybody's pay, and declining the proffered liquor. "Naow," said the historian, "I don't play with no cowboy unless he's a little bit drunk first."

Ere I departed I gathered from more than one man that significant fact that *up to one hundred yards* he felt absolutely secure behind his revolver.

"In England, I understand," quoth a limber youth from the South, "in England a man aren't allowed to play with no firearms. He's got to be taught all that when he enlists. I didn't want much teaching how to shoot straight 'fore I served Uncle Sam. And that's just where it is. But you was talking about your Horse Guards now?"

I explained briefly some peculiarities of equipment connected with our crackest crack cavalry. I grieve to say the camp roared.

"Take 'em over swampy ground. Let 'em run around a bit an' work the starch out of 'em, an' then, Almighty, if we wouldn't plug 'em at ease I'd eat their horses!"

"But suppose they engaged in the open?" said I.

"Engage the Hades. Not if there was a tree-trunk within twenty miles they *couldn't* engage in the open!"

Gentlemen, the officers, have you ever seriously considered the existence on earth of a cavalry who by preference would fight in timber? The evident sincerity of the proposition made me think hard as I moved over to the hotel and joined a party

107

exploration, which, diving into the woods, unearthed a pit pool of burningest water fringed with jet black sand—all the ground near by being pure white. But miracles pall when they arrive at the rate of twenty a day. A flaming dragonfly flew over the pool, reeled and dropped on the water, dying without a quiver of his gorgeous wings, and the pool said nothing whatever, but sent its thin steam wreaths up to the burning sky. I prefer pools that talk.

There was a maiden—a very trim maiden—who had just stepped out of one of Mr. James's novels. She owned a delightful mother and an equally delightful father, a heavy-eyed, slow-voiced man of finance. The parents thought that their daughter wanted change. She lived in New Hampshire. Accordingly, she had dragged them up to Alaska, to the Yosemite Valley, and was now returning leisurely *via* the Yellowstone just in time for the tail-end of the summer season at Saratoga. We had met once or twice before in the Park, and I had been amazed and amused at her critical commendation of the wonders that she saw. From that very resolute little mouth I received a lecture on American literature, the nature and inwardness of Washington society, the precise value of Cable's works as compared with "Uncle Remus" Harris, and a few other things that had nothing whatever to do with geysers, but were altogether delightful. Now an English maiden who had stumbled on a dust-grimed, lime-washed, sun-peeled, collarless wanderer come from and going to goodness knows where, would, her mother inciting her and her father brandishing his umbrella, have regarded him as a dissolute adventurer. Not so those delightful people from New Hampshire. They were good enough to treat me—it sounds almost incredible—as a human being, possibly respectable, probably not in immediate need of financial assistance. Papa talked pleasantly and to the point. The little maiden strove valiantly with the accent of her birth and that of her reading, and mamma smiled benignly in the background.

Balance this with a story of a young English idiot I met knocking about inside his high collars, attended by a valet. He condescended to tell me that "you can't be too careful who you talk to in these parts," and stalked on, fearing, I suppose, every minute for his social chastity. Now that man was a barbarian (I took occasion to tell him so), for he comported himself after the manner of the head-hunters of Assam, who are at perpetual feud one with another.

You will understand that these foolish tales are introduced in order to cover the fact that this pen cannot describe the glories of the Upper Geyser Basin. The evening I spent under the lee of the Castle Geyser sitting on a log with some troopers and watching a baronial keep forty feet high spouting hot water. If the Castle went off first, they said the Giantess would be quiet, and *vice versa;* and then they told tales till the moon got up and a party of campers in the woods gave us all something to eat.

Next morning Tom drove us on, promising new wonders. He pulled up after a few miles at a clump of brushwood where an army was drowning. I could hear the sick gasps and thumps of the men going under, but when I broke through the brushwood the hosts had fled, and there were only pools of pink, black, and white lime, thick as turbid honey. They shot up a pat of mud every minute or two, choking in the effort. It was an uncanny sight. Do you wonder that in the old days the Indians were careful to avoid the Yellowstone? Geysers are permissible, but mud is terrifying. The old lady from Chicago took a piece of it, and in half an hour it died into limedust and blew away between her fingers. All *maya*—illusion—you see! Then we clinked over the sulphur in crystals; there was a waterfall of boiling water; and a road across a level park hotly contested by the beavers. Every winter they build their dam and flood the low-lying land; every summer that dam is torn up by the Government, and for half a mile you must plough axle-deep in water, the willows brushing into the buggy, and little waterways branching off right and left. The road is the main stream—just like the Bolan line in flood. If you turn up a byway, there is no more of you, and the beavers work your buggy into next year's dam.

Then came soft, turfy forest that deadened the wheels, and two troopers—on detachment duty—came noiselessly behind us. One was the Wrap-up-his-Tail man, and we talked merrily while the half-broken horses bucked about among the trees till we came to a mighty hill all strewn with moss agates, and everybody had to get out and pant in that thin air. But how intoxicating it was! The old lady from Chicago clucked like an emancipated hen as she scuttled about the road cramming pieces of rock into her reticule. She sent me fifty yards down the hill to pick up a piece of broken bottle which she insisted was moss agate. "I've some o' that at home an' they shine. You go get it, young feller."

As we climbed the long path the road grew viler and viler till it became without disguise the bed of a torrent; and just when things were at their rockiest we emerged into a little sapphire lake—but never sapphire was so blue—called Mary's Lake; and that between eight and nine thousand feet above the sea. Then came grass downs, all on a vehement slope, so that the buggy following the new-made road ran on to the two off-wheels mostly, till we dipped head-first into a ford, climbed up a cliff, raced along a down, dipped again and pulled up dishevelled at "Larry's" for lunch and an hour's rest. Only "Larry" could have managed that school-feast tent on the lonely hillside. Need I say that he was an Irishman? His supplies were at their lowest ebb, but Larry enveloped us all in the golden glamour of his speech ere we had descended, and the tent with the rude trestle-table became a palace, the rough fare, delicacies of Delmonico, and we, the abashed recipients of Larry's imperial bounty. It was only later that I discovered I had paid eight shillings for tinned beef, biscuits, and beer, but on the other hand Larry had said: "Will I go out an' kill a buffalo?" And I felt that for me and for me alone would he have done it. Everybody else felt that way. Good luck go with Larry!

"An' now you'll all go an' wash your pocket-handkerchiefs in that beautiful hot spring round the corner," said he. "There's soap an' a washboard ready, an' 'tis not every day that ye can get hot water for nothing." He waved us large-handedly to the open downs while he put the tent to rights. There was no sense of fatigue in the body or distance in the air. Hill and dale rode on the eye-ball. I could have clutched the far-off snowy peaks by putting out my hand. Never was such maddening air. Why we should have washed pocket-handkerchiefs

Larry alone knows. It appeared to be a sort of religious rite. In a little valley overhung with gay painted rocks ran a stream of velvet brown and pink. It was hot—hotter than the hand could bear—and it coloured the boulders in its course.

There was the maiden from New Hampshire, the old lady from Chicago, papa, mamma, the woman who chewed gum, and all the rest of them, gravely bending over a washboard and soap. Mysterious virtues lay in that queer stream. It turned the linen white as driven snow in five minutes, and then we lay on the grass and laughed with sheer bliss of being alive. This have I known once in Japan, once on the banks of the Columbia, what time the salmon came in and "California" howled, and once again in the Yellowstone by the light of the eyes of the maiden from New Hampshire. Four little pools lay at my elbow: one was of black water (tepid), one clear water (cold), one clear water (hot), one red water (boiling); my newly washed handkerchief covered them all. We marvelled as children marvel.

"This evening we shall do the grand cañon of the Yellowstone?" said the maiden.

"Together?" said I; and she said yes.

The sun was sinking when we heard the roar of falling waters and came to a broad river along whose banks we ran. And then—oh, then! I might at a pinch describe the infernal regions, but not the other place. Be it known to you that the Yellowstone River has occasion to run through a gorge about eight miles long. To get to the bottom of the gorge it makes two leaps, one of about one hundred and twenty and the other of three hundred feet. I investigated the upper or lesser fall, which is close to the hotel. Up to that time nothing particular happens to the Yellowstone, its banks being only rocky, rather steep, and plentifully adorned with pines. At the falls it comes round a corner, green, solid, ribbed with a little foam and not more than thirty yards wide. Then it goes over still green and rather more solid than before. After a minute or two you, sitting upon a rock directly above the drop, begin to understand that something has occurred; that the river has jumped a huge distance between solid cliff walls and what looks like the gentle froth of ripples lapping the sides of the gorge below

111

is really the outcome of great waves. And the river yells aloud; but the cliffs do not allow the yells to escape.

That inspection began with curiosity and finished in terror, for it seemed that the whole world was sliding in chrysolite from under my feel. I followed with the others round the corner to arrive at the brink of the cañon: we had to climb up a nearly perpendicular ascent to begin with, for the ground rises more than the river drops. Stately pine woods fringe either lip of the gorge, which is—the Gorge of the Yellowstone.

All I can say is that without warning or preparation I looked into a gulf seventeen hundred feet deep with eagles and fish-hawks circling far below. And the sides of that gulf were one wild welter of colour—crimson, emerald, cobalt, ochre, amber, honey splashed with port-wine, snow-white, vermilion, lemon, and silver-grey, in wide washes. The sides did not fall sheer, but were graven by time and water and air into monstrous heads of kings, dead chiefs, men and women of the old time. So far below that no sound of its strife could reach us, the Yellowstone River ran—a finger-wide strip of jade-green. The sunlight took those wondrous walls and gave fresh hues to those that nature had already laid there. Once I saw the dawn break over a lake in Rajputana and the sun set over the Oodey Sagar amid a circle of Holman Hunt hills. This time I was watching both performances going on below me—upside down, you understand—and the colours were real! The cañon was burning like Troy town; but it would burn for ever, and, thank goodness, neither pen nor brush could ever portray its splendours adequately. The Academy would reject the picture for a chromolithograph. The public would scoff at the letter-press for "Daily Telegraphese." "I will leave this thing alone," said I; " 'tis my peculiar property. Nobody else shall share it with me." Evening crept through the pines that shadowed us, but the full glory of the day flamed in that cañon as we went out very cautiously to a jutting piece of rock—blood-red or pink it was—that overhung the deepest deeps of all. Now I know what it is to sit enthroned amid the clouds of sunset. Giddiness took away all sensation of touch or form; but the sense of blinding colour remained. When I reached the main-land again I had sworn that I had been floating. The maid from

112

New Hampshire said no word for a very long time. She then quoted poetry, which was perhaps the best thing she could have done.

"And to think that this show-place has been going on all these days an' none of we ever saw it," said the old lady from Chicago, with an acid glance at her husband.

"No, only the Injuns," said he, unmoved; and the maiden and I laughed long. Inspiration is fleeting, beauty is vain, and the power of the mind for wonder limited. Though the shining hosts themselves had risen choiring from the bottom of the gorge, they would not have prevented her papa and one baser than he from rolling stones down those stupendous rainbow-washed slides. Seventeen hundred feet of steepest pitch and rather more than seventeen hundred colours for log or boulder to whirl through! So we heaved things and saw them gather way and bound from white rock to red or yellow, dragging behind them torrents of colour, till the noise of their descent ceased and they bounded a hundred yards clear at the last into the Yellowstone.

"I've been down there," said Tom that evening. "It's easy to get down if you're careful—just sit and slide; but getting up is worse. An' I found, down below there, two rocks just marked with a pictur of the cañon. I wouldn't sell those rocks not for fifteen dollars."

And papa and I crawled down to the Yellowstone—just above the first little fall—to wet a line for good luck. The round moon came up and turned the cliffs and pines into silver; a two-pound trout came up also, and we slew him among the rocks, nearly tumbling into that wild river.

Then out and away to Livingston once more. The maiden from New Hampshire disappeared; papa and mamma with her disappeared. Disappeared, too, the old lady from Chicago and all the rest, while I thought of all that I had *not* seen—the forest of petrified trees with amethyst crystals in their black hearts; the great Yellowstone Lake where you catch your trout alive in one spring and drop him into another to boil him; and most of all of that mysterious Hoodoo region where all the devils not employed in the geysers live and kill the wandering bear and elk, so that the scared hunter finds in Death Gulch piled carcasses of the dead whom no man has smitten. Hoodoo-land with the overhead noises, the bird and beast and devil-rocks, the mazes and the bottomless pits—all these things I missed. On the return road Yankee Jim and Diana of the Crossways gave me kindly greeting as the train paused an instant before their door, and at Livingston whom should I see but Tom the driver?

"I've done with the Yellowstone and decided to clear out East somewheres," said he. "Your talkin' about movin' round so gay an' careless made me kinder restless; I'm movin' out."

Lord forgie us for our responsibilities one to another!

"And your partner?" said I.

"Here's him," said Tom, introducing a gawky youth with a bundle; and I saw those two young men turn their faces to the East.

"Larry's Lunch Station" at Norris Geyser Basin. Yellowstone Park files

Remington in his New Rochelle, New York studio three years after his trip to Yellowstone. Courtesy of the private collection of Dr. Harold McCracken

Frederic Remington
1893

Frederic Remington was a well-established illustrator when he visited Yellowstone. Eastern publishers respected him as a leading authority on western life. His trip in 1893 was one of many on which he sought picturesque subjects to interpret with pen and brush. In earlier years he had accompanied the cavalry on expeditions against the Sioux and the Apache, so it was only logical he join the troops in "policing the Yellowstone."

Remington's account says little about the Park's famous attractions. He joined Captain George Anderson and his men on patrol of the Park's undeveloped backcountry. Poachers were a constant threat before the turn of the century, so frequent patrols were necessary.[1]

In 1893 Remington weighed "about 240 pounds" and was described as a "huge rollicking animal."[2] With this portrait of Remington in mind, the story of his trip becomes exceptionally vivid. He must have been quite a sight, keeping pace with the soldiers along the tight and winding wilderness trails.

More came of Remington's visit than the article that follows. While in the Park he first met a man with whom he had already been professionally connected. The encounter occurred at Norris Geyser Basin and the man was Owen Wister. Wister (chapter 4) wrote in his journal about the meeting:

Lunch at the Norris Basin where who should I meet but Frederic Remington! When I told him my name he said he had many things to say (he had just illustrated "Balaam and Pedro"). I had many things to say to him and we dined together at Mammoth Hot Springs.[3]

The chance meeting of the two western colorists was the beginning of a long friendship. Though the warmth of the relationship would wax and wane, enthusiasts of western lore would profit much by it.[4]

aptain Anderson—he's the superintendent, you know—started to-day for the south of the Park; some trouble, I believe, down there. A scout thought the buffalo were being disturbed," said Lieutenant Lindsley to me at the Mammoth Hot Springs Hotel, near the entrance to the Park.

"That's unfortunate. Can I overtake him?"

"It's nearly four o'clock, but as I am going down to our camp at the Lower Geyser Basin, we can start now, and by travelling at night we can catch him before he pulls out in the morning, I think," said the yellow-leg.

So putting our belongings into a double surrey, we started hot-foot through the Wonderland, leaving a band of Dakota chicken-shooters standing on the steps waving their adieux. It verified all my predictions—men who shoot chickens belong in a stage-coach—they are a "scrubby wagon outfit," as the cowboys say.

Posed on the trestled road, I looked back at the Golden Gate Pass. It is one of those marvellous vistas of mountain scenery utterly beyond the pen or brush of any man. Paint cannot touch it, and words are wasted. War, storms at sea, and mountain scenery are bigger than any expression little man has ever developed. Mr. Thomas Moran made a famous stagger at this pass in his painting; and great as is the painting, when I contemplated the pass itself I marvelled at the courage of the man who dared the deed. But as the stages of the Park Company run over this road, every tourist sees its grandeur, and bangs away with his kodak.

As we pulled up in front of the tents of the rest camp, one of those mountain thunder-storms set in, and it was as though the New York fire department had concentrated its nozzles on the earth. The place was presided over by a classic Irishman by the name of Larry, who speedily got a roaring-hot beefsteak and some coffee on the table, and then busied himself conducting growing pools of rain-water out of the tent. Larry is justly famous on the road for his *bonhomie* and Celtic wit.

At an early hour we arose and departed—the pale moon shining through the mist of the valley, while around us rose the ghostly pines. We cowered under our great-coats, chilled through, and saddened at remembrances of the warm blankets which we had been compelled to roll out of at this unseemly

119

hour. At 7:30 we broke into one of those beautiful natural parks, the Lower Geyser Basin, with the sun shining on the river and the grass, and spotting the row of tents belonging to D troop, Sixth United States Cavalry. Captain Scott met us at the door, a bluff old trooper in field rig and a welcoming smile. After breakfast a soldier brought up Pat Rooney. Pat was a horse from the ground up; he came from Missouri, but he was a true Irishman nevertheless, as one could tell from his ragged hips, long drooping quarters, and a liberal show of white in his eye, which seemed to say to me, "Aisy, now, and I'm a dray-horse; but spare the brad, or I'll put ye on yer back in the bloomin' dust, I will." The saddle was put on, and I waited, until presently along came the superintendent, with his scout Burgess, three soldiers, and nine pack-mules with their creaking *aparejos,* and their general air of malicious mischief.

Pointing to a range of formidable-looking hills, the captain said, "We will pull in about there," and we mounted and trotted off down the road. What a man really needs when he does the back stretches of the Yellowstone Park is a boat and a balloon, but cavalrymen ride horses in deference to traditions. My mount, Pat, was as big as a stable door, and as light as a puff-ball on his pins. As Mr. Buckram said, "The 'eight of a 'oss 'as nothing to do with 'is size," but Patrick was a horse a man needed two legs for. Besides, he had a mouth like a bull, as does every other animal that wears that impossible bit which Uncle Sam gives his cavalry. We got along swimmingly, and, indeed, I feel considerable gratitude to Pat for the two or three thousand times he saved my life on the trip by his agility and sureness of foot.

Burgess, the scout, was a fine little piece of a man, who had served the government with credit for over thirty years. He had breasted the high divide in a dozen places, had Apache bullets whistle around and through him, and withal was modest about it. He was a quiet person, with his instinct of locality as well developed as an Indian's, and contented with life, since he only wanted one thing—a war. I think he travelled by scent, since it would have been simple enough to have gone over easier places; but Burgess despised ease, and where the fallen timber was thickest and the slopes 60°, there you would find Burgess and his tight little pony picking along.

Both Captains Anderson and Scott have a pronounced weakness for geysers, and were always stopping at every little steamjet to examine it. I suppose they feel a personal responsibility in having them go regularly; one can almost imagine a telegram to "turn on more steam." They rode recklessly over the geyser formation, to my discomfort, because it is very thin and hazardous, and to break through is to be boiled. One instinctively objects to that form of cooking. The most gorgeous colors are observed in this geyser formation; in fact, I have never seen nature so generous in this respect elsewhere. I wondered that the pack-mules did not walk into the sissing holes, but I suspect a mule is a bit of a geologist in his way, and as most of them have been in the government service for thirty or forty years, they have learned how to conserve their well-being. There is a tradition that one was considerably overdone once in a geyserhole, so they may have taken warning. Who can understand a mule? The packer leads the old bell-mare off to a feedingground, and the whole bunch of mules go racing after her, and chains wouldn't hold them. The old bell-mare takes across a nasty chasm or a dirty slough-hole, and as the tinkle of the little cow-bell is losing itself in the timber beyond, one after another they put their ears forward and follow on.

We passed up a cleft in the hills, and were swallowed up in the pine and cedar forest. Presently the cleft ended, and nothing but good honest climbing was in front. There began my first experience in riding over the fallen timber, which obstructs all the northwestern Rocky Mountains. Once up in British Columbia I did it, but had trails, and I childishly imagined that there must also be trails wherever men wanted to go. Crisscross and all about lay the great peeled logs, and travel was slow, toilsome, and with anything but horses trained to it would have been impossible.

A good horse or mule, once accustomed, makes little of it, but on the steep down grades the situation is complicated by fallen logs, which it is necessary to "bucket" over, and then stop dead on an incline of 50°, with a couple of miles of tumble if he fails. The timber grew thicker, and when Burgess would get us in a hopeless sort of place, Captain A. would sing out to Captain S., "Burgess is on the trail now"; and when it was fairly good going, "Now he is off." But nothing could rattle Mr. Burgess, and he continued calmly on his journey, the destination of which, it seemed, could be nothing short of the moon. Finally we found ourselves seemingly so inextricably tangled up that even Burgess had to scratch his head. One mule was hung up hopelessly, while the rest crowded around us into the *chevaux-de-frise* of logs, and merrily wound through the labyrinth the old Sixth Cavalry "gag," "Here's where we trot."

To complete the effect of this passage it began to rain, and shortly to pelt us with hailstones, so we stopped under some trees to let it pass, and two people who should know better dismounted and got their saddles wet, while another, more wise in his generation, sat tight, and was rewarded later for his display of intelligence. By-and-by, wet and tired of fallen timber, we came into the Little Firehole Basin, and found buffalo signs in abundance. We were in great hopes of seeing some of these animals, but I may as well add that only one was seen on the trip, though there was fresh spoor, and they were undoubtedly about. We found no pony tracks either, which was more to the soldiers' liking, since they are intrusted with the protection of the Park against poachers.

In this way squads are sent over the Park, and instructed not to follow the regular trails, but to go to the most unfrequented places, so that they may at any time happen on a malicious person, and perhaps be able to do as one scout did—photograph the miscreant with his own camera.

After a good day's march we made camp by a little lake, and picketed our horses, while the mules ran loose around the bell-mare. Our appetites had been sharpened by a nine hours' fast, when a soldier called us to the "commissaries" which were spread out on a pack canvas. It was the usual military "grub," and no hungry man can find fault with that.

"Any man who can't eat bacon can't fight," as Captain Scott said; so if any reader wants to be a soldier he must have a mania for bacon, it seems. "This is the stuff that makes soldiers brave," he added, as the coffee-pot came around, and we fell to, and left a dreary waste of empty tins for the cook to pick up. We lighted our pipes after the banquet on the grass, and walked down to the shore of the beautiful pond, which seemed so strangely situated up there on the very crest of the Continental Divide. There are only three seasons in these altitudes, which the boys divide into July, August, and Winter, and the nights are always chilly. An inch or two of snow may fall even in mid-summer. In winter the snow covers the ground to a great depth, as we can tell by the trees. Nothing grows but rather stunted fir and pine and a little grass of the most hardy variety. The rounds of the Park are then made by mounting the cavalry on the *ski*, or Norwegian snow-shoe, and with its aid men travel the desolate snow-clad wilderness from one "shack" to another. Small squads of three or four men are quartered in these remote recesses of the savage mountains, and remain for eight months on a stretch. The camps are provisioned for the arctic siege, and what is stranger yet is that soldiers rather like it, and freely apply for this detached service. There is little of the "pomp and vanity" in this soldiering, and it shows good spirit on the part of the enlisted men. They are dressed in fur caps, California blanket coats, leggings, and moccasins—a strange uniform for a cavalryman, and also quite a commentary on what are commonly called the vicissitudes of the service.

In the early morning our tent was pulled down, and our bedding packed off almost before we had disentangled ourselves from its sheltering folds. The well-trained troopers went about their task of breaking camp with method and address. Burgess and a young soldier pulled a reluctant strawberry-blond mule out of the line of pack-animals, and throwing a blind over his face, proceeded to lay the blanket and adjust the *aparejo*. With a heave the *cincha* is hauled tight, and the load laid on, while the expert throws the "diamond hitch," and the mule and pack are integral parts. This packing of nine mules was accomplished with great rapidity, and laying our saddles carefully, we mounted and followed the scouts off down the trail in single file on a toilsome march which would probably not end until three or four o'clock in the afternoon. We wound around the spurs of hills, and then across a marsh, with its yielding treacherous bottom, where the horses floundered, and one mule went down and made the mud and water fly in his struggles, while my apprehensions rose to fever-pitch as I recognized my grip-sack on his load, and not likely to be benefited by the operation. At the head-waters of these rivers—and it may be said that this little purling brook is really the source of the Missouri itself, although not so described—there is abundance of soggy marsh, which makes travel extremely difficult. In one place Captain Anderson's horse went belly-deep on a concealed quag made by a stream coming out of the side of the hill, and rolling back, fell heavily on the captain, and for a time it was rather a question whether the horse would get out or not; but by dint of exertion he regained firm ground. When a big strong horse gets into a slough the dorsal action is terrific, and it is often necessary to dismount quickly to aid him out. We crossed the great divide of the continent at a place where the slope was astonishingly steep and the fallen timber thickly strewn. It was as thoroughly experimental travelling as I have ever seen, unless possibly over a lava-rock formation which I essayed last winter on the western slope of the Sierra Madre, in Chihuahua; and yet there is a fascination about being balanced on those balloonlike heights, where a misstep means the end of horse and rider. I was glad enough, though, when we struck the park-like levels of the Pitchstone plateau as the scene of our further progression. If one has never travelled horseback over the Rocky Mountains there is a new and distinct sensation before him quite as vigorous as his first six-barred gate, or his first yacht-race with the quarter-rail awash.

All through the Park were seen hundreds of wild-geese, so tame that they would hardly fly from us. It was a great temtation to shoot, but the doughty captain said he would run me off the reservation at a turkey-trot if I did shoot, and since I believed him I could restrain myself. The streams and marshes were full of beaver-dams, and the little mud-and-stick houses rose from the pools, while here and there we saw the purl of the quiet water as they glided about. This part is exactly as primitive as when the lonely trapper Coulter made his famous journey through it, and one cannot but wonder what must have been his astonishment at the unnatural steaming and boiling of the geysers, which made the Park known from his descriptions as "Coulter's Hell."

From the breast of the mountains overlooking the great Shoshone Lake there opened up the most tremendous sight as the waters stretched away in their blue placidity to the timbered hills. The way down to the shores was the steepest place I have ever seen horses and mules attempt. In one place, where the two steep sides of the cañon dipped together, it was cut by a nasty seam some six feet deep, which we had to "bucket over" and maintain a footing on the other side. After finding myself safely over, I watched the shower of pack-mules come sliding down and take the jump. One mule was so far overbalanced that for a moment I thought he would lose his centre of gravity, which had been in his front feet, but he sprang across to the opposite slope and was safe. Horses trained to this work do marvels, and old Pat was a "topper" at the business. I gave him his head, and he justified my trust by negotiating all the details without a miss. On a sandy "siding" he spread his feet and slid with an avalanche of detached hillside. Old Pat's ears stuck out in front in an anxious way, as if to say, "If we hit anything solid, I'll stop"; while from behind came the cheery voice of Captain Scott, "Here's where we trot."

On the shores of the Shoshone we camped, and walked over to the famous Union Geysers, which began to boil and sputter, apparently for our especial benefit. In a few minutes two jets of boiling water shot a hundred feet in air, and came down in rain on the other side, while a rainbow formed across it. The roar of the great geysers was awe-inspiring; it was like the exhaust of a thousand locomotives, and Mr. Burgess nudged me and remarked, "Hell's right under here."

Near the geysers, hidden away in a depression, we found a pool of water of a beautiful and curious green, while not twenty feet from it was one of a sulphur yellow. There was a big elk track in the soft mud leading into it, but no counter track coming out. There had been a woodland tragedy there.

The utility of a geyser-hole is not its least attraction to a traveller who has a day's accumulation of dust and sweat on him. I found one near the camp which ran into a little mountain stream, and made a tepid bath, of which I availed myself, and got a cup of hot water, by the aid of which I "policed my face," as the soldiers call shaving.

125

The next day we encountered one of those great spongy mountain meadows, which we were forced to skirt on the rocky timber-strewn hillsides, until finally we ventured into it. We curved and zigzagged through its treacherous mazes, fording and recrossing the stream in search of solid ground. Burgess's little gray pony put his foot forward in a gingerly way, and when satisifed, plunged in and floundered through. The pony had a positive genius for morasses. We followed him into the mud, or plunged off the steep sides into the roaring river, and, to my intense satisfaction, at last struck a good pony trail. "Now Burgess is off the trail!" we cried, whereat the modest little scout grinned cheerfully. From here on it was "fair and easy," until we came to the regular stage-road, to travel on which it seemed to us a luxury.

This expedition is typical of the manner of policing the Park, and it is generally monotonous, toilsome, and uneventful work; and the usefulness of such a *chevauchée* is that it leaves the track of the cavalry horse-shoe in the most remote parts of the preserve, where the poacher or interloper can see it, and become apprehensive in consequence of the dangers which attend his operations. That an old trapper might work quietly there for a long time I do not doubt, if he only visited his line of traps in the early morning or late evening and was careful of his trail, but such damage as he could do would be trivial. Two regiments could not entirely prevent poaching in the mountain wastes of the great reservation, but two troops are successful enough at the task. It is a great game-preserve and breeding-ground, and, if not disturbed, must always give an overflow into Montana, Wyoming, and Idaho, which will make big game shooting there for years to come. The unreasoning antipathy or malicious disregard of the American pioneer for game-laws and game-preservation is somewhat excusable, but the lines of the pioneer are now cast in new places, and his days of lawless *abandon* are done. The regulation for the punishment of Park offenders is inadequate, and should be made more severe. The Park is also full of beasts of prey, the bear being very numerous. A fine grizzly was trapped by some of the superintendent's men and shipped to the Smithsonian Institution while I was there. Near the Fountain Hotel one

126

evening a young army surgeon and myself walked up to within one hundred and fifty yards of a big grizzly, who was not disposed to run off. Being unarmed, we concluded that our point of view was close enough, and as the bear seemed to feel the same way about it, we parted.

Americans have a national treasure in the Yellowstone Park, and they should guard it jealously. Nature has made her wildest patterns here, has brought the boiling waters from her greatest depths to the peaks which bear eternal snow, and set her masterpiece with pools like jewels. Let us respect her moods, and let the beasts she nurtures in her bosom live, and when the man from Oshkosh writes his name with a blue pencil on her sacred face, let him spend six months where the scenery is circumscribed and entirely artificial.

Emerson Hough, driving a covered wagon. From the frontispiece to
The Covered Wagon (New York: Grosset & Dunlap, 1922)

Emerson Hough
1894

In the 1880s and 1890s one of the most potent forces shaping public opinion on conservation was the weekly newspaper *Forest and Stream.* Under the dynamic editorship of George Bird Grinnell, the newspaper took a special interest in Yellowstone's problems, especially those involving wildlife. Hoping to learn more about the wildlife in the Park, Grinnell dispatched Emerson Hough (pronounced "Huff") to the scene, where Hough was just in time to document the capture of the notorious poacher, Ed Howell.

Up to the time of Howell's capture there were only feeble regulations protecting park animals. Poachers could not be fined or jailed, only expelled from the Park. All concerned agreed that what was needed was strong federal legislation to back up the regulations. The publication of the Howell incident, as reported by Hough, was the final catalyst. The resultant public outcry brought a quick response from Congress. Howell was captured on March 12, and the National Park Protective Act became law on May 7.[1]

Emerson Hough was always a vigorous defender of the national parks. He later became a well-known writer of western fiction and outdoor adventure. His support and service was so great that in 1918, after the National Park Service had replaced the army in Yellowstone, he was offered the job of superintendent. By nature outspoken and unpredictable, Hough was ill-suited to such a political post. Luckily, a park service official persuaded him to decline the offer, and Yellowstone was spared what surely would have been a haphazard administration.[2]

The first of the two Hough articles included here was written after the National Park Protective Act was well on its way to passage. The second, recounting the joys and rigors of ski-touring, appeared later in the same series of Hough feature articles on Yellowstone.

The *Forest and Stream* Winter Exploration of the National Park, now just concluded, was a venture singularly fortunate in every respect. Not devoid of certain hardships, and not free from possible dangers of more sorts than one, it was nevertheless brought to a close without illness or accident to any of the party other than of the most trifling sort, and from start till close progressed with the smoothness and merriness, if not the ease and indolence, of a summer picnic. Fortune was kind and raised no obstacle too hard to be overcome. Thus the *Forest and Stream* may truthfully say that it is the first and only paper ever to send a staff man through the Park during the winter time. Schwatka once made 20 miles of this 200 miles winter journey in the interests of the New York *World*. Overcome by his failing, and perhaps discouraged, or disgusted by the amount of unavoidable hard work ahead (for the only possible method of locomotion in those high, rough and snowy regions, is by one's own snowshoes), he allowed his undertaking to come to failure, and returned to his starting point with no results to show. Since him one or two other men have gone to the gates of the Park, looked at the big snow land, and resolved that it was easier to write about the winter scenery of the Park from imagination than from fact. The only man ever successful enough to go through the Park in winter, and intelligent enough to make a newspaper account of it, was Mr. Elwood Hofer, whose stories of his two trips, simply and clearly written, appeared in *Forest and Stream*. Mr. F. Jay Haynes, the able St. Paul photographer who has done so much to make public the beauties of this wonderful region, went through the Park after the collapse of the Schwatka expedition, but never wrote of it, so far as I know. His party was lost on Mount Washburn for three days, and they all came near perishing.

The effort to learn of the winter life of this tremendous and fateful region had hitherto been, let us then say, severely frowned upon by Fortune. When *Forest and Stream*, always rather a favorite of the fickle dame, made the attempt, Fortune relented, and all became possible and plain. To this end, *Forest and Stream* was in the first place highly fortunate in having Mr. Hofer as a member of the party. His guidance, counsel and assistance constituted the difference between success

131

and failure. Without him the trip could not have been what it was, and it is to him, very much more than to its staff representative, that this journal is indebted for the success of the undertaking just completed. What were the obstacles to be overcome before success could be reached, and what were the trials, the pleasures and the incidents of the winter journey through the mountains of the Great Divide, it will be a pleasure to recount later, but the first duty is to tell at first hand, and exclusively, the story of the capture of the man Howell, who was caught in the act of butchering the Park buffalo. This story, taken from *Forest and Stream's* first and exclusive report, has appeared in various forms and in some inaccurate shapes, in the press all over the country, and such is the importance of the occurrence that it has driven Congress to an action delayed years too long. This is undoubtedly the most dramatic and sensational, as well as the most notable and important piece of sporting news which has come up in recent years. It is news which will be historic. The Howell buffalo slaughter marks an epoch, the turning point, let us hope, in the long course of a cruelly wasteful indifference on the part of the United States Government in the matter of one of the most valuable possessions of the American people—a possession growing yearly less and less through this indifference, and which as it has grown less has increased in value, since when once destroyed, it can never by any human power be replaced. Had not *Forest and Stream* been born under a lucky as well as an energetic star, it could not have enjoyed the journalistic good fortune of having a man right on the spot—and a most remote and improbable spot, too—to obtain exclusively for its service this most important piece of news. Now that we are out of the mountains, the first opportunity offers to give the story in accurate detail.

Capt. Anderson, the best superintendent the Park ever had, and one good enough to be retained there for an indefinite term, is a thoroughly fearless and energetic man, and disposed to do all that lies in his power, with the limited means at his disposal, to protect the vast tract of land which lies within the bounds of this peerless reserve of wilderness. How difficult a task this would be with many times the troops and many times the money no one can understand perfectly who does not know the Park, and who does not know what winter in the mountains means. A part of the system of the winter patrol consists of little details, usually a sergeant and two privates, stationed at remote parts of the Park. Thus there is a sub-station of this sort on the east part of the Park, on Soda Butte Creek; one on the west side, known as Riverside Station; one twenty miles from the Post, at Norris Basin; one forty miles from the Post, and near the center of the Park, at the Lower Geyser or Firehole Basin; and one at the extreme south end of the Park, known as Shoshone Station. Communication with these stations can only be made by snowshoe parties. The winter's supplies are carried into the stations by pack trains early in the fall, before the impassable snows have covered all the trails. Under such conditions news would naturally travel slowly. Yet we knew of Howell's capture, some seventy miles from the Post, the very day he was caught in the act of his crime, the news coming by telephone from the Lake Hotel. The Park Association keeps attendants at three hotels within the upper Park, not counting the one at the Mammoth Hot Springs (Fort Yellowstone), on the entrance side of the Park. There is one attendant, or winter keeper, at the Cañon Hotel, one at the Lower Basin Hotel, and a man and his wife at the Lake Hotel. All these hotels are connected by telephone with the Post, elsewise the loneliness and danger of the life of the solitary men thus cut off from the world through the long months of an almost Arctic winter would deter even such hardy spirits from undertaking a service worse than that on a light-house tower at sea. When the telephone line fails to work, as naturally in such a wintry country of mountain and forest it often does, old Snowshoe Peter, the line-man, is sent over the line to locate and repair the damage. He is the only man allowed to go alone through the Park in winter, and he has had some rough and dangerous experiences. When the soldiers of the out-stations wish to report to the Post they go to the nearest hotel, perhaps fifteen, perhaps forty miles, and telephone in, if the telephone happens to be running. Burgess, the only scout whom the munificent U.S. Government provides for the protection of this peerless domain—a domain which any other power on earth would guard jealously as a treasure vault—takes scouts from time to time in all directions through the Park, traveling of course on snowshoes. He may sleep and get supplies at some one of the out-stations, or of one of the three winter keepers of the hotels, or it may be that he will hole up for the night in one of the several shacks built at certain secluded portions of the mountains for this purpose; still again, he may have to lie out in the snow, perhaps without a blanket, perhaps with nothing to eat. This all depends on circumstances. A poacher's trail has to be followed hard and sharp, with no let-up and no returning. It was fortunate for Burgess that he caught his man within a day's march of the Lake Hotel. He brought him in to the Lake Hotel that day and at once telephoned to Capt. Anderson, commanding officer at the Post, Mammoth Hot Springs. The message was received at the Post about 9:30 in the evening, Monday, March 12. This was just before Hofer and I started into the Park from the Post, and as I was the guest of Capt. Anderson at the Post, of course I learned the news at once, and at once put it on the wire for *Forest and Stream,* which had the information within twelve hours of the capture, which latter had occurred 2,000 miles away in the roughest part of the Rocky Mountains, and four days' journey from the nearest telegraph station, by the only possible means of travel. The next day *Forest and Stream* was represented in Washington. Within thirty days the Lacey bill had passed the House. To *Forest and Stream,* born under a lucky, as well as an energetic, star, will be due more than to any other one agency the thanks of the public for the ultimate preservation of one of the public's most valuable heritages. No other paper has made the fight for the Park that this one has, and it deserves the utmost success which now seems certain to attend it. When the people finally come to look upon an undivided National Park, and one tenanted once more with some specimens at least of its grand though vanishing animals, they may thank all the men who nobly and fearlessly worked for that and so carried out the actual will of the people—they may thank all these friends of intelligence and justice and public honor and decency; but they will have only one newspaper on earth to thank, and that one will be *Forest and Stream.*

When Capt. Anderson came in after hearing the news of this capture, he was positively jubilant through every inch of his 6 ft. 2 in. of muscular and military humanity. He couldn't sit still, he was so glad.

It was some time before I could get from him the story of the plans leading up to the capture.

"I knew that Howell had been in the Park," said he, "and had an idea that he was over on Pelican Valley somewhere. I sent Burgess in after sign once before this winter, but Burgess broke his axe and had to come back. I told Burgess this time that I wanted him to come back this time with a whole axe and a whole prisoner, if possible. I knew that Howell had come out of the Park for supplies, not long ago. He came out from Cooke City, where he hails from. He brought out his toboggan, and took back a load of supplies with him. I knew he must leave a broad trail, and knew that if Burgess could strike his trail and follow it into the Park, not out of it, he could catch him sure. Burgess has been scouting on Pelican, as directed. He says, by telephone, that he found the trail early in the morning, and followed it till he found a *cache* of six buffalo heads, hung up in the trees. Then he followed the trail a good distance till he found Howell's tepee. While he was there he heard shots. Approaching carefully, he saw Howell skinning out the head of one of five buffalo he had just killed. Making a careful run over the 400 yds. of open ground between Howell and the timber he got the drop on Howell. Burgess had with him no one whatever but one private, Troike, who was not armed and who stayed back in the timber. Capt. Scott, Lieut. Forsyth and party were at the Lake Hotel not engaged in this scout at all. I must say that Burgess's action has been in every way highly courageous and commendable, and I shall be glad to commend him publicly. He made his arrest alone and brought his man into the Lake Hotel to report for orders. I have ordered him to bring his prisoner on in to the Post as quickly as he can. To-morrow I start out a party on snowshoes from here to bring in all the heads and hides of the buffalo killed. I have ordered Howell's tepee and supplies burned. His arms and outfit will be confiscated, and I will sock him just as far and as deep into the guard-house as I know how when I get him, and he won't get fat there, either. That is all I can do under the regulations. I shall report to the Secretary of the Interior and in due course the Secretary of the Interior will order me to set the prisoner free. There is no law governing this Park except the military regulations. There is no punishment that can be inflicted on this low-down fellow. I only wish I had the making of the law and the devising of the penalty. I'll bet you this man wouldn't soon go at large if I did have."

This was Capt. Anderson's story of the plan that led to the capture, a plan evidently wise and well laid. But how wide a difference there remained between this plan and the actual arrest I never knew until I had seen the Park itself in all its immensity, its impenetrableness, its forbidding and awful regions of forest, precipice and crag, until I had traversed with weary feet some of those endless miles of bottomless snow; until I learned how utterly small, lonely and insignificant a man looks and feels in the midst of solitude so vast, so boundless, so tremendous and so appalling. Then I knew that the man Howell was in his brutal and misguided way a hero in self-reliance, and that Scout Burgess was also in courage and self-reliance a hero, nothing less. Howell, or any like him, I hate instinctively, but I salute him. To Burgess the salute will come more easily from any man who knows the facts and knows what a winter trail in the Rockies means.

Burgess's story of the capture, as told by himself, simply and modestly, would make it out no great thing. This story I heard from Burgess himself at Norris Station, which point he had reached, coming out with his prisoner at the same time the *Forest and Stream* party made it, going in. We spent the night there together.

"I expect probably I was pretty lucky," said he. "Everything seemed to work in my favor. I got out early and hit the trail not long after daybreak. After I had found the *cache* of heads and the tepee, over on Astringent Creek, in the Pelican Valley, I heard the shooting, six shots. The six shots killed five buffalo. Howell made his killing out in a little valley, and when I saw

him he was about 400 yds. away from the cover of the timber.
I knew I had to cross that open space before I could get him
sure. I had no rifle, but only an army revolver, .38 cal., the
new model. You know a revolver isn't lawfully able to hold
the drop on a man as far as a rifle. I wouldn't have needed to
get so close with a rifle before ordering him to throw up his
hands. Howell's rifle was leaning against a dead buffalo, about
15 ft. away from him. His hat was sort of flapped down over
his eyes, and his head was toward me. He was leaning over,
skinning on the head of one of the buffalo. His dog, though
I didn't know it at first, was curled up under the hindleg of the
dead buffalo. The wind was so the dog didn't smell me, or
that would have settled it. That was lucky, wasn't it? Howell
was going to kill the dog, after I took him, because the dog
didn't bark at me and warn him. I wouldn't let him kill it.
That's the dog outside—a bob-tailed, curly, sort of half-
shepherd. It can get along on a snowshoe trail the best of any
dog I ever saw, and it had followed Howell all through the
journey, and was his only companion.

"I thought I could maybe get across without Howell seeing
or hearing me, for the wind was blowing very hard. So I started
over from cover, going as fast as I could travel. Right square
across the way I found a ditch about 10 ft. wide, and you know
how hard it is to make a jump with snowshoes on level ground.
I had to try it, anyhow, and some way I got over. I ran up to
within 15 ft. of Howell, between him and his gun, before I
called to him to throw up his hands, and that was the first
he knew of any one but him being anywhere in that country.
He kind of stopped and stood stupid like, and I told him to
drop his knife. He did that and then I called Troike, and we got
ready to come on over to the hotel. It was so late by the time
I found Howell—you see he was a long way from his *cache* or
his camp—that we didn't stop to open up any of the dead
buffalo. We tried to bring in some heads, but we found we
couldn't, so we left them.

"Howell had been in camp over there for a long time. I
only found 6 heads cached. He wrapped them up in gunny
sacks and then hoisted them up in trees so the wolves couldn't
get at them. He had a block and tackle, so that he could run a

heavy head up into a tree without much trouble. He was fixed for business.

"Howell said to me that if he had seen me first, I 'would never have taken him.' I asked him why, and he said, 'Oh, I'd have got on my shoes and run away, of course.' I don't know what he meant by that, but he'd have been in bad shape if he had, unless he had taken his rifle along, for I had already found his camp."

Howell was, we found, a most picturesquely ragged, dirty and unkempt looking citizen. His beard had been scissored off. His hair hung low on his neck, curling up like a drake's tail. His eye was blue, his complexion florid. In height he seemed about 5 ft. 10 in. His shoulders were broad, but sloping. His neck stooped forward. His carriage was slouchy, loose-jointed and stooping, but he seemed a powerful fellow. Thick, protruding lips and large teeth completed the unfavorable cast of an exterior by no means prepossessing. He was dressed in outer covering of dirty, greasy overalls and jumper. He had no shoes, and he had only a thin and worthless pair of socks. He wrapped his feet and legs up in gunny sacking, and put his feet when snowshoeing into a pair of meal sacks he had nailed on to the middle of his snowshoes. The whole bundle he tied with thongs. His snowshoes (*skis*) were a curiosity. They were 12 ft. long, narrow, made of pine (or spruce), Howell himself being the builder of them. The front of one had its curve supplemented by a bit of board, wired on. All sorts of curves existed in the bottoms of the shoes. He had them heavily covered with resin to keep the snow from sticking to them. To cap the climax he had broken one shoe while in the Park— a mishap often very serious indeed, as one must have two shoes to walk with, and elsewise cannot walk at all. With the ready resources of a perfect woodsman, Howell took his axe, went to a fir tree, hewed out a three-cornered splice about 5 ft. long, nailed it fast to the bottom of his broken shoe, picked out some pieces of resin, coated the shoe well with it, and went on his way as well as ever. He said he could travel as far in a day on those shoes as any man in the party could with any other pair, and I presume that is true. Moreover, Howell pulled a toboggan behind him all the way from Cooke City with a load of 180 lbs.

None of us could pull a toboggan behind *skis,* and we would not wear web shoes. Howell's toboggan was 10 ft. long, and had wide runners, like *skis.* He said a flat-bottomed Canadian model toboggan was no good, as it pulled too heavy.

At the Cañon Hotel Howell ate twenty-four pancakes for breakfast. He seemed to enjoy the square meals of captivity. At Norris he was always last at table. He was very chipper and gay, and willing to talk to the officers, Capt. Scott and Lieut. Forsyth, on about any subject that came up, though the officers mostly looked over his head while he was talking. He was apparently little concerned about his capture, saying, as I have already mentioned, that he stood to make $2,000, and could only lose $26.75. He knew he could not be punished, and was only anxious lest he should be detained until after the spring sheep shearing in Arizona. He is an expert sheep shearer, sometimes making $10 and $15 a day. He has money always, and was not driven to poaching by want or hunger.

"Yes," Howell said, in reply to our questions, "I'm going to take a little walk up to the Post, but I don't think I'll be there long. About my plans? Well, I haven't arranged any plans yet for the future. I may go back into the Park again, later on, and I may not. No, I will not say who it was contracted to buy the heads of me. I had been camped over on Pelican since September. It was pretty rough, of course. If you don't think it's a hard trail from Cooke City to Pelican Valley, you just try pulling a toboggan over Specimen Ridge.

"If I'd seen Burgess first, he'd never had arrested me. I'd have got away from him. It was so windy and stormy, I never heard him till he got right up against me and hollered for me to put up my hands. He was sort of blowin', and was nervous like. I see I was subjec' to the drop, so I let go my knife and came along."

Larsen, one of the men Capt. Anderson sent in with our party, talked with Howell later in the day, when most of us were away, and Howell was freer with him. Larsen says that Howell told him he had been camped in the Park since September and that at first he had a partner, a man by name of Noble, but that they had a falling out and he run Noble out of the camp. Noble went out at the south end of the Park, not going back to Cooke City. Howell said there was nothing in being arrested, they couldn't do anything to him. Howell also said he "supposed them—fellers would want to get a photograph of him in the morning, but he wasn't going to let them." (Nevertheless, one had already been made of him and in the morning I got a shot at him without his consent, while he was stooping over and fastening his shoes. He tried to spoil the picture by rising and coming toward me. He had told me previously that he would not have any pictures taken and I was sorry to be so impolite about it. Capt. Scott, who had at that time gone on down the trail with Lieut. Forsyth, had said to me that if I preferred it he would give me the privilege of photographing Howell standing on his head. On the whole I believe that would have been nicer, if Howell could have been induced to look pleasant. The negative is not yet developed, but my impression is that he wasn't looking so very pleasant over the surreptitious *Forest and Stream* shot at him.)

The party sent out by Capt. Anderson to bring in the heads and hides of the slaughtered buffalo consisted of Sergt. Kellner and two privates. They passed the in-coming party between Norris and the Cañon, and pushed on down at a hot pace to the remote corner of the Park where the butchery took place. The second day out from Norris found them near the spot, but it was two days later before the animals were found, a fall of snow having covered them up, and Troike, the private who was with Burgess at the capture, having lost his head entirely about the localities. If it was so hard a spot to locate among the interminable mountains, even after a man had been there but a few days before, how much harder must it be to locate a poacher whose whereabouts is not known at all, but who has the whole great winter wilderness of the Park to surround him and his doings? The only wonder is that arrests can be made at all, where the country is so great and so difficult, and the special police of the Park limited to just one scout. The need of more scouts is too apparent to require comment.

When finally the butcher's work had been found again, it was learned that most of the robes and some of the heads were ruined for lack of proper care, Howell having been stopped too early in his work for this. The scene of the butchery was a sad sight enough for any one who has the least thoughtfulness in his make-up. The great animals lay slaughtered in the deep snow in which they had wallowed and plunged in their efforts to escape. To run up to them on the *skis* and to shoot them down one by one—only six shots to kill the five buffalo outright—was the work of the clumsiest butcher. In the snow these animals are absolutely defenseless. Howell could have killed more of the band, if there had been more, and he would not have stopped had there been more to kill. As I shall show later, I think he had killed far more than the eleven head discovered. I think his partner, Noble, left the camp of his own free will, and took out a load of heads at the lower end of the Park. I do not consider it impossible, from news I had after I left the Park, that Howell took out some heads with him when he went out to Cooke City after supplies. As *Forest and Stream* has said, he was killing cows and calves in this last killing. He had been in camp since September, and he was killing cows and calves. I cannot evade the belief that he would kill any buffalo he could get to. He could prepare and hang up a good many in five months.

The heads and the available robes were brought first into the Lake Hotel. Capt. Anderson sent another party over the long trail from the Post, and the spoils were finally received at the Post the first week of April. The capture of Howell had required two trips by Burgess, aggregating 250 to 300 miles, one trip by the first detail of three men, nearly 150 miles, and a final trip of a little less than the latter distance by the detail who carried in the plunder. The heavy heads and hides all had to be packed in on the backs of the men. Every foot of the way had to be traveled on snowshoes. No men but just these hardy ones could do this work. For a time the Park had more men in it than it ever had in winter time before. The stir was all over this miserable specimen of humanity who was heartless enough to kill all he could of the few remaining buffalo left alive on earth do-day. These bare words convey no idea whatever of the hardships and dangers incurred in the winter patrolling of the Park. To criticize the military, or to say that Capt. Anderson should have caught the fellow sooner, is to display a total ignorance of the conditions, and to be absurdly

141

unjust as well as ignorant. For such ignorance and injustice we must look first in just the quarters where it should not exist. Nowhere can we find an ignorance and indifference on this subject equal to that which has so long existed in the halls of Congress. It is time the change should come.

Let us remember, then, first, that Howell was killing cows and yearlings; second, that the few buffalo left are helpless when pursued in the snow; third, that for a crime of this sort Congress *provides no penalty!* As this is written the word comes that the Secretary of the Interior has ordered the release of Howell from custody. On this old basis he can now go into the Park again and kill more buffalo, and have another hunt made after him by the U.S. Army. Let us hope that by the time this shall be in print there will have been a new basis established by Congress, so that such villainy as this shall obtain a punishment, prompt, adequate and just. Kill a Government mule and try what the U.S. Government will do to you. Yet a mule can be replaced. A buffalo cannot be replaced. This is the end. But kill a Government buffalo, and what does the U.S. Government do? Nothing! Absolutely nothing! This is the old basis. Let us sincerely hope that the new basis will come soon and that it will be widely different. Gentlemen of Congress can surely only need to have the matter called to their attention, and this has been done in the various measures this year submitted by the members who know the facts.

In a later article I shall advance the facts on which I base the firm belief that half the buffalo of the Park have been killed, and that not over 200 now remain alive. The Howell killing above described has been only a part of the total. Nineteen head were killed by Indians southeast of the Park last fall. Seven heads were offered to a Bozeman taxidermist for sale (not of these 19 heads) from Idaho this winter. We found what we supposed to be 6 or 8 dead buffalo in the Hayden Valley. I have track of several other heads that have this year appeared in Montana towns. No one knows how many heads have been quietly bought by Sheard or another Livingston taxidermist. Certain it is, that the traceable total of buffalo killed this year in the Park is alarmingly, appallingly large. There are not very many more now left to kill.

The method of work in scouting for a poacher is simple if arduous. The scout must know the country and the course likely to be taken in the Park. He circles to cut the trail of the man he wants. The snowshoes leave a deep, plain trail on any ordinary snow (except crust), and this will remain for weeks. Even if covered by later snow, the trail will eventually become evident again. The trail packs the snow under the line of the shoes. In the spring when the snow begins to melt, a snowshoe trail will not melt and sink, but will show up in the form of a little ridge above the level of the snow, the other snow melting and sinking below it. The poacher can get in in no possible way but on snowshoes, and he cannot travel without leaving a trail which for the rest of the season will endure, though part of the time it may be invisible under new snow.

I can not leave this description of the Howell capture without mentioning one fact showing the indomitable grit of the scout Burgess who brought Howell in. We were all looking out over the trail when Burgess and his prisoner came in sight. Howell, of course, was ahead, but we noticed that Burgess was limping very badly. How he was able to travel at all was a wonder. When he got in by the fire he said nothing, but took off his heavy socks, showing a foot on which the great toe was inflamed and swollen to four times its natural size. The whole limb above was swollen and sore, with red streaks of inflammation extending up to the thigh. How the man ever walked I can not see. I noticed that Burgess had lost the two toes next to the great toe, and that the scar of the cut ran half way through the great toe. He told me, quietly, that the Crow Indians did that for him. They made him put his foot on a log, and amused themselves by cutting off his toes, taking two off clean and nearly cutting off the great toe. Since then the circulation had been bad in that member, and he had frozen it more than once. It had been frozen again on this trip, and was now in bad shape. Yet in spite of this injury, which would have disabled most men, Burgess passed the evening calmly playing whist, and the following morning again took the trail, making the twenty miles to the Post before evening, and delivering his prisoner safely. The post surgeon, Dr. Gandy, after making examination of Burgess's foot, at once amputated the great toe, thus finishing what the Indians had less skillfully begun some years before.

––––––––

In the first article of this series I made the statement that no one except Mr. Hofer had ever made the winter trip through the Park and written a newspaper account of it. Mr. F. Jay Haynes, the well-known St. Paul photographer, who has long been official artist for the Northern Pacific Road, and who has done so much to set forth the beauties of the Park in a pictorial way, calls my attention to the fact that the story of his winter trip, mentioned in my first article, was written by himself and printed in a Chicago paper, *Harper's Weekly,* also running full illustrations of it. This I did not know. Mr. Haynes adds that he took with him four men of the unfortunate Schwatka party, and made the circuit of the Park, regardless of trails, and passing over Mount Washburn, as I stated. It was on Mount Washburn that this party were caught in a storm and nearly lost their lives. On that trip Mr. Haynes did not try for any game pictures, but this winter, as I stated last week, he went into the Park again after game pictures. We met the Haynes party at the Cañon very pleasantly as I shall later mention.

The Schwatka expedition, as is well known, was sent out by the New York *World,* and it made a magnificent and elaborate failure. Schwatka had along enough baggage to supply an army. He had long-tailed reindeer coats, plenty of furs, sledges, etc., and in short was equipped for an Arctic trip. Unfortunately one cannot sit in a sledge and be hauled by dog team through the Park, because the snow is too soft and it snows too much and too often there, and the hills are too high and steep. The only way to go is by one's own muscle. Schwatka got his big party and all his lumber into the Park just 20 miles, and then he found he had enough of it, and so marched down the hill

144

again. The *Forest and Stream* outfit, the first and only staff party ever to go through the Park in winter, did not wear long-tailed reindeer coats. They only wore short-tailed canvas jumpers, but they got there just the same.

One thing is certain; at the time of which I was writing last week I had never been through the Park in my life. Another thing is certain, and that is that I had never been on *skis* in my life. Therefore two startling experiences in my life remained ahead of me.

Billy took' me out where the snow was about 11 ft. deep and introduced me to a pair of long, low, rakish, piratical-looking things, with a good deal of overhang forward, and—as I learned later—without any centerboard, keel or moral principles anywhere in their composition. You can talk about a vessel being a "thing of life," and "instinct with soul," and all that sort of thing, but she isn't in it with the lowly *ski,* not for a minute. A pair of *skis* make about the liveliest way of locomotion, if you give them a chance, of anything on earth, and if you don't think they are alive and full of soul, you just try them and see. They've got a howling, malignant devil in every inch of their slippery surface, and the combination will give the most blasé and motionless man on earth a thrill a minute for a good many minutes. You don't want to go in for the sport of *ski*-running, not on a hill, anyhow, unless you want to be carried away with it.

Billy started me in on a hill, and I was quite carried away. They dug me out of the snow, somewhere down along the hill, I don't remember just where, and we started back up again, to do it some more. It was then I discovered that a *ski* is like a poor rule, because it won't work both ways. My *skis* had been bright and cheerful when it was suggested that we go down hill, but when we talked about going up hill they became ugly and rebellious. They would slip backward down hill, but wouldn't go up. I began to reflect then that I had 200 miles ahead of me, every inch of it up hill according to accounts, and I was thoughtful.

"Slap your shoe down hard on the snow," said Billy, "and take up all the weight you can with your pole. Lean forward, and don't lift your heel."

Billy is one of the best snowshoers in the mountains, having learned the art while carrying mail for years among the mining camps of Colorado. Moreover, Billy is a philosopher, and disposed to find out the theory of things. Moreover again, he is not disposed to excessive and untimely mirth on serious occasions like this. So, watching Billy, and trying to get close enough to smash him one with the pole if he got too gay, I found I could get up the hill a little by using industry and economy. Pretty soon we came to a steep pitch, which even Billy could not walk up.

"Here we have to 'corduroy,'" said he. "You turn your shoes at right angles to the trail, this way, instead of straight along the way you want to go. That keeps you from slipping down hill. Now you side-step up the hill, lifting the shoe clear from the snow each time. You go right on up sideways, this way, one foot after the other, getting up only a foot or so at a step. Keep your shoes at an angle up the hill, just all the angle they will stand till they begin to slide back down hill, and keep on side-stepping up the hill, on the angle, this way, till you get to where the natural bite of the shoe on the snow will allow you to go straight ahead again. That's 'corduroying.' Some folks use clogs, which they buckle around their shoes. With a clog, you slap your foot down and go straight ahead. You can tie a knotted piece of gunny sack under the shoe and get the same result. It's a nuisance, though, to be stopping putting such things on and off all the time, at every little hill. You will find that the best *ski* runners don't use any clogs, but depend on 'corduroying' up the steep places. Some fellows can go straight up steep hills, without 'corduroying,' where other fellows can't. It's a good deal in the way the shoe is planted down on the snow, and left clinging there without breaking the hold till the other foot has been shoved forward. But any fellow has to corduroy sometimes, and his average in speed per hour depends on his ability to do it fast, without slipping, and without losing anything out of his uphill angle. You want to keep your shoes at just all the uphill angle they'll stand, and you want to side-step as high up hill as you can each time, and you don't want to lose any time slipping back, or plunging or crossing your shoes, or trying to recover yourself.

146

Just take it easy and regular. Time in snowshoeing is made by keeping at it steadily, not stopping and not taking spurts."

All this was plain enough, and I got up the hill. I found, however, that the awkwardness of using the unskilled muscles required in the work, brought on a profuse perspiration, though it was a cold winter day. It was at the top of this hill that I found out I wasn't going to be able to wear my nice new fireman's shirt, because it was too warm.

"You'll find muscles in you you never dreamed of," said Billy, "and you'll find you don't need much clothing while you're on the trail."

Over the hill, I became exalted in spirit, for I had discovered that the way to do was not to lift the whole 10 ft. of shoe off the snow, but to slide it along on the snow, letting it carry its own weight, and dragging it forward by the toe strap. I was going at a great gait, like a boy with a new pair of galluses, right along in front of D company barracks, and rather glad a lot of blue-coated gladiators were out watching the tenderfoot learn to *ski*-go, when all at once I learned something more. I got my feet crossed, somehow, and right at the critical moment I went end over end in the snow, with the *skis* fairly braided around my neck in the most extraordinary and inexplicable fashion in the world. The *skis* got away the best of that fall. D company laughed long and hearty, as one man. A company always does that way, I suppose, owing to the army discipline, but I felt like trying to lick D company, while Billy was trying to untackle and unbraid me and get me dug out again.

It would seem easy to get up after falling in the snow, but let one try this in deep, soft snow, and he will find that his hand and arm sink deep down, but afford him no support when he tries to raise himself. He can get no bearing until he gets above his *skis,* which do not sink in the snow. He must therefore get his *skis* under him, somehow. That somehow is best understood after a wrestle or two in trying to get one's feet untangled and located once more intelligibly. Getting up from a fall in soft snow or a steep side hill is a very delicate operation.

Billy and I made our way up the mountain side where lies that marvelous geyser formation known as the Minerva Terrace. Earth has no mammoth hot spring to compare with this one,

147

whose giant stairway now lay before us, and the year holds no time like that of midwinter to see it at its best. The graded pools rose one above another like jewels on a cloth of white. The snow, yards deep, made a setting for each pool. Out of the pools the water sparkled, boiling hot, cut through the snow, melted the ice, bid defiance to winter. Evidently, nature's plans beneath the surface of the earth were at variance with those about it. The paradox was startling. Billy and I crawled on our *skis* close along the edge of the giant pools, crossed some of the rocks on foot where it was too hot for the snow to lie, and at length, bracing ourselves from slipping into the hot bath, we stood over 10 ft. of snow on a rock which overlooked the ultimate pool, whose blue, scalding flood pours up eternally through an unfathomable crevice in the mountain side. Around us swept the incomparable panorama of the snow-clad hills. Surely the scene was an impressive one and one such as should win forgiveness for a brief feeling of emotion and of sentiment.

I know a fellow oughtn't to "spill over," and oughtn't to "make a scene," because it isn't good form. Yet I hope I should be forgiven for the thought which came to me as I gazed into that ceaseless fountain of red hot water which flows forever, day and night, summer and winter. What a place for Mr. Armour! What a place for scalding hogs!

I commend this thought to those who wish to cut apart the Park, who wish to put railroads through it, who wish to ruin and make common its wonders. It has been suggested that a railroad through the Park would be a useful thing to some few men who wish to carry freight. I believe it has not yet been brought to their minds that the hot springs might be made useful in scalding hogs. By all means let us do away with horses and vehicles in the Park. Let us make the trip in two days. Let us have an electrical railroad, and a grand national pork concern, thus utilizing the hot water nature has evidently provided with the design of scalding hogs. Niagara is harnessed. Why not the Park? National Pork! There is a music in the sound, a similitude in the form, and a close fit in the thought behind the form. It will do for a label. By all means let us have in the railroads at once. And over the gate which lets them in let us have the fitting announcement and the fitting epitaph

for the desecrated wonderland—National Pork! Would Congress
then know the difference in the sign, and would it then realize
what the design of this last instance of national porkism had
been from first to last?

"Come," said Billy, "and I will have some fun with you."

He did, he did, and let no man say to the contrary. He took
me through the heavy pines up to the top of a steep rise above
the terrace, and politely requested me to follow my leader,
saying which, he let go and slid off down the hill like a bird,
calling back to me to "keep my feet together and put on
brakes with the pole." This I did as nearly as I could, and in a
moment, with an ease and precision which pleased us both,
I also was at the foot of the hill, but upside down, with the
skis on top.

"We'll try another one," said Billy, who wasn't near as
much discouraged as I was. "There's a pretty swift little pitch
over here a way, and you can ride your pole down there."

"Riding the pole" I learned to be sitting astride of it, with
the rear end of the pole dropping deep in the snow behind and
thus serving as a brake. I was rejoiced to see by this means I
could regulate the speed a little bit, so that I didn't feel so
much as if I was going to get off the earth. Billy was pleased
to be flattering when he saw that I was on top of the *skis* at
the bottom of the hill, instead of their being on top of me.

"Now we'll take one steeper yet," said he. "I'll show you the
way to do where it's too steep to stand up. Come ahead."

Billy stopped at the head of a sharp little pitch, which was
so steep that we couldn't see to the bottom of it. All we could
see was a rounded curve of white dropping down, apparently
off into the blue substance which the poets call aether. Here
Billy unbuckled the straps of his shoes, took the shoes off,
put them together, pointed them down hill, and sat down on
the middle of the two, on top of the shoe-straps. Then he gave
a push or so with his hands, started, gathered speed, and whish!
he was over into the unknown, apparently sliding on the seat
of his overalls.

As I knew of no way of getting out of there except by doing
the way Billy did, I also took off my shoes and sat down on
them, putting them carefully in the tracks left by Billy's. I

was looking thoughtfully at the carved dragon heads on the ends of my *skis,* and wondering how far off the end of that hill was, when all at once the malignant creatures took a slip and a start and away I went. There was an astonishing slipping past of trees stuck on a broad ribbon of snow, then a feeling of keen exhilaration at the smooth, even flight through the air; then came a second of still more winged flight, clear out into the air, and a smother of something white and soft. The dragon-headed *skis* and the eagle-eyed newspaper man had gone clear over a 30 ft. bank of snow, and buried themselves in the soft drift at its base. I had taken my first *ski*-jump, and taken it sitting down, at the take-off and the landing.

"It was steeper than I thought," said Billy, when he could undouble himself from laughing, "and the fact is, I did just what you did. I had to hurry to get out of the drift, or you'd have lit right on top of me.

"Now you've seen the gaits," continued he, "and you see how it's done. The rest you'll have to learn from practice. We'll go home now, for you don't want to get too tired at first."

The next day, thanks to a muscular system already in pretty fair order from the training I had gone into preparatory for the trip, I was not so very stiff, though I found the new muscles Billy had prophesied, more especially some north of my knees. The dreadful *mal de raquette* of which I had read in books, I never felt at all. That day we took a rather slow run down the hill to the Boiling River a mile or so, the snow being sticky. This concluded my entire experience on the *skis* before we started on our journey, less than half a day in all. I remember that I thought it a great feat to get down the Boiling River hill. When I saw the same hill, on coming out of the Park after the trip, it seemed a very innocent and tame affair.

Wednesday morning, that of our start, dawned bright and fair enough. The two privates, Larsen and Holte, detailed by Capt. Anderson to accompany us, reported in due season, and Billy, as chief pack master, was early busy in arranging the packs we were to carry. Larsen and Holte took absolutely no blankets, saying they would rather not carry them. Billy took only one blanket, and generously insisted on my taking his

150

light sleeping bag, made of wildcat skins, and weighing only about 6 lbs. We had also a light canvas lodge-lining, about 6 ft. by 15 ft. Billy's camera, the special long-range outfit made for him by the Smithsonian Institution, weighed 25½ lbs. without the plate holders, and made all the load Billy could carry. The holders, plates, rolls of films, ruby lantern, etc. which belonged with this camera, made a goodly part of the other packs. My camera, weighing about 10½ lbs., made a good basis for a third pack. We had a light and very excellent camp axe. The men carried their army revolvers. They had in their packs extra socks, and also the warm muskrat skin caps issued by the army, which latter they rarely wore. Billy and I had extra underwear and plenty of socks, of course, and each had a heavy woolen shirt extra, to which I added a sweater. We carried each an extra pair of overshoes, and we were careful to have each an extra pair of colored goggles, an important precaution, for to be without some protection for the eyes in that snowy glare, is to practically go blind. I had along a pair of moccasins in my pack—which I am most thankful I carried in spite of Billy's injunction to cut down weight. Billy had a few screws, in case of a broken *ski,* I had a needle and thread, and we had plenty of wax for the shoes. Of course we had plenty of good matches. We carried lunch enough for two meals, intending to make the soldiers' quarters at Norris Basin, 20 miles out, and to replenish there. We had some tea, the very best we could buy; Billy said we must not drink coffee, but tea, as tea was "better to work on." In this the miners and lumbermen nearly all agree with him, but I am such a coffee drinker myself that I became mutinous after the first day out, and finished the trip on coffee. We had two of the army quart tin cups, the sole dishes or utensils that we carried. As I have said, Billy and I carried no weapon but our scabbard-knives. Item, the men had their tobacco. I put in my kit some such simple remedies as vaseline, quinine, etc., and we also carried a pint of brandy. This was all the spirits we took along, and we had about half of that when we got back, thus establishing a marked difference between our own and the Schwatka outfit.

The above, with a most scanty allowance of toilet articles, constituted all of our simple baggage, yet one will be surprised

151

to learn that made up into four packs it made each pack weigh between 15 and 30 lbs. Billy, one of the most experienced packers in the mountains, soon made up two solid, oblong packs for the soldier boys, adjusting them with soft whang leather carrying-straps. Billy had a carrying harness—and an abominably stiff and awkward one, too—attached to his camera. Sometimes I carried that camera to give Billy a chance for his life, and I always wished the Smithsonian man who invented that harness had it around his neck. For myself, in spite of Billy's entreaties, I stuck to the Lake Superior pack bag, made in Duluth, which I had in long trips through the pine woods previously found so roomy and so easy to carry. This bag was made of heavy canvas, and weighed 3½ lbs., but its straps, "tote" strap (the head strap by which alone Indians will carry a pack) and shoulder straps are put on this bag so understandingly that one can carry additional weight and not feel it as he would with ordinary straps. We found this bag handy for the loose small articles. Of course, being not new at packing, we carried our packs lying well down along the spine, so that shoulders and hips shared the weight. We found a breast strap, of leather or gunny sacking, passed across the front and pulling the shoulder straps a trifle together, made the carrying easier. For this I usually engaged my silk handkerchief. We all carried strips of gunny sacking at our belts. Billy had made two sets of snowshoe clogs. We carried these three miles and threw them away.

At 9 o'clock the last pack had been lashed, the last strap adjusted, the last grunt of protest uttered by the human pack train Billy was cinching up, and we were on our way up the first slopes of the great Golden Gate hill, beyond which lay the wonders and the trials of the wild region of the upper Park. The journey was on. Since I was a boy and used to lie awake all night before the days when my father was going to take me with him on a fishing trip or camp hunt, I can not remember ever to have felt so keen a thrill of curiosity and anticipation as I did then. In anticipation, it was the trip of a lifetime, and in the realization it proved all and more than I had hoped.

The Golden Gate hill rises about 1,500 ft. or so in three and a half miles, and it isn't so awfully particular how it does it, either. It is the terror of the soldiers and scouts who have to snowshoe in the Park, and is considered about the hardest climb in the Park. Certainly it constitutes a delightful place to break in a greenhorn on the *skis* with a 30 lbs. pack on his back and a reputation for dignity to sustain.

The worst of it was the snow stuck to our shoes and made it hard going even on the places where we didn't want to slip back any. We paused at the end of the first half hour or so and scraped off our shoes. The day was cold, but we were all perspiring with the work.

"Put on your glasses," said Billy to me. "Your eyes aren't bigger than slits in a blanket already. Do you want to go blind? And stop eating that snow. Whatever you do, and no matter how thirsty you get, you must not eat snow. If you get heated up and take one drink of cold water, that knocks you out worse than four hours of work. It weakens you right away. You must not drink between meals, and you mustn't eat snow."

This struck me as being hard luck, for just then I would rather have eaten snow than do anything, but I obeyed. We pushed on up the sharp grades the best we could, or rather the best I could, for of course the others could leave me as they liked. We let the two privates go ahead, with instructions to build a fire at the top of the hill, opposite the magnificent Cathedral Rock. They were joined further on by the detail sent out by Capt. Anderson to bring in the poacher Howell, who had just been caught—Sergt. Kellner and two privates, all good shoers. At last Billy and I made the last rise—I'm sure I don't know how—and in a moment more we were beside our little fire, melting snow to make tea. I drank about a quart of strong tea—and nearly met a Waterloo by doing it, for it made me sick. We ate also a bite of lunch, and fixed up our shoes, heating them scorching hot and then rubbing them quickly with wax. Billy showed me how, enjoining me by no means ever to allow a drop of water to fall on either surface of the *skis,* as it would freeze and cause the snow to stick to it. The theory of the *ski* is to slip over and through the snow without

153

dragging any along. It is quite an art to learn all the tricks of *ski* work, and keeping the *skis* in order is one of the most important ones.

Travelers through the Park will remember the rock cut, the trestle and the bridge just below the entrance of the Golden Gate proper. Above the wall of rock rises straight up and on the left as one ascends the mountain side drops sheer off into the cañon which makes down below the Cathedral Rock. This is a pretty bit of road in summer. As we saw it there was no road at all, but a drift of snow filling the road 30 ft. deep. We had to leave the road at a point above the trestle, take off our *skis* and make our way the best we could along the mountain side, climbing up steps cut in the snow to the point right at the last little bridge, under the rail of which we crawled. Then, after this ticklish piece of business was over, we put on the *skis,* pushed around the corner, ran up the last faint rise and lo! Before us lay the wide and storm-swept plain of the Swan Lake Flats.

Big white mountains hemmed in this high plateau—Electric Peak, Sepulcher Peak, Joseph Peak, Quadrant Mountain, Antler Peak, Trilobite Point, Mount Holmes; all these could be seen standing sentry. White Mount Washburn, highest peak of the Park, could be seen far off in the wild central region of the Park. We could even see over to the Yellowstone range toward Cooke City. Certainly it was a most impressive landscape and rendered not the less forbidding by the stalking pillars of snow which went in procession across the wind-swept plateau which made the near foreground.

Billy now told me that we had eight miles more to go before we could make the Crystal Springs "shack," the only practicable stopping place this side of Norris quarters. It was so late, and the shoeing was so bad, that he had given up all hope of making Norris that night. He added that the eight miles was not so hard as the three miles we had just passed, and bade me of good cheer. Larsen and Holte, whom we found to be excellent *ski* men, as befitted their Scandinavian ancestry, Billy advised to go ahead and turn in at the Crystal Springs, as we did not wish to hold them back. They hit off a swinging gait at this, and were soon mere specks on the other side of the

flat. Billy could have kept up with them, of course, but remained with me, who equally of course could not go such a pace
my first day on the *skis*.

If Billy had not stayed back with me, it is very probable
I should never have gotten into camp that night or any other
night. That he did so was only what he would in mountain
honor consider himself bound to do, but none the less the fact
that he did has always left a soft spot in my heart for Billy,
and a feeling that if he were in a tight place I should like to
stay with him in turn. Certainly he helped me through a tight
enough place—about as bad as afternoon as I care to put in.

On the windy flats the snow was hard and made fair shoeing,
and I plodded along behind Billy's shoes methodically enough,
and did not really feel so very tired. At the Gardner River,
however, four and a half miles still from the shack, I was taken
desperately faint and sick, so that at length I fairly toppled
over off my *skis*. I don't know what it was, unless the unusual
exertion, combined with the unusual altitude, caused the
stomach to resent the unusual dose of bitter tea I had given it.
Anyhow, I got desperately weak, and pretty soon I didn't
care a copper whether I went anywhere or not. Billy would
not let me stop for more than a moment, however, knowing
the effects of a chilling through. He fished out the brandy
bottle and for almost the only time on the trip I drank a little
of it—about a thimbleful was Billy's idea of a plenty. This
braced me up a little, but for over an hour I was so weak, and
moreover so dull and apathetic, that it seems to me I know
how it must feel to be left on the trail. In my belief a fellow
wouldn't care much about it, one way or another, if he got
much further along than I was. Billy was anxious, I know, for
the day was waning, and it had come on to snow most dis-
mally. Worse still, the snow began to stick to the shoes when
we entered the dense forest, and it was hard plugging for a
man even at his best. We worried along over one little hill
after another, not daring to stop long enough to build a fire
and wax our shoes. Once in a while we would turn from the
trail, tramp a hole down in the snow—which was 8 ft. deep on
the level here—and sit for a moment resting, with our packs
leaning on the snow. Then we would cut a pine bough and

155

rub the *skis* hard with the resinous tips and needles. This would help the shoes for a way, when perhaps we would cut off another bough, throw it on the snow and drag the *skis* across that to cut off the adhering snow, and "slick" the shoes a little. Billy would not let me sit down long at a time, but kept me moving; and at length toward evening I began to get stronger.

"It's only three-quarters of a mile further now," said Billy finally. "Can you make it?"

"Betcherlife, Billy," I said, making an awful bluff.

"Come on, then," he said, and so set out at a better pace. But it transpired that he had feared I could not go even that distance, for it was not a quarter of a mile further before he turned out to the left from the trail, into a deep thicket of pines that fringed a little stream.

"Brace up, old man," said he, "we're home now."

And home it was, a very blessed one, this little shack of rough boards, buried roof deep in the snow which folded the whole forest in like a great white blanket. There was a blue wisp of smoke rising, and there were voices of welcome as we came in sight, and that is the most of home.

We learned that Kellner's party had been unable to make Norris quarters that day, owing to the stickiness of the shoeing, and it therefore became necessary for all seven of us to pass the night in the little shack, not over 9 ft. square. This, however, we found not an unwelcome prospect. Everything in life is relative. For my part I threw myself down on a board somebody had propped up off the floor, and for over half an hour I knew nothing of what was going on. This might have been sleep, or it might have been sheer exhaustion. I heard somebody say, "That feller's purty tired." Then somebody gave me a warm sandwich with corned beef hash in it, and a tin cup of coffee. This combination saved my life, and pretty soon I got quite peart again. The boys cut a lot of boughs and put down on the floor, and brought in plenty of wood for the old cook stove which Uncle Sam had left in there against just such an emergency as this. Not one of the party but Billy and myself had a blanket, for the soldiers declare they would rather sit up by a fire all night than pack a blanket all day. Billy spread

156

down his piece of canvas and his one blanket, insisting on my taking the sleeping bag, and so we all turned in the best we could, the soldier men squatting, lying or crouching about the stove as the taste and fancy of each dictated.

This ended my first day on the *skis,* and it served at least to teach me what a snowshoe trip through the Park meant, how serious a thing it might become and how impossible help would be in case of sickness or accident. When I lay down to sleep that night I had not the slightest idea that I would be able to travel the next day, for I thought I would be too stiff and sore. I never could understand what the trouble really was, nor how it was that I got over it so easily. Certain it is that the next morning I awoke rested and refreshed, stiff and a bit sore, of course, but only triflingly so by comparison. I got on my shoes all right, and from that time on clear through the trip I never did have any more trouble. I took coffee and corned beef hash in mine after that every time I got a chance, and attribute my later success to those remedies. That one first bruising day—it was a nightmare of a time—made the beginning and the end of the grief. After that the art of shoeing grew easier and easier every day, and the trip more and more delightful. But I have not yet forgotten how Billy stayed with me when I was disposed to lie down and join the golden choir.

The men who first reached the Swan Lake Flats that day saw four elk off to the right of the trail. No other game was seen. Billy and I noticed elk pawings in the snow on the hills north of the Golden Gate, but no very large band was indicated.

The thermometer went nearly to zero that night.

Charles Dudley Warner a few years before his death in 1900. Courtesy
of the Stowe-Day Foundation, Hartford, Connecticut

Charles Dudley Warner
1896

Charles Dudley Warner was a popular essayist-humorist-journalist whose career spanned the last four decades of the nineteenth century. Very little of his work has survived in print to the present. His most enduring book, *The Gilded Age,* probably owes its longevity to the co-authorship of his friend, Mark Twain.

Though he wrote much fiction, he was at his best in his essays. He published many collections of these, traveling widely for subject matter. From 1884 to 1898 he was a contributing editor of *Harper's New Monthly Magazine,* in which this account appeared.

While most of Warner's fiction is deservedly forgotten, a number of his essays on wilderness and camp life are worthy of a better fate. His book *In The Wilderness,* published in 1878, is a delightful series of sketches about his misadventures in the Adirondack region of New York. It is hoped that some of his work will someday be republished, if only to satisfy regional interests, such as those of present-day Adirondack enthusiasts.

I

Lady said that the central portion of the Rocky Mountain region—that is, the Yellowstone Park—is the safety-valve of the United States. There are the vent-holes of its internal fires and explosive energies, and but for the relief they afford, the whole country might be shaken with earthquakes and be blown up in fragments. There is the smoking and vomiting chimney of the continent. There issue the stream, the hot water in fountains and rivers, the explosive gases, the dissolved and triturated minerals and earths, generated in the incandescent bowels of the earth. I heard a soldier say that if the Old Faithful geyser did not go off every sixty-five minutes, he should be alarmed, and should fear to stay in that neighborhood, for no one could tell where this suppressed force might not break out. The mountains look pretty solid around there, though some of them—like the Roaring Mountain, which is so full of steam-vents that it looks like a hill on fire—do not seem promising places to plant vineyards (if grapes would grow 7500 feet above the sea); the great basins of Hell, the Devil, and other unpleasant names, upon which the steam whirls in clouds, driving over the red-hot ponds and boiling pot-holes, have usually a thin crust, upon which people walk with some courage; but there arises a general want of confidence in the stability of the whole region. It is not encouraging to feel the crust made hot under your feet, and to have to be careful not to step into holes of boiling water, and fissures of unknown depth which vomit steam, fat-frying kettles, boiling pots of paint and mud, and to have to run away from a caldron which suddenly sends into the air a great column of hot water.

All the world knows, from the pens of a thousand descriptive writers and from the photographs, the details of these marvels, so that I need not enter upon them. But I suppose their effect is different upon different persons. How beautiful many of the "formations" are that have been slowly built up by the overflow of these limpid waters which carry so many salts in solution! What a sense of power there is in the spouting geysers! How exquisite in iridescent colors are some of the burning lakes! How lovely the pools of deep emerald, of sapphire! and the graceful steam floating about over this burning world! But it is hot, and it has a sickening smell, like steam from a dirty laundry. I learned to call it the Park smell, so constant it is in the hell-fire regions. It is exciting to watch for the spouting of the geysers, and the recurrence of other intermitting phenomena; but many disagreeable things do not intermit. The pools and pots are always boiling, streams of hot water never stop, and there are steam-vents that roar as constantly as blast-furnaces. One I recall which sends out laterally as from a funnel, with an awful roar, a great volume of super-heated steam, night and day, year after year, in extravagant rage and prodigality. Steam enough is wasted here to run all the Western railways. Where does it come from? This one never takes a day or an hour off, like many of the uneasy friers and spouters in the basin below it. These displays, however, are wholesome in comparison with what is called the mud-geyser, which is, I suppose, the most disgusting object in nature. This horrible thing is not in any of the geyser basins, but has a place to itself on the road between the Lake and the Yellowstone Cañon. On the side of a hill, at the bottom of a deep sloping pit, is a sort of cave, like the lair of a wild beast, which perpetually vomits a compound of mud, putty, nastiness. Over the mouth seems to be a concave rock, which prevents the creature from spouting his filth straight up like a geyser. Against this obstacle, with a thud, every moment the vile fluid is flung, as if the beast were in a rage, and growling because he could not get out, and then through the orifice the mud is flung in spiteful spits and gushes of nastiness. And the most disgusting part of it is that this awful mixture cannot get out, and the creature has to swallow it again, and is perpetually sick to nausea. It is the most fascinatingly loathsome thing in the world. I recalled the dragon and his cave in Wagner's *Siegfried.* There, the reader remembers, is a dark cave, out of which issue volumes of steam and an animal noise. Presently a dragon protrudes his horrid scaly head and fore paws, and from his jaws come flame and steam. The contrivance seems to have been suggested by this mud-geyser. In this geyser I have no doubt there is a dragon, but he can never get his head out. You can only hear him rage, and you can see the nastiness he vomits out.

II

Bewildering as all this spectacle is to one's idea of a normal and orderly world, I was more impressed by what I could not see than by these strange surface phenomena. It is what is underneath this thin crust, it is the state of things underground, that appeals to the imagination. Where does all this inexhaustible supply of steam and limpid hot water and dissolved salts and paint and liquid mud come from? The crust is hot and trembling. We must be walking, amid boiling pots and pits, over a terrible furnace. How far below is this furnace? Are these hot substances thrown up from the centre, or is the earth, only a little distance under us, all molten and fluid and a raging hell? Why does it not burst up everywhere and blow this whole mountain region sky-high? Here and there in this vast territory one sees frightful fields and ravines of shapeless, contorted rocks, as if in those places the interior had exploded, and created and left ruin. And yet there is a process of creation in sight, going on daily and yearly, the slow formation of terraces and mounds and well-curbs, all exquisitely sculptured, now like lace-work, now like the chiselling of a sculptor. Are these lovely things created only to be destroyed in a great upheaval of the internal forces? Will the "formations" at the Mammoth Hot Springs and in the geyser basins some day, any day, go up in a vast explosion, and be destroyed and buried in mud, as were recently the similar terraces and formations in New Zealand? What insurance company would take a risk on these things?

In the presence of this immense energy and fiery agitation we seem to be witnesses of the processes of creation, of the primitive evolutionary forces that are making the planet. Of course I know that the earth is not yet created. The lower Mississippi region is now being made before our eyes, as the Nile delta is. What I should like to know is whether the Yellowstone region is now in process of creation, whether it is to be within certain calculable periods greatly changed in form, or whether we are witnessing now the expiring energies of a world gradually cooling down into rigidity and death. The intermittent geysers would seem to intimate that the internal forces are weakening. The great Excelsior geyser, which was so active in 1889, which shook the whole region when it went off, and deluged the neighborhood with an immense flow of hot water, and liberated itself by tearing open an orifice of half an acre in area, is a horrible pit of boiling water and steam, and its opening is now so large that it will probably not be able to send up a column of water again. Still there is no doubt energy here enough to outlast our time, and perhaps our nation, and there can be little doubt that this region acts as a safety-valve of the continent, which would be shaken with earthquakes if these vents were stopped up.

III

These glooms and wonders, however, do not depress the spirits of the traveller in this glorious Yellowstone Park, which the government is so wisely protecting from vandalism. It would take more than these to depress him in this rare, splendid atmosphere, on the top of the world. The pure dry air brings life in all his tingling veins, and under the deepest of blue skies the fir and aspen forests, the swift fish-full streams, the lakes reflecting the blue of the high skies, and the shapely encircling mountains, with patches of snow even in August, are a heavenly vision to eyes tired of cities and the conventionalities of slashed and cultivated regions deformed by bad taste. The Yellowstone Lake, irregular in form, and some forty miles long by twenty broad, is a much finer sheet of water than I expected, and with its placid surface and fair shores, and noble ranges of purple mountains, it seems civilized and habitable, and is a most restful place after the tour in the infernal regions. Its outflow, the Yellowstone River, leads naturally to the culmination of the wonders of the Park, the Falls and the Grand Cañon. That has been so much described and painted that it is unnecessary to say much about it. Comparisons of great natural wonders are always misleading, and generally futile. It suffices to be lost in amazement and admiration before each one. It is enough to say that the Yellowstone Cañon is unique as it is impressive in form and depth, and gorgeous in color. The Falls would be more impressive if they were not enclosed in such gigantic walls. The Upper Fall is about seventy-five feet in height, and the Lower some three hundred and sixty. Both are dark green in color, full, graceful, powerful, with masses of foam at the bottom which takes occasionally a violet hue. The walls of the Canon, which is here about three miles long, are from twelve hundred to fifteen hundred feet in height, sometimes almost perpendicular, and winding, with noble juttings and buttresses of rock at the turns and angles, and the roaring river is a narrow green ribbon at the bottom. Three miles below the Falls, at Inspiration Point, is the greatest view of the Cañon. From this point is the finest display of color. The main body of color is yellow, but of all shades, and intermingled with it is much brown and red, spots of deep red and vermilion and white, astonishingly brilliant. The slopes of the Cañon are of friable, decadent, crumbling rock, and the colors run much together, so that you get often an iridescent appearance. There are some fine buttresses and towers—several round isolated towers I saw with each an osprey's nest on top, with the fearless bird sitting on her nest—but generally the rock is too far decayed to form very picturesque or sculptural or architectural imitations of man's work. The magnificence is in the great depth, and the supernal beauty in the brilliant color. The scene is mightily impressive and unwearying. The different shades in morning and evening light, in a gray sky and in the bright sunlight, are so varied that the picture is always new, and the more wonderful the more one gets to know it. I should say that it is the sort of spectacle that would grow upon one the longer and the oftener he saw it.

I was asked many times there, and I have been asked many times since, how this compares with the Grand Cañon of the Colorado. I am reluctant to make any comparison, for there is none. It is partly a matter of magnitude. If I were forced to answer, I should be compelled to say that the Yellowstone would be only a lateral fissure in the Colorado system. You would have to look long to find it. There is no scenery on earth to compare with the Colorado Cañon; and, indeed, the word cañon applied to it is not descriptive. From the brink where I saw the Colorado you look perpendicularly down six thousand feet to the thread of a river, but you look also away over twelve miles of high formation, all full of color, and upon rocks and mountains, the tops of which rise to the level of the eye, that are solidly built into all the architectural forms you have ever seen or can conceive of. You see all the strata of the geological periods lying upon each other in order six thousand feet high. In my recollection the color at the

164

Yellowstone is more brilliant—that is, more brilliant in spots—
and also more mixed. The color at the Colorado is in greater
masses, more orderly and more subdued in tone, but, by reason
of its great mass and extent, and even greater variety in
moderate tones, quite as effective. And when you come to
speak of rock sculpture and architectural forms, Occidental,
Oriental, and fantastic, the Yellowstone with its crumbling
walls has nothing whatever to show in the comparison. And
yet the Yellowstone is undoubtedly one of the wonders of
the world.

IV

Due appreciation of what this magnificent reserve is to the
people of the United States will not be gained by merely visiting the sights and wonders I have spoken of. By the original
act the Yellowstone Park was somewhat smaller than the State
of Connecticut; by the recent addition of timber reserves,
strips on the east and south, it is larger than Connecticut.
The prime object of the first reservation was to preserve from
desecration and destruction one of the wonders of the world,
and to keep intact a magnificent pleasure-ground for the use of
all the people and prevent its destruction by the lawless few;
the addition of the timber reserve was to increase the second
value of the Park, as a source of water supply. Denuded of its
forests, this mountainous region would have ceased to be of
use as a reservoir for irrigation purposes to the surrounding
territory.

The most magnificent scenery is now outside of the roads
that lead to the special sights, and can only be seen by some
labor and endurance of some hardship. The southern part of
the Park, Heart Lake, Jackson Lake, Snake River, and the
Tetons, is inaccessible except by rough trails and the use of
pack-trains. The same may be said of the western part of the
Park, out of which flow the Gibbon and the Madison. The
whole eastern part is almost inaccessible, except in the north,
towards Soda Butte and Cooke City, by horrible wagon roads,
and south of that by the wildest trails. When the government
shall appropriate money to open these regions some notion
will be had of the grandeur and beauty of this Rocky Mountain

country, and its infinite variety as a pleasure-ground. Road surveys have been made in these regions, and roads and bridges are in process of construction, so that year by year the travel can take a wider sweep, and the thousands of camping parties can visit new scenes. But with the heavy snows and the spring thaws the highways are much injured, and the main part of the government's small appropriation is necessarily expended in repairs. The able superintendent, however, contrives to save some money for improvements. A bridge is just built over the Madison, and the survey is nearly complete, and portions of the new road are built between the Mammoth Hot Springs and Cooke City. This road of fifty miles, which is used by teams for hauling ore and supplies, and by camping parties who enter the Park at Cooke City, goes through some of the finest scenery in the country—great grassy uplands, where the antelope and the deer and the elk roam, and splendid rock mountains ten and eleven thousand feet high—crossing the Yellowstone and many clear and beautiful streams. This road is about the worst road that I ever saw horses and mules attempt to haul wagons over. Road-making is, however, carried on with a great deal of energy. The superintendent has a soldier's and surveyor's eye for feasible routes, and some passable roads are made at small cost where to the ordinary eye road-building seems almost impracticable. His theory is that it is better for the accommodation of the public to build twenty miles of good road with fair grades than to use up his money in one mile of macadam, and consume twenty years in opening the Park to the public. I must say, however, that the Park roads are uncommonly good, and would be so considered anywhere. They are not free from dust, but the surface is smooth and the grades are fair. If the superintendent is permitted to carry out his intelligent and economical plans, the Park will year by year be more accessible and attractive.

The forests of the Park are of small trees, for its average altitude is over seven thousand feet. These are mainly firs, pines, balsams, and aspens—few if any large trees—but the growth is essential to the beauty of the Park and its use as a water-storer. Under the civil administration frequent and extensive fires occurred, and the country is literally full of fallen dead timber. If a fire starts, and in the dry time gets into the tree-tops, it will run over a vast area in spite of human efforts. The main anxiety of the Park guardians in the summer is on account of forest fires. The Park is full of game. All the streams abound in fish, mainly varieties of trout, the best being those transplanted there from our Eastern trout streams. Wild geese and ducks and pelicans and gulls abound on all the lakes and ponds. Since game has been preserved it has multiplied exceedingly. There are a few buffaloes left, but in the warm season they go up the mountains to the snow patches; and so do the thousands and thousands of elk. Antelopes are also abundant. I saw many of these graceful animals on the mountain slopes. Deer are equally numerous. There are many mountain-sheep. There are enough of other wild animals, such as the coyote, the porcupine, and the woodchuck, many singing-birds, and everywhere hawks, ospreys, and eagles. The air and the waters are alive with animal life. The bear of course, black and cinnamon. The bear is domestically inclined, and since he is not shot at, he has not only multiplied his kind, but become pleasantly familiar. He is a regular boarder at some of the hotels, and he likes to come around the camps for food. He is a humorous kind of beast, and being well treated, he seems inclined to cause little trouble, though sometimes he does make a mess of people's kitchens. I should not forget to speak of the prodigality and brilliancy of the wild flowers. Think of acres of blue gentians, bluebells, wild sunflowers, wild geraniums, asters, marguerites, golden-rods of many varieties, and countless other exquisite and bright blooms!

Since the Park has passed under military control fires are infrequent, poaching is suppressed, the "formations" are no longer defaced, roads are improved, and the region is saved with its natural beauty for the enjoyment of all the people. The Interior Department made stringent rules, with adequate penalties for their infraction, and the military arm in command has enforced them splendidly. The good citizen rejoices that there is at least one spot in the United States where law is promptly enforced. In this respect Yellowstone Park is a moral lesson of the highest value to the United States. The lawless and the marauders are promptly caught, tried (by a civil officer), fined, and ejected. For six years Captain George S. Anderson, a West-Pointer, and of the cavalry service, has been superintendent of the Park. He has two companies of cavalry; one of them is stationed at the Mammoth Hot Springs, and the other, during the summer, at the Upper Basin. The latter is under the immediate command of Captain Scott, a very energetic officer. Outposts of a sergeant and two to four men are stationed at various out-lying places. All the roads are patrolled, the trails are watched, the "formations" and all the "wonders" are guarded, and all the few passes and entrances to the Park are under inspection. All who enter the Park are registered, and all are liable to be searched for fire-arms. Arms are taken away from travellers and camping parties, and hunters going through the Park for game south of it have their guns sealed until they pass out of the Park. There is rigid discipline, but it is only for the protection of the Park and for the benefit of the great mass of law-abiding people. Fishing is absolutely free to everybody. There is abundance of dead fallen timber for camp-fires. No check is put upon its use. But there is a heavy penalty for any one who leaves a fire unextinguished when he moves on. There is another stringent rule about defacing the "formations" by writing or scratching or cutting names on them, and against breaking off or carrying away specimens of any sort. Vandalism in this respect is stopped. When Captain Anderson took command the most beautiful "formations" were defaced by names written or scratched over them. He set his soldiers to chiselling and rubbing out these offensive names and inscriptions. Only in this way could the guardians see if new names were added. This is the only place in the wide world that I know where vulgar and lawless people are really restrained from writing their names in conspicuous places, and from thus defacing monuments and natural objects. As an American, I am exceedingly proud of this achievement of Captain Anderson and his officers. When I drove over the regular road to the Cañon I met one party of roughs being escorted out of the Park by a soldier for leaving a camp-fire burning, and another of three men in a canvas-covered wagon also being escorted to Mammoth for trial for writing their names on the "formations" at the Upper Basin. Whoever is caught in any act of vandalism is turned back by the road he came, and not allowed to see the rest of the Park. I will not say that this Rocky Mountain region is the only part of the country where this lesson of obedience to law is badly needed, but it is one of them. I may be permitted to add, as an impartial spectator, that the Park is now in excellent hands. The intelligent rules of the Interior Department could only be carried out by military discipline, and I sincerely hope not only that the present very energetic and efficient and wise management will not be disturbed in its work, but that the government will, for the benefit of the people visiting the Park, be a little more liberal in money appropriations. If Captain Anderson is left to carry out his excellent and economical plans, and to protect the region by aid of the capable officers with him, the whole country will have reason to be proud of the Yellowstone Park and its condition.

The transportation service in the Park is managed by one company, and the hotels, lunch-houses, and supply of food by another. It is proper to say that the whole transportation service is excellent—very comfortable coaches and carriages, good horses, expert and civil drivers—and that the whole service is prompt and agreeable. The same praise can be as emphatically given to the entire hotel and lunch service. I was surprised to find uniformly such good fare in this remote mountain region—very obliging attendants; excellent, well-cooked food in abundant variety; everywhere plenty of good milk and fruits. The management of these two departments matches the good general management of the Park. As an American, as I said before, I feel inclined to boast of these things.

The lady who said that the Rocky Mountain region is a safety-valve for the United States, in respect to its internal energies, might have said also that the Mountain West is another kind of vent, for the restlessness and love of adventure of that part of our population which is always on the move, likes the excitement of an unrestrained life, and always expects "to strike it rich" by speculation and chance enterprises, and not by patient, thrifty cultivation of the soil. The State of Illinois, especially the middle and southern part, was some forty years ago little more than a treeless prairie, dotted over with cabins, in which were fever-stricken settlers. It is now tree-planted, full of pretty villages, thriving farms, comfortable and pretty houses, with neat gardens, flowers, fruits, and domestic peace. Emigration was restrained this side the Mississippi long enough for the country to get cultivated and civilized. There can be no satisfactory civilization without careful cultivation of the soil, with thrift and economy. The theme is a fruitful one for the political economist and the student of sociology.

Speaking of law and the enforcement of discipline in Yellowstone Park, I heard the story of a bear there, which I consider exceedingly important not only as a comment on the discipline of the Park, but as a moral lesson to parents in domestic obedience. The story is literally true, and if it were not I should not repeat it, for it would have no value. Mr. Kipling says "the law of the jungle is—Obey." This also seems to be the law of Yellowstone Park. There is a lunch station at the Upper Basin, near Old Faithful, kept by a very intelligent and ingenious man. He got acquainted last year with a she-bear, who used to come to his house every day and walk into the kitchen for food for herself and her two cubs. The cubs never came. The keeper got on very intimate terms with the bear, who was always civil and well-behaved, and would take food from his hand (without taking the hand). One day towards sunset the bear came to the kitchen, and having received her portion, she went out of the back door to carry it to her cubs. To her surprise and anger, the cubs were there waiting for her. She laid down the food, and rushed at her infants and gave them a rousing spanking. "She did not cuff them; she spanked them," and then she drove them back into the woods, cuffing them and knocking them at every step. When she reached the spot where she had told them to wait, she left them there and returned to the house. And there she stayed in the kitchen for two whole hours, making the disobedient children wait for their food, simply to discipline them and teach them obedience. The explanation is very natural. When the bear leaves her young in a particular place and goes in search of food for them, if they stray away in her absence she has great difficulty in finding them. The mother knew that the safety of her cubs and her

170

own peace of mind depended upon strict discipline in the family. O that we had more such mothers in the United States!

Stage arriving at Mammoth Hotel, ca. 1904. Warner wrote that "the whole transportation service is excellent—very comfortable coaches and carriages, good horses, expert and civil drivers." Yellowstone Park files

George Anderson. Yellowstone Park files

George Anderson
1897

In 1886, when the U.S. Cavalry arrived in Yellowstone to administer and care for the Park, Yellowstone's prospects were bleak. Some congressmen were disenchanted with the Park, and its natural wonders were being destroyed by the careless and malicious. The cavalry provided the necessary order and discipline, putting the Park back on the right track.

The first third of the army's three-year stay was by far the most critical. By 1896 congressional disillusionment had faded. In its place was a growing recognition of Yellowstone's place in the American leisure tradition.

George Anderson, the third military superintendent (these officers were known as "acting superintendents," as their supervision of the Park was long regarded as a temporary expedient), had a broad background that prepared him well for the job. He had been a road engineer, an international traveler, and a West Point philosophy instructor, besides being an active conservationist; he was an associate member of The Boone and Crockett Club, an influential group of conservation-minded sportsmen organized by George Bird Grinnell and Theodore Roosevelt.[1]

Testimonials on behalf of Anderson's competence appear in chapters 6, 7, and 8. His enthusiasm for the Park was boundless. When the Park budget proved inadequate, he funded poacher patrols from his own pocket.[2] While he may underestimate the work of his civilian predecessors in this article, there is no doubt that his own contributions to the Park's welfare were tremendous. Crusaders like Grinnell and Roosevelt found a very capable champion in Captain Anderson. He helped turn their ideals into the reality of a sound park management.

efore entering upon the subject proper, it will be well to give a short resumé of the history of the Park, and to show by what process the cavalry becomes a part of the legal machinery for enforcement of order there.

The organic act of the Park bears date March 1, 1872. The first superintendent was appointed on May 10th of that same year. He received no compensation, did not live in or near the Park, and afforded it little or no protection. On April 18, 1877, he was relieved by a successor, who served under the same conditions until July 5, 1878, after which date he received a salary of $1,500 a year, and spent at least a portion of each year within the Park.

This superintendent was removed February 2, 1882. He paid little or no attention to the protection of the game, and was himself one of the leading vandals in breaking up and carrying away the beautiful incrustations about the springs and geysers, and in despoiling the petrified forests. In succession to him were three others, whose joint incumbency covered the period from February 2, 1882, to August 1, 1886. During all this time there was no law for the government of the Park, and all acts of the superintendent were arbitrary and legally unauthorized.

In March, 1883, the Sundry Civil Bill provided that the Secretary of War be *"directed,"* on the request of the Secretary of the Interior, to make details of troops to prevent the destruction of game and objects of interest. Congress, however, failed to properly provide for the execution of this act, and the Interior Department did not seem to desire the assistance of troops; so no action was taken under it for several years. Meanwhile the destruction of the Park was going on at an accelerated rate, until in 1884 the Legislature of Wyoming, then a Territory, passed a law for its protection. The law was strict enough, and its penalties were ample, but the machinery for its enforcement was most defective.

The assistant superintendents of the Park (Federal officials) were given appointments as justices and constables under this law, and eked out their small salaries by levying a species of blackmail on the traveling public. Finally the law was repealed in March, 1886, and the Park reverted to previous conditions. The repeal was brought about in this way: In 1885 a Member of

Congress from Illinois was arrested and fined $50.00 for leaving his camp-fire unextinguished. To the justice of the peace he looked about like a man who would probably have $50.00 in his pockets. Had he paid it, the money would have been divided between the justice and the constable, and all would have been well; but this time they had the wrong man. Under the law an appeal lay to the Wyoming courts. This Member of Congress made a motion for an appeal, and asked them to fix the bond. Such proceedings had never been heard of in their court, and an adjournment was taken for consultation—and drinks.

The justice had never heard of an "appeal bond," but he was resourceful. Could he not put the amount out of reach; make it $100,000, and still get the $50.00 in cash? That was his method; but it did not work. The prisoner offered as bonds Mr. G.M. Pullman, Mr. Story and Mr. Armour, and other friends who were with him, who offered to qualify for several millions.

The guardians of the Park had evidently hit too deep; they took another adjournment—the justice and the constable—and returned with a verdict of "not guilty"; but this the prisoner would not agree to accept. This begat more trouble. The results of it all were that from the Sundry Civil Bill for 1886 the pay for the superintendent and his ten assistants was struck out and, strange to say, they all vacated their offices at the end of that year. It was then that the act of March 3, 1883, came in play, and in accordance with its provisions the Interior Department asked for the army.

Major Moses Harris, then captain First Cavalry, was sent with his troop from Fort Ellis, Mont., and became the first military ruler of the Park, with the title of "acting superintendent," while at the same time he was the military commander of the troops, under army regulations. He arrived and assumed charge in August, 1886, and the Park has been under military rule, and cavalry rule, ever since that date.

Until June, 1894, there was no law to protect officers and troops in the exercise of their onerous duties under Park regulations, but for the last three years all has been properly provided for by the "Yellowstone Park Protective Act" of May 7, 1894.

The military garrison at first consisted of a single troop of cavalry, which remained here the entire year, assisted by a second one (or a detachment) from June 1st to October 1st; this second one always summered in camp at the geyser basins.

In 1891, upon my arrival here, the construction of a new post was begun. This post was intended to replace the old, temporary one, built by Major Harris in 1886. The new post was occupied in November, 1891, and in May, 1892, a second troop arrived here and has remained ever since, spending the summers in camp and the winters in the old post.

The Park proper is about fifty-four miles from north to south and about sixty-two miles from east to west, giving an area of about 3,350 square miles. In 1891 the President declared a forest reserve, in shape like an "L," on the east and south of the Park—about twenty-five miles on the east and ten miles on the south. This area was placed under the control of the superintendent of the Park, "with the same rules and regulations as were in force in the Park itself," but of course it was not under Park *law.* This added about 2,000 square miles to the area to be guarded, making the entire domain longer than the State of Connecticut. This tract is situated on the very summit of the Rocky Mountains. Fort Yellowstone, which is nearly the lowest point within it, is about 6,300 feet altitude. The most of the Park plateau is near 1,500 feet higher, and the peaks rise to 11,000 to 13,000 feet. The whole area is well watered, which results in a heavy snow-fall. There are large sections near the Yellowstone Lake, over which the year's snow-fall is fully twenty feet. At least four-fifths of the Park is covered with a dense growth of highly resinous pine trees, too small for lumber, but perfectly adapted to conserve the snow and allow it to gradually melt and pursue its belated course to the ocean.

There are few treeless tracts, but wherever such are found the grass is luxuriant, and there the game seeks its winter sustenance.

As might be supposed, the climate is very severe, yet in many ways it is enjoyable. Thermometer records have been kept since Major Harris came in 1886, and a hasty inspection of them shows that here, at Fort Yellowstone, the thermometer has been as low as zero every month in the year but May, June, July and August, and that it has been below freezing every month in the year. In the higher levels, which include most of the Park area, we expect at least ten degrees lower. At the time of this writing the registered thermometer at this post has not been above zero for over five days, and one day showed a record of twenty-nine degrees below. In spite of all this, we enjoy delightful weather most of the time, for we are spared the winds which make low temperature unbearable.

The works of "protection" which have fallen to the cavalry may be generally grouped under three heads. 1st. Protection of the beauties and wonders of the Park from destruction by tourists and sight-seers; this work is confined almost entirely to the four months of travel—June, July, August and September—while hotels are open and transportation service running. 2d. Protection of the forests from fires; this work is largely limited to the camping season, which is, generally speaking, July, August and part of September. 3d. Protection of the game from the ravages of poachers.

In addition to the post proper a number of out-stations are established. Four of these stations remain the same summer and winter. One is at Norris Geyser Basin, twenty miles south of here; a second is at Riverside, about twenty-five miles southwest of Norris and near the west line of the Park; a third is on Snake River, one hundred miles south of here and near the south boundary, and the fourth is at Soda Butte, forty miles east of here and near the northeast corner of the Park. Norris is on the main circuit of tourist travel; the other three are on the only routes by which it is possible to enter the Park by wagon.

A non-commissioned officer and three men are kept at each place during the entire year. They have good, comfortable log houses, with fairly comfortable stables. The horses are left at all of them, except Snake River, during the winter, but on account of deep snow they cannot, as a rule, be used between December 1st and May 1st. The Snake River horses are turned into post in November and sent down as soon as practicable

178

in the spring. We have generally found it impossible to get to this station with supplies before July 1st.

The main work of these men is to examine all parties entering and leaving the Park, register their names, destination, transportation, arms, etc. If entering with guns, the mechanism is so tied with red tape as not to be capable of movement, and the knot in the tape filled with red sealing wax. Each party is then passed on to the next station that it will meet on its way.

All violations of Park regulations are looked after, and particular attention is given to the prevention of forest fires. For this purpose a mounted man leaves each station every day during the season, soon after his breakfast. He rides leisurely along the road, carefully examining all recently abandoned camps. Should unextinguished fires be found, the guilty parties are arrested and brought here for trial. At a point about half way to the next station a man from that post is met; the two eat luncheon and spend an hour or two together, and in the afternoon they retrace their steps, exercising the same vigilance as in the forenoon.

But it is in winter that their hardest and most perilous work comes. All must be done on snowshoes, and the Norwegian ski is the one always used. The work at this time is entirely under the third head—the protection of game. As blankets, subsistence, and all necessaries must be carried on the back, I have established a number of small huts, with fireplaces, at different places known to the men on station, and in the autumn these are stocked with cut wood and certain staple articles of food, such as flour, hard bread, bacon, coffee, sugar, etc., properly protected in tin-lined boxes. There are few trips now made where the men cannot spend the night in one of these.

For bedding a man generally carries a fur-lined sleeping bag, and in case they have to spend the night out of doors, one must sleep while the other keeps up the fire. It is always necessary to carry an axe, and I never permit a man to go alone on any snowshoe trip.

I require monthly reports from these stations, giving names of men on trips, date of departure and return, number of miles traveled—on horseback and on skis—object of the trip and results accomplished. The mileage reported from these stations runs from 200 to 500 per month on skis, and more when they go on horseback.

In addition to these stations, I have a winter station at the site of the summer camp of the troop, at the Lower Geyser Basin, and a winter station near the Hayden Valley, and summer stations at the Upper Geyser Basin, Cañon, Lake and Thumb. The main object of these summer stations is to regulate the tourist travel, keep it orderly, prevent forest fires, and prevent the mutilation of everything beautiful by scribbling names upon it. The deposits of the hot springs soon cover a name, written in pencil, so it can not be rubbed off, but the material is so transparent that the name is visible through it for a number of years.

In 1891 there were so many names that I found it impossible to recognize a new one and thus arrest the offender, but I caused them all to be chiseled out, and on the appearance of a name it was sure to be new and the culprit was easily caught by reference to the hotels' and campers' registers, and by use of the telegraph line, which connects all the hotels in the Park.

A very picturesque figure is a sentimental youth at twilight as he transmits his name to fame by writing it upon the "formations"—the hot springs deposits. A much more interesting figure is this same youth at sunrise the next morning, when, followed by a mounted soldier he proceeds, scrub-brush and soap in hand, to the same spot and removes the perishable evidence of his late presence. Each year a good many trials and convictions are had under the law of 1894 for this act as well as for leaving camp-fires unextinguished and for breaking or mutilating objects of interest or wonder.

Owing to the rigors of the climate, the winter work is ever accompanied by danger. In March, 1894, a private of "D" Troop, Sixth Cavalry, left Riverside for the Lower Basin, for the mail. The sergeant in charge of the station went about six or eight miles on the road with him, and he was then over the half of his journey. He was never seen or heard of after, until his remains were found a year and a half later, ten miles or more from where he was last seen, entirely out of his proper direction and in a place where he must have forded at least one large stream to reach. He either became lost and wandered about until he perished from cold, or he met with some of our good neighbors, the poachers, and they gave him his quietus. The latter theory is not at all unlikely. One or two other men have perished of cold since my arrival here, and at present there is a man in hospital whose feet were badly frozen on a recent snowshoe trip to the buffalo country.

During the ten years of occupancy of this post, only six deaths have occurred among the soldiers here, and five of these were from violence. The records show this to be the most healthy post in the army, in spite of the very large percentage of frost cases. For the most part the men are thoroughly satisfied on stations, and it is never difficult to get men to volunteer for these places. The main trouble is to get non-commissioned officers suitable for the duties. It requires much tact, judgment and firmness in dealing with tourists; and it requires energy, push, courage and knowledge of the country, and the ways and habits of poachers in dealing with their winter problems. They have as a rule been faithful to their duties, honest, reliable and worthy of all praise.

As a consequence of their good work, the beauties of the Park are no longer defaced; no fires have ravaged the forests; poaching has diminished to a small percentage of what it was ten years ago; and more than all, order exists everywhere, and there are no more fake courts in session for the blackmailing of innocent travelers.

The government truly recovers a large interest on this small investment.

Theodore Roosevelt in Yellowstone Park. Yellowstone Park files

Theodore Roosevelt
1903

Theodore Roosevelt's interest in nature and outdoor recreation
is well known, but his role in the early conservation movement
is well-nigh legendary. Yellowstone was a special interest of
his, even in the 1880s when he first visited the Park. Throughout his public career he supported the Park's goals and defended it
against destruction and overdevelopment. According to one [his-
torian] it was because of a special interest in Yellowstone Park
that Roosevelt began "his career as an active conservationist."[1]

The famous 1903 visit was part of a grand western tour that
also included Yosemite National Park in California. In spite
of the pressures of publicity, Roosevelt was determined to
avoid the customary presidential fanfare while in Yellowstone.
His party was small. Roosevelt and John Burroughs were
accompanied by a few staff members and a modest force of
soldiers. This was in marked contrast to the lordly entourage
of President Arthur, who, twenty years earlier, enjoyed the
Park in company with a small pack of dignitaries and a large
train of elegant camp furnishings. Roosevelt knew that the
spontaneity and informality of a small group would give him
the freedom he needed to absorb himself in the study of Park
wildlife.

His article then is primarily an account of his camping and
watching. Beyond the recitals of animal numbers and anecdotes

about tramping through the woods, however, he offers us something more. "Wilderness Reserves"—the book from which this essay is taken—is his personal testimonial, an appreciation of and an appeal for inviolate wildlife sanctuaries like Yellowstone Park.[2]

Roosevelt and Burroughs on a sleigh in Yellowstone. Courtesy of the American Museum of Natural History

he most striking and melancholy feature in connection with American big game is the rapidity with which it has vanished. When, just before the outbreak of the Revolutionary War, the rifle-bearing hunters of the backwoods first penetrated the great forests west of the Alleghanies, deer, elk, black bear, and even buffalo, swarmed in what are now the States of Kentucky and Tennessee, and the country north of the Ohio was a great and almost virgin hunting-ground. From that day to this the shrinkage has gone on, only partially checked here and there, and never arrested as a whole. As a matter of historical accuracy, however, it is well to bear in mind that many writers, in lamenting this extinction of the game, have from time to time anticipated or overstated the facts. Thus as good an author as Colonel Richard Irving Dodge spoke of the buffalo as practically extinct, while the great Northern herd still existed in countless thousands. As early as 1880 sporting authorities spoke not only of the buffalo, but of the elk, deer, and antelope as no longer to be found in plenty; and recently one of the greatest living hunters has stated that it is no longer possible to find any American wapiti bearing heads comparable with the red deer of Hungary. As a matter of fact, in the early eighties there were still large regions where every species of game that had ever been known within historic times on our continent was still to be found as plentifully as ever. In the early nineties there were still big tracts of wilderness in which this was true of all game except the buffalo; for instance, it was true of the elk in portions of northwestern Wyoming, of the blacktail in northwestern Colorado, of the whitetail here and there in the Indian Territory, and of the antelope in parts of New Mexico. Even at the present day there are smaller, but still considerable, regions where these four animals are yet found in abundance; and I have seen antlers of wapiti shot since 1900 far surpassing any of which there is record from Hungary. In New England and New York, as well as New Brunswick and Nova Scotia, the whitetail deer is more plentiful than it was thirty years ago, and in Maine (and to an even greater extent in New Brunswick) the moose, and here and there the caribou, have, on the whole, increased during the same period. There is yet

185

ample opportunity for the big game hunter in the United States, Canada and Alaska.

While it is necessary to give this word of warning to those who, in praising time past, always forget the opportunities of the present, it is a thousandfold more necessary to remember that these opportunities are, nevertheless, vanishing; and if we are a sensible people, we will make it our business to see that the process of extinction is arrested. At the present moment the great herds of caribou are being butchered, as in the past the great herds of bison and wapiti have been butchered. Every believer in manliness, and therefore in manly sport, and every lover of nature, every man who appreciates the majesty and beauty of the wilderness and of wild life, should strike hands with the far-sighted men who wish to preserve our material resources, in the effort to keep our forests and our game beasts, game birds, and game fish—indeed, all the living creatures of prairie, and woodland, and seashore—from wanton destruction.

Above all, we should realize that the effort toward this end is essentially a democratic movement. It is entirely in our power as a nation to preserve large tracts of wilderness, which are valueless for agricultural purposes and unfit for settlement, as playgrounds for rich and poor alike, and to preserve the game so that it shall continue to exist for the benefit of all lovers of nature, and to give reasonable opportunities for the exercise of the skill of the hunter, whether he is or is not a man of means. But this end can only be achieved by wise laws and by a resolute enforcement of the laws. Lack of such legislation and administration will result in harm to all of us, but most of all in harm to the nature lover who does not possess vast wealth. Already there have sprung up here and there through the country, as in New Hampshire and the Adirondacks, large private preserves. These preserves often serve a useful purpose, and should be encouraged within reasonable limits; but it would be a misfortune if they increased beyond a certain extent or if they took the place of great tracts of wild land, which continue as such either because of their very nature, or because of the protection of the State exerted in the form of making them state or national parks or reserves. It is foolish

186

to regard proper game laws as undemocratic, unrepublican. On the contrary, they are essentially in the interests of the people as a whole, because it is only through their enactment and enforcement that the people as a whole can preserve the game and can prevent its becoming purely the property of the rich, who are able to create and maintain extensive private preserves. The wealthy man can get hunting anyhow, but the man of small means is dependent solely upon wise and well-executed game laws for his enjoyment of the sturdy pleasure of the chase. In Maine, in Vermont, in the Adirondacks, even in parts of Massachusetts and on Long Island, people have waked up to this fact, particularly so far as the common white-tail deer is concerned, and in Maine also as regards the moose and caribou. The effect is shown in the increase in these animals. Such game protection results, in the first place, in securing to the people who live in the neighborhood permanent opportunities for hunting; and in the next place, it provides no small source of wealth to the locality because of the visitors which it attracts. A deer wild in the woods is worth to the people of the neighborhood many times the value of its carcass, because of the way it attracts sportsmen, who give employment and leave money behind them.

True sportsmen, worthy of the name, men who shoot only in season and in moderation, do no harm whatever to game. The most objectionable of all game destroyers is, of course, the kind of game butcher who simply kills for the sake of the record of slaughter, who leaves deer and ducks and prairie-chickens to rot after he has slain them. Such a man is wholly obnoxious; and, indeed, so is any man who shoots for the purpose of establishing a record of the amount of game killed. To my mind this is one very unfortunate feature of what is otherwise the admirably sportsmanlike English spirit in these matters. The custom of shooting great bags of deer, grouse, partridges, and pheasants, the keen rivalry in making such bags, and their publication in sporting journals, are symptoms of a spirit which is most unhealthy from every standpoint. It is to be earnestly hoped that every American hunting or fishing club will strive to inculcate among its own members, and in the minds of the general public, that anything like an excessive bag, any destruction for the sake of making a record, is to be severely reprobated.

But after all, this kind of perverted sportsman, unworthy though he be, is not the chief actor in the destruction of our game. The professional skin or market hunter is the real offender. Yet he is of all others the man who would ultimately be most benefited by the preservation of the game. The frontier settler, in a thoroughly wild country, is certain to kill game for his own use. As long as he does no more than this, it is hard to blame him; although if he is awake to his own interests he will soon realize that to him, too, the live deer is worth far more than the dead deer, because of the way in which it brings money into the wilderness. The professional market hunter who kills game for the hide, or for the feathers, or for the meat, or to sell antlers and other trophies; the market men who put game in cold storage; and the rich people, who are content to buy what they have not the skill to get by their own exertions— these are the men who are the real enemies of game. Where there is no law which checks the market hunters, the inevitable result of their butchery is that the game is completely destroyed, and with it their own means of livelihood. If, on the other hand, they were willing to preserve it, they could make much more money by acting as guides. In northwestern Colorado, at the present moment, there are still blacktail deer in abundance, and some elk are left. Colorado has fairly good game laws, but they are indifferently enforced. The country in which the game is found can probably never support any but a very sparse population, and a large portion of the summer range is practically useless for settlement. If the people of Colorado generally, and above all the people of the counties in which the game is located, would resolutely cooperate with those of their own number who are already alive to the importance of preserving the game, it could, without difficulty, be kept always as abundant as it now is, and this beautiful region would be a permanent health resort and playground for the people of a large part of the Union. Such action would be a benefit to every one, but it would be a benefit most of all to the people of the immediate locality.

The practical common sense of the American people has been in no way made more evident during the last few years than by the creation and use of a series of large land reserves—situated for the most part on the great plains and among the mountains of the West—intended to keep the forests from destruction, and therefore to conserve the water supply. These reserves are, and should be, created primarily for economic purposes. The semi-arid regions can only support a reasonable population under conditions of the strictest economy and wisdom in the use of the water supply, and in addition to their other economic uses the forests are indispensably necessary for the preservation of the water supply and for rendering possible its useful distribution throughout the proper seasons. In addition, however, to this economic use of the wilderness, selected portions of it have been kept here and there in a state of nature, not merely for the sake of preserving the forests and the water, but for the sake of preserving all its beauties and wonders unspoiled by greedy and short-sighted vandalism. What has been actually accomplished in the Yellowstone Park affords the best possible object-lesson as to the desirability and practicability of establishing such wilderness reserves. This reserve is a natural breeding-ground and nursery for those stately and beautiful haunters of the wilds which have now vanished from so many of the great forests, the vast lonely plains, and the high mountain ranges, where they once abounded.

On April 8, 1903, John Burroughs and I reached the Yellowstone Park, and were met by Major John Pitcher of the Regular Army, the Superintendent of the Park. The Major and I forthwith took horses; he telling me that he could show me a good deal of game while riding up to his house at the Mammoth Hot Springs. Hardly had we left the little town of Gardiner and gotten within the limits of the Park before we saw prongbuck. There was a band of at least a hundred feeding some distance from the road. We rode leisurely toward them. They were tame compared to their kindred in unprotected places; that is, it was easy to ride within fair rifle range of them; and though they were not familiar in the sense that we afterwards found the bighorn and the deer to be familiar, it was extraordinary to find them showing such familiarity almost literally in the streets of a frontier town. It spoke volumes for the good sense and law-abiding spirit of the people of the town. During the two hours following my entry into the Park we rode around the plains and lower slopes of the foothills in the neighborhood of the mouth of the Gardner and we saw several hundred—probably a thousand all told—of these antelopes. Major Pitcher informed me that all the pronghorns in the Park wintered in this neighborhood. Toward the end of April or the first of May they migrate back to their summering homes in the open valleys along the Yellowstone and in the plains south of the Golden Gate. While migrating they go over the mountains and through forests if occasion demands. Although there are plenty of coyotes in the Park, there are no big wolves, and save for very infrequent poachers the only enemy of the antelope, as indeed the only enemy of all the game, is the cougar.

Cougars, known in the Park, as elsewhere through the West, as "mountain lions," are plentiful, having increased in numbers of recent years. Except in the neighborhood of the Gardner River, that is within a few miles of Mammoth Hot Springs, I found them feeding on elk, which in the Park far outnumbered all other game put together, being so numerous that the ravages of the cougars are of no real damage to the herds. But in the neighborhood of the Mammoth Hot Springs the cougars are noxious because of the antelope, mountain sheep, and deer which they kill; and the Superintendent has imported some hounds with which to hunt them. These hounds are managed by Buffalo Jones, a famous old plainsman, who is now in the Park taking care of the buffalo. On this first day of my visit to the Park I came across the carcass of a deer and of an antelope which the cougars had killed. On the great plains cougars rarely get antelope, but here the country is broken so that the big cats can make their stalks under favorable circumstances. To deer and mountain sheep the cougar is a most dangerous enemy—much more so than the wolf.

The antelope we saw were usually in bands of from twenty to one hundred and fifty, and they travelled strung out almost in single file, though those in the rear would sometimes bunch up. I did not try to stalk them, but got as near them as I could on horseback. The closest approach I was able to make was to

190

within about eighty yards of two which were by themselves—
I think a doe and a last year's fawn. As I was riding up to them,
although they looked suspiciously at me, one actually lay down.
When I was passing them at about eighty yards' distance the big
one became nervous, gave a sudden jump, and away the two
went at full speed.

Why the prongbucks were so comparatively shy I do not
know, for right on the ground with them we came upon deer,
and, in the immediate neighborhood, mountain sheep, which
were absurdly tame. The mountain sheep were nineteen in
number, for the most part does and yearlings with a couple
of three-year-old rams, but not a single big fellow—for the big
fellows at this season are off by themselves, singly or in little
bunches, high up in the mountains. The band I saw was tame to
a degree matched by but few domestic animals.

They were feeding on the brink of a steep washout at the
upper edge of one of the benches on the mountain-side just
below where the abrupt slope began. They were alongside a
little gully with sheer walls. I rode my horse to within forty
yards of them, one of them occasionally looking up and at once
continuing to feed. Then they moved slowly off and leisurely
crossed the gully to the other side. I dismounted, walked
around the head of the gully, and moving cautiously, but in
plain sight, came closer and closer until I was within twenty
yards, when I sat down on a stone and spent certainly twenty
minutes looking at them. They paid hardly any attention to
my presence—certainly no more than well-treated domestic
creatures would pay. One of the rams rose on his hind legs,
leaning his fore-hoofs against a little pine tree, and browsed the
ends of the budding branches. The others grazed on the short
grass and herbage or lay down and rested—two of the yearlings
several times playfully butting at one another. Now and then
one would glance in my direction without the slightest sign of
fear—barely even of curiosity. I have no question whatever but
that with a little patience this particular band could be made to
feed out of a man's hand. Major Pitcher intends during the
coming winter to feed them alfalfa—for game animals of several
kinds have become so plentiful in the neighborhood of the Hot
Springs, and the Major has grown so interested in them, that he

wishes to do something toward feeding them during the severe weather. After I had looked at the sheep to my heart's content, I walked back to my horse, my departure arousing as little interest as my advent.

Soon after leaving them we began to come across blacktail deer, singly, in twos and threes, and in small bunches of a dozen or so. They were almost as tame as the mountain sheep, but not quite. That is, they always looked alertly at me, and though if I stayed still they would graze, they kept a watch over my movements and usually moved slowly off when I got within less than forty yards of them. Up to that distance, whether on foot or on horseback, they paid but little heed to me, and on several occasions they allowed me to come much closer. Like the bighorn, the blacktails at this time were grazing, not browsing; but I occasionally saw them nibble some willow buds. During the winter they had been browsing. As we got close to the Hot Springs we came across several whitetail in an open, marshy meadow. They were not quite as tame as the blacktail, although without any difficulty I walked up to within fifty yards of them. Handsome though the blacktail is, the whitetail is the most beautiful of all deer when in motion, because of the springy, bounding grace of its trot and canter, and the way it carries its head and white flag aloft.

Before reaching the Mammoth Hot Springs we also saw a number of ducks in the little pools and on the Gardner. Some of them were rather shy. Others—probably those which, as Major Pitcher informed me, had spent the winter there—were as tame as barn-yard fowls.

Just before reaching the post the Major took me into the big field where Buffalo Jones had some Texas and Flathead Lake buffalo—bulls and cows—which he was tending with solicitous care. The original stock of buffalo in the Park have now been reduced to fifteen or twenty individuals, and their blood is being recruited by the addition of buffalo purchased out of the Flathead Lake and Texas Panhandle herds. The buffalo were at first put within a wire fence, which, when it was built, was found to have included both blacktail and whitetail deer. A bull elk was also put in with them at one time, he having met with some accident which made the Major and

Buffalo Jones bring him in to doctor him. When he recovered his health he became very cross. Not only would he attack men, but also buffalo, even the old and surly master bull, thumping them savagely with his antlers if they did anything to which he objected. The buffalo are now breeding well.

When I reached the post and dismounted at the Major's house, I supposed my experiences with wild beasts were ended for the day; but this was an error. The quarters of the officers and men and the various hotel buildings, stables, residences of the civilian officials, etc., almost completely surround the big parade-ground at the post, near the middle of which stands the flag-pole, while the gun used for morning and evening salutes is well off to one side. There are large gaps between some of the buildings, and Major Pitcher informed me that throughout the winter he had been leaving alfalfa on the parade-grounds, and that numbers of blacktail deer had been in the habit of visiting it every day, sometimes as many as seventy being on the parade-ground at once. As springtime came on the numbers diminished. However, in mid-afternoon, while I was writing in my room in Major Pitcher's house, on looking out of the window I saw five deer on the parade-ground. They were as tame as so many Alderney cows, and when I walked out I got within twenty yards of them without any difficulty. It was most amusing to see them as the time approached for the sunset gun to be fired. The notes of the trumpeter attracted their attention at once. They all looked at him eagerly. One of them resumed feeding, and paid no attention whatever either to the bugle, the gun or the flag. The other four, however, watched the preparations for firing the gun with an intent gaze, and at the sound of the report gave two or three jumps; then instantly wheeling, looked up at the flag as it came down. This they seemed to regard as something rather more suspicious than the gun, and they remained very much on the alert until the ceremony was over. Once it was finished, they resumed feeding as if nothing had happened. Before it was dark they trotted away from the parade-ground back to the mountains.

The next day we rode off to the Yellowstone River, camping some miles below Cottonwood Creek. It was a very pleasant camp. Major Pitcher, an old friend, had a first-class pack-train,

193

so that we were as comfortable as possible, and on such a trip there could be no pleasanter or more interesting companion than John Burroughs—"Oom John," as we soon grew to call him. Where our tents were pitched the bottom of the valley was narrow, the mountains rising steep and cliff-broken on either side. There were quite a number of blacktail in the valley, which were tame and unsuspicious, although not nearly as much so as those in the immediate neighborhood of the Mammoth Hot Springs. One mid-afternoon three of them swam across the river a hundred yards above our camp. But the characteristic animals of the region were the elk—the wapiti. They were certainly more numerous than when I was last through the Park twelve years before.

In the summer the elk spread all over the interior of the Park. As winter approaches they divide, some going north and others south. The southern bands, which, at a guess, may possibly include ten thousand individuals, winter out of the Park, for the most part in Jackson Hole—though of course here and there within the limits of the Park a few elk may spend both winter and summer in an unusually favorable location. It was the members of the northern band that I met. During the wintertime they are nearly stationary, each band staying within a very few miles of the same place, and from their size and the open nature of their habitat it is almost as easy to count them as if they were cattle. From a spur of Bison Peak one day, Major Pitcher, the guide Elwood Hofer, John Burroughs and I spent about four hours with the glasses counting and estimating the different herds within sight. After most careful work and cautious reduction of estimates in each case to the minimum the truth would permit, we reckoned three thousand head of elk, all lying or feeding and all in sight at the same time. An estimate of some fifteen thousand for the number of elk in these northern bands cannot be far wrong. These bands do not go out of the Park at all, but winter just within its northern boundary. At the time when we saw them, the snow had vanished from the bottoms of the valleys and the lower slopes of the mountains, but remained as continuous sheets farther up their sides. The elk were for the most part found up on the snow slopes, occasionally singly or in small

194

gangs—more often in bands of from fifty to a couple of hundred. The larger bulls were highest up the mountains and generally in small troops by themselves, although occasionally one or two would be found associating with a big herd of cows, yearlings, and two-year-olds. Many of the bulls had shed their antlers; many had not. During the winter the elk had evidently done much browsing, but at this time they were grazing almost exclusively, and seemed by preference to seek out the patches of old grass which were last left bare by the retreating snow. The bands moved about very little, and if one were seen one day it was generally possible to find it within a few hundred yards of the same spot the next day, and certainly not more than a mile or two off. There were severe frosts at night, and occasionally light flurries of snow; but the hardy beasts evidently cared nothing for any but heavy storms, and seemed to prefer to lie in the snow rather than upon the open ground. They fed at irregular hours throughout the day, just like cattle; one band might be lying down while another was feeding. While travelling they usually went almost in single file. Evidently the winter had weakened them, and they were not in condition for running; for on the one or two occasions when I wanted to see them close up I ran right into them on horseback, both on level plains and going up hill along the sides of rather steep mountains. One band in particular I practically rounded up for John Burroughs, finally getting them to stand in a huddle while he and I sat on our horses less than fifty yards off. After they had run a little distance they opened their mouths wide and showed evident signs of distress.

We came across a good many carcasses. Two, a bull and a cow, had died from scab. Over half the remainder had evidently perished from cold or starvation. The others, including a bull, three cows and a score of yearlings, had been killed by cougars. In the Park the cougar is at present their only animal foe. The cougars were preying on nothing but elk in the Yellowstone Valley, and kept hanging about the neighborhood of the big bands. Evidently they usually selected some outlying yearling, stalked it as it lay or as it fed, and seized it by the head and throat. The bull which they killed was in a little open valley by himself, many miles from any other elk. The cougar which killed it, judging from its tracks, was a big male. As the elk were evidently rather too numerous for the feed, I do not think the cougars were doing any damage.

Coyotes are plentiful, but the elk evidently have no dread of them. One day I crawled up to within fifty yards of a band of elk lying down. A coyote was walking about among them, and beyond an occasional look they paid no heed to him. He did not venture to go within fifteen or twenty paces of any one of them. In fact, except the cougar, I saw but one living thing attempt to molest the elk. This was a golden eagle. We saw several of these great birds. On one occasion we had ridden out to the foot of a sloping mountain side, dotted over with bands and strings of elk amounting in the aggregate probably to a thousand head. Most of the bands were above the snow-line— some appearing away back toward the ridge crests, and looking as small as mice. There was one band well below the snow-line, and toward this we rode. While the elk were not shy or wary, in the sense that a hunter would use the words, they were by no means as familiar as the deer; and this particular band of elk, some twenty or thirty in all, watched us with interest as we approached. When we were still half a mile off they suddenly started to run toward us, evidently frightened by something. They ran quartering, and when about four hundred yards away we saw that an eagle was after them. Soon it swooped, and a yearling in the rear, weakly, and probably frightened by the swoop, turned a complete somersault, and when it recovered its feet stood still. The great bird followed the rest of the band across a little ridge, beyond which they disappeared. Then it returned, soaring high in the heavens, and after two or three wide circles, swooped down at the solitary yearling, its legs hanging down. We halted at two hundred yards to see the end. But the eagle could not quite make up its mind to attack. Twice it hovered within a foot or two of the yearling's head, again flew off and again returned. Finally the yearling trotted off after the rest of the band, and the eagle returned to the upper air. Later we found the carcass of a yearling, with two eagles, not to mention ravens and magpies, feeding on it; but I could not tell whether they had themselves killed the yearling or not.

Here and there in the region where the elk were abundant we came upon horses, which for some reason had been left out through the winter. They were much wilder than the elk. Evidently the Yellowstone Park is a natural nursery and breeding-ground of the elk, which here, as said above, far out-number all the other game put together. In the winter, if they cannot get to open water, they eat snow; but in several places where there had been springs which kept open all winter, we could see by the tracks that they had been regularly used by bands of elk. The men working at the new road along the face of the cliffs beside the Yellowstone River near Tower Falls informed me that in October enormous droves of elk coming from the interior of the Park and travelling northward to the lower lands had crossed the Yellowstone just above Tower Falls. Judging by their description, the elk had crossed by thousands in an uninterrupted stream, the passage taking many hours. In fact nowadays these Yellowstone elk are, with the exception of the Arctic caribou, the only American game which at times travel in immense droves like the buffalo of the old days.

A couple of days after leaving Cottonwood Creek—where we had spent several days—we camped at the Yellowstone Canyon below Tower Falls. Here we saw a second band of mountain sheep, numbering only eight—none of them old rams. We were camped on the west side of the canyon; the sheep had their abode on the opposite side, where they had spent the winter. It has recently been customary among some authorities, especially the English hunters and naturalists who have written of the Asiatic sheep, to speak as if sheep were naturally creatures of the plains rather than mountain climbers. I know nothing of the Old World sheep, but the Rocky Mountain big-horn is to the full as characteristic a mountain animal, in every sense of the word, as the chamois, and, I think, as the ibex. These sheep were well known to the road builders, who had spent the winter in the locality. They told me they never went back on the plains, but throughout the winter had spent their days and nights on the top of the cliff and along its face. This cliff was an alternation of sheer precipices and very steep inclines. When coated with ice it would be difficult to imagine an uglier

197

bit of climbing; but throughout the winter, and even in the wildest storms, the sheep had habitually gone down it to drink at the water below. When we first saw them they were lying sunning themselves on the edge of the canyon, where the rolling grassy country behind it broke off into the sheer descent. It was mid-afternoon and they were under some pines. After a while they got up and began to graze, and soon hopped unconcernedly down the side of the cliff until they were half-way to the bottom. They then grazed along the sides, and spent some time licking at a place where there was evidently a mineral deposit. Before dark they all lay down again on a steeply inclined jutting spur midway between the top and bottom of the canyon.

Next morning I thought I would like to see them close up, so I walked down three or four miles below where the canyon ended, crossed the stream, and came up the other side until I got on what was literally the stamping-ground of the sheep. Their tracks showed that they had spent their time for many weeks, and probably for all the winter, within a very narrow radius. For perhaps a mile and a half, or two miles at the very outside, they had wandered to and fro on the summit of the canyon, making what was almost a well-beaten path; always very near and usually on the edge of the cliff, and hardly ever going more than a few yards back into the grassy plain-and-hill country. Their tracks and dung covered the ground. They had also evidently descended into the depths of the canyon wherever there was the slightest break or even lowering in the upper line of the basalt cliffs. Although mountain sheep often browse in winter, I saw but few traces of browsing here; probably on the sheer cliff side they always get some grazing.

When I spied the band they were lying not far from the spot in which they had lain the day before, and in the same position on the brink of the canyon. They saw me and watched me with interest when I was two hundred yards off, but they let me get up within forty yards and sit down on a large stone to look at them, without running off. Most of them were lying down, but a couple were feeding steadily throughout the time I watched them. Suddenly one took the alarm and dashed straight over the cliff, the others all following at once. I ran after them to

198

the edge in time to see the last yearling drop off the edge of the basalt cliff and stop short on the sheer slope below, while the stones dislodged by his hoofs rattled down the canyon. They all looked up at me with great interest, and then strolled off to the edge of a jutting spur and lay down almost directly underneath me and some fifty yeards off. That evening on my return to camp we watched the band make its way right down to the river bed, going over places where it did not seem possible a four-footed creature could pass. They halted to graze here and there, and down the worst places they went very fast with great bounds. It was a marvellous exhibition of climbing.

After we had finished this horseback trip we went on sleds and skis to the upper Geyser Basin and the Falls of the Yellowstone. Although it was the third week in April, the snow was still several feet deep, and only thoroughly trained snow horses could have taken the sleighs along, while around the Yellowstone Falls it was possible to move only on snowshoes. There was little life in those woods. In the upper basin I caught a meadow mouse on the snow; I afterwards sent it to Hart Merriam, who told me it was of a species he had described from Idaho, *Microtus nanus;* it had not been previously found in the Yellowstone region. We saw an occasional pine squirrel, snowshoe rabbit or marten; and in the open meadows around the hot waters there were Canada geese and ducks of several species, and now and then a coyote. Around camp Clark's crows and Stellar's jays, and occasionally magpies, came to pick at the refuse; and of course they were accompanied by the whiskey jacks, which behaved with their usual astounding familiarity. At Norris Geyser Basin there was a perfect chorus of bird music from robins, western purple finches, juncos and mountain bluebirds. In the woods there were mountain chickadees and pygmy nuthatches, together with an occasional woodpecker. In the northern country we had come across a very few blue grouse and ruffed grouse, both as tame as possible. We had seen a pygmy owl no larger than a robin sitting on the top of a pine in broad daylight, and uttering at short intervals a queer un-owl-like cry.

The birds that interested us most were the solitaires, and especially the dippers or water-ousels. We were fortunate

199

enough to hear the solitaires sing not only when perched on trees, but on the wing, soaring over a great canyon. They are striking birds in every way, and their habit of singing while soaring, and their song, are alike noteworthy. Once I heard a solitaire singing at the top of a canyon, and an ousel also singing but a thousand feet below him; and in this case I thought the ousel sang better than his unconscious rival. The ousels are to my mind wellnigh the most attractive of all our birds, because of their song, their extraordinary habits, their whole personality. They stay through the winter in the Yellowstone because the waters are in many places open. We heard them singing cheerfully, their ringing melody having a certain suggestion of the winter wren's. Usually they sang while perched on some rock on the edge or in the middle of the stream; but sometimes on the wing; and often just before dipping under the torrent, or just after slipping out from it onto some ledge of rock or ice. In the open places the Western meadow lark was uttering its beautiful song; a real song as compared to the plaintive notes of its Eastern brother, and though short, yet with continuity and tune as well as melody. I love to hear the Eastern meadow lark in the early spring; but I love still more the song of the Western meadow lark. No bird escaped John Burroughs' eye; no bird note escaped his ear.

I cannot understand why the Old World ousel should have received such comparatively scant attention in the books, whether from nature writers or poets; whereas our ousel has greatly impressed all who know him. John Muir's description comes nearest doing him justice. To me he seems a more striking bird than for instance the skylark; though of course I not only admire but am very fond of the skylark. There are various pipits and larks in our own country which sing in highest air, as does the skylark, and their songs, though not as loud, are almost as sustained; and though they lack the finer kind of melody, so does his. The ousel, on the contrary, is a really brilliant singer, and in his habits he is even farther removed from the commonplace and the uninteresting than the lark himself. Some birds, such as the ousel, the mocking-bird, the solitaire, show marked originality, marked distinction; others do not; the chipping sparrow, for instance, while in no way objectionable (like the imported house sparrow), is yet a hope-lessly commonplace little bird alike in looks, habits and voice.

On the last day of my stay it was arranged that I should ride down from Mammoth Hot Springs to the town of Gardiner, just outside the Park limits, and there make an address at the laying of the cornerstone of the arch by which the main road is to enter the Park. Some three thousand people had gathered to attend the ceremonies. A little over a mile from Gardiner we came down out of the hills to the flat plain; from the hills we could see the crowd gathered around the arch waiting for me to come. We put spurs to our horses and cantered rapidly toward the appointed place, and on the way we passed within forty yards of a score of blacktails, which merely moved to one side and looked at us, and within almost as short a distance of half a dozen antelope. To any lover of nature it could not help being a delightful thing to see the wild and timid creatures of the wilderness rendered so tame; and their tameness in the immediate neighborhood of Gardiner, on the very edge of the Park, spoke volumes for the patriotic good sense of the citizens of Montana. At times the antelope actually cross the Park line to Gardiner, which is just outside, and feed unmolested in the very streets of the town; a fact which shows how very far advanced the citizens of Gardiner are in right feeling on this subject; for of course the Federal laws cease to protect the antelope as soon as they are out of the Park. Major Pitcher informed me that both the Montana and Wyoming people were cooperating with him in zealous fashion to preserve the game and put a stop to poaching. For their attitude in this regard they deserve the cordial thanks of all Americans interested in these great popular playgrounds, where bits of the old wilder-ness scenery and the old wilderness life are to be kept un-spoiled for the benefit of our children's children. Eastern people, and especially Eastern sportsmen, need to keep steadily in mind the fact that the westerners who live in the neighbor-hood of the forest preserves are the men who in the last resort will determine whether or not these preserves are to be permanent. They cannot in the long run be kept as forest and game reservations unless the settlers roundabout believe in them and heartily support them; and the rights of these settlers

201

must be carefully safeguarded, and they must be shown that the movement is really in their interest. The Eastern sportsman who fails to recognize these facts can do little but harm by advocacy of forest reserves.

It was in the interior of the Park, at the hotels beside the lake, the falls, and the various geyser basins, that we would have seen the bears had the season been late enough; but unfortunately the bears were still for the most part hibernating. We saw two or three tracks, but the animals themselves had not yet begun to come about the hotels. Nor were the hotels open. No visitors had previously entered the Park in the winter or early spring, the scouts and other employees being the only ones who occasionally traverse it. I was sorry not to see the bears, for the effect of protection upon bear life in the Yellowstone has been one of the phenomena of natural history. Not only have they grown to realize that they are safe, but, being natural scavengers and foul feeders, they have come to recognize the garbage heaps of the hotels as their special sources of food supply. Throughout the summer months they come to all the hotels in numbers, usually appearing in the late afternoon or evening, and they have become as indifferent to the presence of men as the deer themselves—some of them very much more indifferent. They have now taken their place among the recognized sights of the Park, and the tourists are nearly as much interested in them as in the geysers. In mussing over the garbage heaps they sometimes get tin cans stuck on their paws, and the result is painful. Buffalo Jones and some of the other scouts in extreme cases rope the bear, tie him up, cut the tin can off his paw, and let him go again. It is not an easy feat, but the astonishing thing is that it should be performed at all.

It was amusing to read the proclamations addressed to the tourists by the Park management, in which they were solemnly warned that the bears were really wild animals, and that they must on no account be either fed or teased. It is curious to think that the descendants of the great grizzlies which were the dread of the early explorers and hunters should now be semi-domesticated creatures, boldly hanging around crowded hotels for the sake of what they can pick up, and quite harmless so long as any reasonable precaution is exercised. They are much safer, for instance, than any ordinary bull or stallion, or even ram, and, in fact, there is no danger from them at all unless they are encouraged to grow too familiar or are in some way molested. Of course among the thousands of tourists there is a percentage of fools; and when fools go out in the afternoon to look at the bears feeding they occasionally bring themselves into jeopardy by some senseless act. The black bears and the cubs of the bigger bears can readily be driven up trees, and some of the tourists occasionally do this. Most of the animals never think of resenting it; but now and then one is run across which has its feelings ruffled by the performance. In the summer of 1902 the result proved disastrous to a too inquisitive tourist. He was travelling with his wife, and at one of the hotels they went out toward the garbage pile to see the bears feeding. The only bear in sight was a large she, which, as it turned out, was in a bad temper because another party of tourists a few minutes before had been chasing her cubs up a tree. The man left his wife and walked toward the bear to see how close he could get. When he was some distance off she charged him, whereupon he bolted back toward his wife. The bear overtook him, knocked him down and bit him severely. But the man's wife, without hesitation, attacked the bear with that thoroughly feminine weapon, an umbrella, and frightened her off. The man spent several weeks in the Park hospital before he recovered. Perhaps the following telegram sent by the manager of the Lake Hotel to Major Pitcher illustrates with sufficient clearness the mutual relations of the bears, the tourists, and the guardians of the public weal in the Park. The original was sent me by Major Pitcher. It runs:

"Lake. 7-27-'03. Major Pitcher, Yellowstone: As many as seventeen bears in an evening appear on my garbage dump. Tonight eight or ten. Campers and people not of my hotel throw things at them to make them run away. I cannot, unless there personally, control this. Do you think you could detail a trooper to be there every evening from say six o'clock until dark and make people remain behind danger line laid out by Warden Jones? Otherwise I fear some accident. The arrest of one or two of these campers might help. My own guests do pretty well as they are told. James Barton Key. 9 A.M."

Major Pitcher issued the order as requested.

At times the bears get so bold that they take to making inroads on the kitchen. One completely terrorized a Chinese cook. It would drive him off and then feast upon whatever was left behind. When a bear begins to act in this way or to show surliness it is sometimes necessary to shoot it. Other bears are tamed until they will feed out of the hand, and will come at once if called. Not only have some of the soldiers and scouts tamed bears in this fashion, but occasionally a chambermaid or waiter girl at one of the hotels has thus developed a bear as a pet.

This whole episode of bear life in the Yellowstone is so extraordinary that it will be well worth while for any man who has the right powers and enough time, to make a complete study of the life and history of the Yellowstone bears. Indeed, nothing better could be done by some of our out-door faunal naturalists than to spend at least a year in the Yellowstone, and to study the life habits of all the wild creatures therein. A man able to do this, and to write down accurately and interestingly what he has seen, would make a contribution of permanent value to our nature literature.

In May, after leaving the Yellowstone, I visited the Grand Canyon of the Colorado, and then went through the Yosemite Park with John Muir—the companion above all others for such a trip. It is hard to make comparisons among different kinds of scenery, all of them very grand and very beautiful; but nothing that I have ever seen has impressed me quite as much as the desolate and awful sublimity of the Grand Canyon of the Colorado. I earnestly wish that Congress would make it a national park, and I am sure that such course would meet the approbation of the people of Arizona. The people of California with wise and generous forethought have given the Yosemite Valley to the National Government to be kept as a national park, just as the surrounding country, including some of the groves of giant trees, has been kept. The flower-clad slopes of the Sierras—golden with the blazing poppy, brilliant with lilies and tulips and red-stemmed Manzinita bush—are unlike anything else in this country. As for the giant trees, no words can describe their majesty and beauty.

John Muir and I, with two packers and three pack mules, spent a delightful three days in the Yosemite. The first night was clear, and we lay in the open, on beds of soft fir boughs, among the huge, cinnamon-colored trunks of the sequoias. It was like lying in a great solemn cathedral, far vaster and more beautiful than any built by hand of man. Just at nightfall I heard, among other birds, thrushes which I think were Rocky Mountain hermits—the appropriate choir for such a place of worship. Next day we went by trail through the woods, seeing some deer—which were not wild—as well as mountain quail and blue grouse. Among the birds which we saw was a white-headed woodpecker; the interesting carpenter woodpeckers were less numerous than lower down. In the afternoon we struck snow, and had considerable difficulty in breaking our trails. A snow-storm came on toward evening, but we kept warm and comfortable in a grove of splendid firs—rightly named "magnificent"—near the brink of the wonderful Yosemite Valley. Next day we clambered down into it and at nightfall camped in its bottom, facing the giant cliffs over which the waterfalls thundered.

Surely our people do not understand even yet the rich heritage that is theirs. There can be nothing in the world more beautiful than the Yosemite, the groves of giant sequoias and redwoods, the Canyon of the Colorado, the Canyon of the Yellowstone, the Three Tetons; and our people should see to it that they are preserved for their children and their children's children forever, with their majestic beauty all unmarred.

John Burroughs. Yellowstone Park files

John Burroughs
1903

"I would like to visit the Yellowstone Park for a fortnight this spring," Theodore Roosevelt wrote to John Burroughs in 1903, "I wonder whether you could not come along?"[1] Roosevelt's choice of Burroughs as a traveling companion was a good one. Not only was the sixty-five-year-old naturalist one of the most popular wildlife writers of the day, he was truly a kindred spirit, a fellow lover of the wild.

"Roosevelt has a good deal of the boy in him. I suppose that makes him like me," Burroughs commented as the presidential party made its way west.[2] Though he felt familiar enough with the boy in Roosevelt, he was frequently awed by the man, often by the attention he found himself getting from the Chief Executive: "Yesterday I stood talking to Governor Van Zandt of Minn., near the President, when I dropped one of my gloves. Quick as a flash the President picked it up and handed it to me . . . . I am elbowing with governors and senators and mayors. They no doubt think the President a man of queer tastes."[3]

In his account of their Park tour, Burroughs, though he yielded to his tendency to adulate, provided us with yet another reason Roosevelt was wise in choosing "Oom John" to accompany him. There is something preciously human in Burroughs' story of the President interrupting his morning shave and hurrying "coatless, hatless, but not latherless," to observe some bighorn sheep near camp.[4] Time and again Burroughs revealed to his readers the private side of the President, the naturalist-turned-politician who was quite a fine traveling companion himself.

Roosevelt and Burroughs in camp at Yellowstone. Courtesy of the American Museum of National History

have said that I stood in dread of the necessity of snow-shoeing in the Park, and, in lieu of that, of horseback riding. Yet when we reached Gardiner, the entrance to the Park, on that bright, crisp April morning, with no snow in sight save that on the mountain-tops, and found Major Pitcher and Captain Chittenden at the head of a squad of soldiers, with a fine saddle-horse for the President, and an ambulance drawn by two span of mules for me, I confess that I experienced just a slight shade of mortification. I thought they might have given me the option of the saddle or the ambulance. Yet I entered the vehicle as if it was just what I had been expecting.

The President and his escort, with a cloud of cowboys hovering in the rear, were soon off at a lively pace, and my ambulance followed close, and at a lively pace, too; so lively that I soon found myself gripping the seat with both hands. "Well," I said to myself, "they are giving me a regular Western send-off"; and I thought, as the ambulance swayed from side to side, that it would suit me just as well if my driver did not try to keep up with the presidential procession. The driver and his mules were shut off from me by a curtain, but, looking ahead out of the sides of the vehicle, I saw two good-sized logs lying across our course. Surely, I thought (and barely had time to think), he will avoid these. But he did not, and as we passed over them I was nearly thrown through the top of the ambulance. "This *is* a lively send-off," I said, rubbing my bruises with one hand, while I clung to the seat with the other. Presently I saw the cowboys scrambling up the bank as if to get out of our way; then the President on his fine gray stallion scrambling up the bank with his escort, and looking ominously in my direction, as we thundered by.

"Well," I said, "this is indeed a novel ride; for once in my life I have side-tracked the President of the United States! I am given the right of way over all." On we tore, along the smooth, hard road, and did not slacken our pace till, at the end of a mile or two, we began to mount the hill toward Fort Yellowstone. And not till we reached the fort did I learn that our mules had run away. They had been excited beyond control by the presidential cavalcade, and the driver, finding he could not hold them, had aimed only to keep them in the road, and we very soon had the road all to ourselves.

209

Fort Yellowstone is at Mammoth Hot Springs, where one gets his first view of the characteristic scenery of the Park,— huge, boiling springs with their columns of vapor, and the first characteristic odors which suggest the traditional infernal regions quite as much as the boiling and steaming water does. One also gets a taste of a much more rarefied air than he has been used to, and finds himself panting for breath on a very slight exertion. The Mammoth Hot Springs have built themselves up an enormous mound that stands there above the village on the side of the mountain, terraced and scalloped and fluted, and suggesting some vitreous formation, or rare carving of enormous, many-colored precious stones. It looks quite unearthly, and, though the devil's frying pan, and ink pot, and the Stygian caves are not far off, the suggestion is of something celestial rather than of the nether regions,—a vision of jasper walls, and of amethyst battlements.

With Captain Chittenden I climbed to the top, stepping over the rills and creeks of steaming hot water, and looked at the marvelously clear, cerulean, but boiling, pools on the summit. The water seemed as unearthly in its beauty and purity as the gigantic sculpturing that held it.

The Stygian caves are still farther up the mountain,—little pockets in the rocks, or well-holes in the ground at your feet, filled with deadly carbon dioxide. We saw birds' feathers and quills in all of them. The birds hop into them, probably in quest of food or seeking shelter, and they never come out. We saw the body of a martin on the bank of one hole. Into one we sank a lighted torch, and it was extinguished as quickly as if we had dropped it into water. Each cave, or niche is a death valley on a small scale. Near by we came upon a steaming pool, or lakelet, of an acre or more in extent. A pair of mallard ducks were swimming about in one end of it,—the cool end. When we approached, they swam slowly over into the warmer water. As they progressed, the water got hotter and hotter, and the duck's discomfort was evident. Presently they stopped, and turned toward us, half appealingly, as I thought. They could go no farther; would we please come no nearer? As I took another step or two, up they rose and disappeared over the

210

hill. Had they gone to the extreme end of the pool, we could have had boiled mallard for dinner.

Another novel spectacle was at night, or near sundown, when the deer came down from the hills into the streets and ate hay, a few yards from the officers' quarters, as unconcernedly as so many domestic sheep. This they had been doing all winter, and they kept it up till May, at times a score or more of them profiting thus on the government's bounty. When the sundown gun was fired a couple of hundred yards away, they gave a nervous start, but kept on with their feeding. The antelope and elk and mountain sheep had not yet grown bold enough to accept Uncle Sam's charity in that way.

The President wanted all the freedom and solitude possible while in the Park, so all newspaper men and other strangers were excluded. Even the secret service men and his physician and private secretaries were left at Gardiner. He craved once more to be alone with nature; he was evidently hungry for the wild and the aboriginal,—a hunger that seems to come upon him regularly at least once a year, and drives him forth on his hunting trips for big game in the West.

We spent two weeks in the Park, and had fair weather, bright, crisp days, and clear, freezing nights. The first week we occupied three camps that had been prepared, or partly prepared, for us in the northeast corner of the Park, in the region drained by the Gardner River, where there was but little snow, and which we reached on horseback.

The second week we visited the geyser region, which lies a thousand feet or more higher, and where the snow was still five or six feet deep. This part of the journey was made in big sleighs, each drawn by two span of horses.

On the horseback excursion, which involved only about fifty miles of riding, we had a mule pack train, and Sibley tents and stoves, with quite a retinue of camp laborers, a lieutenant and an orderly or two, and a guide, Billy Hofer.

The first camp was in a wild, rocky, and picturesque gorge on the Yellowstone, about ten miles from the fort. A slight indisposition, the result of luxurious living, with no wood to chop or to saw, and no hills to climb, as at home, prevented me from joining the party till the third day. Then Captain Chittenden drove me eight miles in a buggy. About two miles from camp we came to a picket of two or three soldiers, where my big bay was in waiting for me. I mounted him confidently, and, guided by an orderly, took the narrow, winding trail toward camp. Except for an hour's riding the day before with Captain Chittenden, I had not been on a horse's back for nearly fifty years, and I had not spent as much as a day in the saddle during my youth. That first sense of a live, spirited, powerful animal beneath you, at whose mercy you are,—you, a pedestrian all your days,—with gullies and rocks and logs to cross, and deep chasms opening close beside you, is not a little disturbing. But my big bay did his part well, and I did not lose my head or my nerve, as we cautiously made our way along the narrow path on the side of the steep gorge, with a foaming torrent rushing along at its foot, nor yet when we forded the rocky and rapid Yellowstone. A misstep or a stumble on the part of my steed, and probably the first bubble of my confidence would have been shivered at once; but this did not happen, and in due time we reached the group of tents that formed the President's camp.

The situation was delightful,—no snow, scattered pine trees, a secluded valley, rocky heights, and the clear, ample, trouty waters of the Yellowstone. The President was not in camp. In the morning he had stated his wish to go alone into the wilderness. Major Pitcher very naturally did not quite like the idea, and wished to send an orderly with him.

"No," said the President. "Put me up a lunch, and let me go alone. I will surely come back."

And back he surely came. It was about five o'clock when he came briskly down the path from the east to the camp. It came out that he had tramped about eighteen miles through a very rough country. The day before, he and the major had located a band of several hundred elk on a broad, treeless hillside, and his purpose was to find those elk, and creep up on them, and eat his lunch under their very noses. And this he did, spending an hour or more within fifty yards of them. He came back looking as fresh as when he started, and at night, sitting before the big camp fire, related his adventure, and talked with his usual emphasis and copiousness of many things. He told me of

212

the birds he had seen or heard; among them he had heard one
that was new to him. From his description I told him I thought
it was Townsend's solitaire, a bird I much wanted to see and
hear. I had heard the West India solitaire,—one of the most
impressive songsters I ever heard,—and I wished to compare
our Western form with it.

The next morning we set out for our second camp, ten or a
dozen miles away, and in reaching it passed over much of the
ground the President had traversed the day before. As we came
to a wild, rocky place above a deep chasm of the river, with a
few scattered pine trees, the President said, "It was right here
that I heard that strange bird song." We paused a moment.
"And there it is now!" he exclaimed.

Sure enough, there was the solitaire singing from the top of
a small cedar,—a bright, animated, eloquent song, but without
the richness and magic of the song of the tropical species. We
hitched our horses, and followed the bird up as it flew from
tree to tree. The President was as eager to see and hear it as I
was. It seemed very shy, and we only caught glimpses of it. In
form and color it much resembles its West India cousin, and
suggests our catbird. It ceased to sing when we pursued it. It
is a bird found only in the wilder and higher parts of the
Rockies. My impression was that its song did not quite merit
the encomiums that have been pronounced upon it.

At this point, I saw amid the rocks my first and only Rocky
Mountain woodchucks, and, soon after we had resumed our
journey, our first blue grouse,—a number of them like larger
partridges. Occasionally we would come upon blacktailed deer,
standing or lying down in the bushes, their large ears at
attention being the first thing to catch the eye. They would
often allow us to pass within a few rods of them without
showing alarm. Elk horns were scattered all over this part of the
Park, and we passed several old carcasses of dead elk that had
probably died a natural death.

In a grassy bottom at the foot of a steep hill, while the
President and I were dismounted, and noting the pleasing
picture which our pack train of fifteen or twenty mules made
filing along the side of a steep grassy slope,—a picture which
he has preserved in his late volume, "Out-Door Pastimes of an

American Hunter,"—our attention was attracted by plaintive, musical, bird-like chirps that rose from the grass about us. I was almost certain it was made by a bird; the President was of like opinion; and we kicked about in the tufts of grass, hoping to flush the bird. Now here, now there, arose this sharp, but bird-like note. Finally, we found that it was made by a species of gopher, whose holes we soon discovered. What its specific name is I do not know, but it should be called the singing gopher.

Our destination this day was a camp on Cottonwood Creek, near "Hell-Roaring Creek." As we made our way in the afternoon along a broad, open, grassy valley, I saw a horseman come galloping over the hill to our right, startling up a band of elk as he came; riding across the plain, he wheeled his horse, and, with the military salute, joined our party. He proved to be a government scout, R.A. Waagner, called the "Duke of Hell Roaring,"—an educated officer from the Austrian army, who, for some unknown reason, had exiled himself here in this out-of-the-way part of the world. He was a man in his prime, of fine, military look and bearing. After conversing a few moments with the President and Major Pitcher, he rode rapidly away.

Our second camp, which we reached in mid-afternoon, was in the edge of the woods on the banks of a fine, large trout stream, where ice and snow still lingered in patches. I tried for trout in the head of a large, partly open pool, but did not get a rise; too much ice in the stream, I concluded. Very soon my attention was attracted by a strange note, or call, in the spruce woods. The President had also noticed it, and, with me, wondered what made it. Was it bird or beast? Billy Hofer said he thought it was an owl, but the sound in no way suggested an owl, and the sun was shining brightly. It was a sound such as a boy might make by blowing in the neck of an empty bottle. Presently we heard it beyond us on the other side of the creek, which was pretty good proof that the creature had wings.

"Let's go run that bird down," said the President to me.

So off we started across a small, open, snow-streaked plain, toward the woods beyond it. We soon decided that the bird was on the top of one of a group of tall spruces. After much

214

skipping about over logs and rocks, and much craning of our necks, we made him out on the peak of a spruce. I imitated his call, when he turned his head down toward us, but we could not make out what he was.

"Why did we not think to bring the glasses?" said the President.

"I will run and get them," I replied.

"No," said he, "you stay here and keep that bird treed, and I will fetch them."

So off he went like a boy, and was very soon back with the glasses. We quickly made out that it was indeed an owl,—the pigmy owl, as it turned out,—not much larger than a blue-bird. I think the President was as pleased as if we had bagged some big game. He had never seen the bird before.

bird

Throughout the trip I found his interest in bird life very keen, and his eye and ear remarkably quick. He usually saw the bird or heard its note as quickly as I did,—and I had nothing else to think about, and had been teaching my eye and ear the trick of it for over fifty years. Of course, his training as a big-game hunter stood him in good stead, but back of that were his naturalist's instincts, and his genuine love of all forms of wild life.

I have been told that his ambition up to the time he went to Harvard had been to be a naturalist, but that there they seem to have convinced him that all the out-of-door worlds of natural history had been conquered, and that the only worlds remaining were in the laboratory, and to be won with the microscope and the scalpel. But Roosevelt was a man made for action in a wide field, and laboratory conquests could not satisfy him. His instincts as a naturalist, however, lie back of all his hunting expeditions, and, in a large measure, I think, prompt them. Certain it is that his hunting records contain more live natural history than any similar records known to me, unless it be those of Charles St. John, the Scotch naturalist-sportsman.

The Canada jays, or camp-robbers, as they are often called, soon found out our camp that afternoon, and no sooner had the cook begun to throw out peelings and scraps and crusts than the jays began to carry them off, not to eat, as I observed, but to hide them in the thicker branches of the spruce trees. How tame they were, coming within three or four yards of one! Why this species of jay should everywhere be so familiar, and all other kinds so wild, is a puzzle.

In the morning, as we rode down the valley toward our next camping-place, at Tower Falls, a band of elk containing a hundred or more started along the side of the hill a few hundred yards away. I was some distance behind the rest of the party, as usual, when I saw the President wheel his horse off to the left, and, beckoning to me to follow, start at a tearing pace on the trail of the fleeing elk. He afterwards told me that he wanted me to get a good view of those elk at close range, and he was afraid that if he sent the major or Hofer to lead me, I would not get it. I hurried along as fast as I could, which was not fast; the way was rough,—logs, rocks, spring runs, and a tenderfoot rider.

Now and then the President, looking back and seeing what slow progress I was making, would beckon to me impatiently, and I could fancy him saying, "If I had a rope around him, he would come faster than that!" Once or twice I lost sight of both him and the elk; the alititude was great, and the horse was laboring like a steam engine on an upgrade. Still I urged him on. Presently, as I broke over a hill, I saw the President pressing the elk up the opposite slope. At the brow of the hill he stopped, and I soon joined him. There on the top, not fifty yards away, stood the elk in a mass, their heads toward us and their tongues hanging out. They could run no farther. The President laughed like a boy. The spectacle meant much more to him than it did to me. I had never seen a wild elk till on this trip, but they had been among the notable game that he had hunted. He had traveled hundreds of miles, and undergone great hardships, to get within rifle range of these creatures. Now here stood scores of them with lolling tongues, begging for mercy.

After gazing at them to our hearts' content, we turned away to look up our companions, who were nowhere within sight. We finally spied them a mile or more away, and, joining them, all made our way to an elevated plateau that commanded an open landscape three or four miles across. It was high noon, and the sun shone clear and warm. From this lookout we saw

216

herds upon herds of elk scattered over the slopes and gentle valleys in front of us. Some were grazing, some were standing or lying upon the ground, or upon the patches of snow. Through our glasses we counted the separate bands, and then the numbers of some of the bands or groups, and estimated that three thousand elk were in full view in the landscape around us. It was a notable spectacle. Afterward, in Montana, I attended a council of Indian chiefs at one of the Indian agencies, and told them, through their interpreter, that I had been with the Great Chief in the Park, and of the game we had seen. When I told them of these three thousand elk all in view at once, they grunted loudly, whether with satisfaction or with incredulity, I could not tell.

In the midst of this great game amphitheatre we dismounted and enjoyed the prospect. And the President did an unusual thing, he loafed for nearly an hour,—stretched himself out in the sunshine upon a flat rock, as did the rest of us, and, I hope, got a few winks of sleep. I am sure I did. Little, slender, striped chipmunks, about half the size of ours, were scurrying about; but I recall no other wild things save the elk.

From here we rode down the valley to our third camp, at Tower Falls, stopping on the way to eat our luncheon on a washed boulder beside a creek. On this ride I saw my first and only badger; he stuck his striped head out of his hole in the ground only a few yards away from us as we passed.

Our camp at Tower Falls was amid the spruces above a cañon of the Yellowstone, five or six hundred feet deep. It was a beautiful and impressive situation,—shelter, snugness, even cosiness,—looking over the brink of the awful and the terrifying. With a run and a jump I think one might have landed in the river at the bottom of the great abyss, and in doing so might have scaled one of those natural obelisks or needles of rock that stand up out of the depths two or three hundred feet high. Nature shows you what an enormous furrow her plough can open through the strata when moving horizontally, at the same time that she shows you what delicate and graceful columns her slower and gentler aerial forces can carve out of the piled strata. At the Falls there were two or three of these columns, like the picket-pins of the elder gods.

Across the cañon in front of our camp, upon a grassy plateau which was faced by a wall of trap rock, apparently thirty or forty feet high, a band of mountain sheep soon attracted our attention. They were within long rifle range, but were not at all disturbed by our presence, nor had they been disturbed by the road-builders who, under Captain Chittenden, were constructing a government road along the brink of the cañon. We speculated as to whether or not the sheep could get down the almost perpendicular face of the chasm to the river to drink. It seemed to me impossible. Would they try it while we were there to see? We all hoped so; and sure enough, late in the afternoon the word came to our tents that the sheep were coming down. The President, with coat off and a towel around his neck, was shaving. One side of his face was half shaved, and the other side lathered. Hofer and I started for a point on the brink of the cañon where we could have a better view.

"By Jove," said the President, "I must see that. The shaving can wait, and the sheep won't."

So on he came, accoutred as he was,—coatless, hatless, but not latherless, nor towelless. Like the rest of us, his only thought was to see those sheep do their "stunt." With glasses in hand, we watched them descend those perilous heights, leaping from point to point, finding a foothold where none appeared to our eyes, loosening fragments of the crumbling rocks as they came, now poised upon some narrow shelf and preparing for the next leap, zigzagging or plunging straight down till the bottom was reached, and not one accident or misstep amid all that insecure footing. I think the President was the most pleased of us all; he laughed with the delight of it, and quite forgot his need of a hat and coat till I sent for them.

In the night we heard the sheep going back; we could tell by the noise of the falling stones. In the morning I confidently expected to see some of them lying dead at the foot of the cliffs, but there they all were at the top once more, apparently safe and sound. They do, however, occasionally meet with accidents in their perilous climbing, and their dead bodies have been found at the foot of the rocks. Doubtless some point of rock to which they had trusted gave way, and crushed them in the descent, or fell upon those in the lead.

The next day, while the rest of us went fishing for trout in the Yellowstone, three or four miles above the camp, over the roughest trail that we had yet traversed on horseback, the President, who never fishes unless put to it for meat, went off alone again with his lunch in his pocket, to stalk those sheep as he had stalked the elk, and to feel the old sportsman's thrill without the use of firearms. To do this involved a tramp of eight or ten miles down the river to a bridge and up the opposite bank. This he did, and ate his lunch near the sheep, and was back in camp before we were.

We took some large cut-throat trout, as they are called, from the yellow mark across their throats, and I saw at short range a blacktailed deer bounding along in that curious, stiff-legged, mechanical, yet springy manner, apparently all four legs in the air at once, and all four feet reaching the ground at once, affording a very singular spectacle.

We spent two nights in our Tower Falls camp, and on the morning of the third day set out on our return to Fort Yellowstone, pausing at Yancey's on our way, and exchanging greetings with the old frontiersman, who died a few weeks later.

While in camp we always had a big fire at night in the open near the tents, and around this we sat upon logs or campstools, and listened to the President's talk. What a stream of it he poured forth! and what a varied and picturesque stream! —anecdote, history, science, politics, adventure, literature; bits of his experience as a ranchman, hunter, Rough Rider, legislator, civil service commissioner, police commissioner, governor, president—the frankest confessions, the most telling criticisms, happy characterizations of prominent political leaders, or foreign rulers, or members of his own Cabinet; always surprising by his candor, astonishing by his memory, and diverting by his humor. His reading has been very wide, and he has that rare type of memory which retains details as well as mass and generalities. One night something started him off on ancient history, and one would have thought he was just fresh from his college course in history, the dates and names and events came so readily. Another time he discussed palæontology, and rapidly gave the outlines of the science, and the main facts, as if he had been reading up on the subject

219

that very day. He sees things as wholes, and hence the relation of the parts comes easy to him.

At dinner, at the White House, the night before we started on the expedition, I heard him talking with a guest,—an officer of the British army, who was just back from India. And the extent and variety of his information about India and Indian history and the relations of the British government to it were extraordinary. It put the British major on his mettle to keep pace with him.

One night in camp he told us the story of one of his Rough Riders who had just written him from some place in Arizona. The Rough Riders, wherever they are now, look to him in time of trouble. This one had come to grief in Arizona. He was in jail. So he wrote the President, and his letter ran something like this:—

"Dear Colonel,—I am in trouble. I shot a lady in the eye, but I did not intend to hit the lady; I was shooting at my wife."

And the presidential laughter rang out over the tree-tops. To another Rough Rider, who was in jail, accused of horse stealing, he had loaned two hundred dollars to pay counsel on his trial, and, to his surprise, in due time the money came back. The ex-Rough wrote that his trial never came off. *"We elected our district attorney"*; and the laughter again sounded, and drowned the noise of the brook near by.

On another occasion we asked the President if he was ever molested by any of the "bad men" of the frontier, with whom he had often come in contact. "Only once," he said. The cowboys had always treated him with the utmost courtesy, both on the round-up and in camp; "and the few real desperadoes I have seen were also perfectly polite." Once only was he maliciously shot at, and then not by a cowboy nor a *bona fide* "bad man," but by a "broad-hatted ruffian of a cheap and common-place type." He had been compelled to pass the night at a little frontier hotel where the bar-room occupied the whole lower floor, and was, in consequence, the only place where the guests of the hotel, whether drunk or sober, could sit. As he entered the room, he saw that every man there was being terrorized by a half-drunken ruffian who stood in the middle of the floor with a revolver in each hand, compelling different ones to treat.

"I went and sat down behind the stove," said the President, "as far from him as I could get; and hoped to escape his notice. The fact that I wore glasses, together with my evident desire to avoid a fight, apparently gave him the impression that I could be imposed upon with impunity. He very soon approached me, flourishing his two guns, and ordered me to treat. I made no reply for some moments, when the fellow became so threatening that I saw something had to be done. The crowd, mostly sheep-herders and small grangers, sat or stood back against the wall, afraid to move. I was unarmed, and thought rapidly. Saying, 'Well, if I must, I must,' I got up as if to walk around him to the bar, then, as I got opposite him, I wheeled and fetched him as heavy a blow on the chin-point as I could strike. He went down like a steer before the axe, firing both guns into the ceiling as he went. I jumped on him, and, with my knees on his chest, disarmed him in a hurry. The crowd was then ready enough to help me, and we hog-tied him and put him in an outhouse." The President alludes to this incident in his "Ranch Life," but does not give the details. It brings out his mettle very distinctly.

He told us in an amused way of the attempts of his political opponents at Albany, during his early career as a member of the Assembly, to besmirch his character. His outspoken criticisms and denunciations had become intolerable to them, so they laid a trap for him, but he was not caught. His innate rectitude and instinct for the right course saved him, as it has saved him many times since. I do not think that in any emergency he has to debate with himself long as to the right course to be pursued; he divines it by a kind of infallible instinct. His motives are so simple and direct that he finds a straight and easy course where another man, whose eye is less single, would flounder and hesitate.

One night he entertained us with reminiscences of the Cuban War, of his efforts to get his men to the firing line when the fighting began, of his greenness and general ignorance of the whole business of war, which in his telling was very amusing. He has probably put it all in his book about the war, a work I have not yet read. He described the look of the slope of Kettle Hill when they were about to charge up it, how the grass was combed and rippled by the storm of rifle bullets that swept down it. He said, "I was conscious of being pale when I looked at it and knew that in a few moments we were going to charge there." The men of his regiment were all lying flat upon the ground, and it became his duty to walk along their front and encourage them and order them up on their feet. "Get up, men, get up!" One big fellow did not rise. Roosevelt stooped down and took hold of him and ordered him up. Just at that moment a bullet struck the man and went the entire length of him. He never rose.

On this or on another occasion when a charge was ordered, he found himself a hundred yards or more in advance of his regiment, with only the color bearer and one corporal with him. He said they planted the flag there, while he rushed back to fetch the men. He was evidently pretty hot. "Can it be that you flinched when I led the way!" and then they came with a rush. On the summit of Kettle Hill he was again in advance of his men, and as he came up, three Spaniards rose out of the trenches and deliberately fired at him at a distance of only a few paces, and then turned and fled. But a bullet from his revolver stopped one of them. He seems to have been as much exposed to bullets in this engagement as Washington was at Braddock's defeat, and to have escaped in the same marvelous manner.

The President unites in himself powers and qualities that rarely go together. Thus, he has both physical and moral courage in a degree rare in history. He can stand calm and unflinching in the path of a charging grizzly, and he can confront with equal coolness and determination the predaceous corporations and money powers of the country.

He unites the qualities of the man of action with those of the scholar and writer,—another very rare combination. He unites the instincts and accomplishments of. the best breeding and culture with the broadest democratic sympathies and affiliations. He is as happy with a frontiersman like Seth Bullock as with a fellow Harvard man, and Seth Bullock is happy, too.

He unites great austerity with great good nature. He unites great sensibility with great force and will power. He loves solitude, and he loves to be in the thick of the fight. His love of nature is equaled only by his love of the ways and marts of men.

He is doubtless the most vital man on the continent, if not on the planet, to-day. He is many-sided, and every side throbs with his tremendous life and energy; the pressure is equal all around. His interests are as keen in natural history as in economics, in literature as in statecraft, in the young poet as in the old soldier, in preserving peace as in preparing for war. And he can turn all his great power into the new channel on the instant. His interest in the whole of life, and in the whole life of the nation, never flags for a moment. His activity is tireless. All the relaxation he needs or craves is a change of work. He is like the farmer's fields, that only need a rotation of crops. I once heard him say that all he cared about being President was just "the big work."

During this tour through the West, lasting over two months, he made nearly three hundred speeches; and yet on his return Mrs. Roosevelt told me he looked as fresh and unworn as when he left home.

We went up into the big geyser region with the big sleighs, each drawn by four horses. A big snow-bank had to be shoveled through for us before we got to the Golden Gate, two miles above Mammoth Hot Springs. Beyond that we were at an altitude of about eight thousand feet, on a fairly level course that led now through woods, and now through open country, with the snow of a uniform depth of four or five feet, except as we neared the "formations," where the subterranean warmth kept the ground bare. The roads had been broken and the snow packed for us by teams from the fort, otherwise the journey would have been impossible.

The President always rode beside the driver. From his youth, he said, this seat had always been the most desirable one to him. When the sleigh would strike the bare ground, and begin to drag heavily, he would bound out nimbly and take to his heels, and then all three of us—Major Pitcher, Mr. Childs, and myself—would follow suit, sometimes reluctantly on my part.

223

Walking at that altitude is no fun, especially if you try to keep pace with such a walker as the President is. But he could not sit at his ease and let those horses drag him in a sleigh over bare ground. When snow was reached, we would again quickly resume our seats.

As one nears the geyser region, he gets the impression from the columns of steam going up here and there in the distance—now from behind a piece of woods, now from out a hidden valley—that he is approaching a manufacturing centre, or a railroad terminus. And when he begins to hear the hoarse snoring of "Roaring Mountain," the illusion is still more complete. At Norris there is a big vent where the steam comes tearing out of a recent hole in the ground with terrific force. Huge mounds of ice had formed from the congealed vapor all around it, some of them very striking.

The novelty of the geyser region soon wears off. Steam and hot water are steam and hot water the world over, and the exhibition of them here did not differ, except in volume, from what one sees by his own fireside. The "Growler" is only a boiling tea-kettle on a large scale, and "Old Faithful" is as if the lid were to fly off, and the whole contents of the kettle should be thrown high into the air. To be sure, boiling lakes and steaming rivers are not common, but the new features seemed, somehow, out of place, and as if nature had made a mistake. One disliked to see so much good steam and hot water going to waste; whole towns might be warmed by them, and big wheels made to go round. I wondered that they had not piped them into the big hotels which they opened for us, and which were warmed by wood fires.

At Norris the big room that the President and I occupied was on the ground floor, and was heated by a huge box stove. As we entered it to go to bed, the President said, "Oom John, don't you think it is too hot here?"

"I certainly do," I replied.

"Shall I open the window?"

"That will just suit me." And he threw the sash, which came down to the floor, all the way up, making an opening like a doorway. The night was cold, but neither of us suffered from the abundance of fresh air.

224

The caretaker of the building was a big Swede called Andy. In the morning Andy said that beat him: "There was the President of the United States sleeping in that room, with the window open to the floor, and not so much as one soldier outside on guard."

The President had counted much on seeing the bears that in summer board at the Fountain Hotel, but they were not yet out of their dens. We saw the track of only one, and he was not making for the hotel. At all the formations where the geysers are, the ground was bare over a large area. I even saw a wild flower—an early buttercup, not an inch high—in bloom. This seems to be the earliest wild flower in the Rockies. It is the only fragrant buttercup I know.

As we were riding along in our big sleigh toward the Fountain Hotel, the President suddenly jumped out, and, with his soft hat as a shield to his hand, captured a mouse that was running along over the ground near us. He wanted it for Dr. Merriam, on the chance that it might be a new species. While we all went fishing in the afternoon, the President skinned his mouse, and prepared the pelt to be sent to Washington. It was done as neatly as a professed taxidermist would have done it. This was the only game the President killed in the Park. In relating the incident to a reporter while I was in Spokane, the thought occurred to me, Suppose he changes that *u* to an *o*, and makes the President capture a moose, what a pickle I shall be in! Is it anything more than ordinary newspaper enterprise to turn a mouse into a moose? But, luckily for me, no such metamorphosis happened to that little mouse. It turned out not to be a new species, as it should have been, but a species new to the Park.

I caught trout that afternoon, on the edge of steaming pools in the Madison River that seemed to my hand almost blood-warm. I suppose they found better feeding where the water was warm. On the table they did not compare with our Eastern brook trout.

I was pleased to be told at one of the hotels that they had kalsomined some of the rooms with material from one of the devil's paint-pots. It imparted a soft, delicate, pinkish tint, not at all suggestive of things satanic.

One afternoon at Norris , the President and I took a walk to observe the birds. In the grove about the barns there was a great number, the most attractive to me being the mountain bluebird. These birds we saw in all parts of the Park, and at Norris there was an unusual number of them. How blue they were,—breast and all! In voice and manner they were almost identical with our bluebird. The Western purple finch was abundant here also, and juncos, and several kinds of sparrows, with an occasional Western robin. A pair of wild geese were feeding in the low, marshy ground not over one hundred yards from us, but when we tried to approach nearer they took wing. A few geese and ducks seem to winter in the Park.

The second morning at Norris one of our teamsters, George Marvin, suddenly dropped dead from some heart affection, just as he had finished caring for his team. It was a great shock to us all. I never saw a better man with a team than he was. I had ridden on the seat beside him all the day previous. On one of the "formations" our teams had got mired in the soft, putty-like mud, and at one time it looked as if they could never extricate themselves, and I doubt if they could have, had it not been for the skill with which Marvin managed them. We started for the Grand Cañon up the Yellowstone that morning, and, in order to give myself a walk over the crisp snow in the clear, frosty air, I set out a little while in advance of the teams. As I did so, I saw the President, accompanied by one of the teamsters, walking hurriedly toward the barn to pay his last respects to the body of Marvin. After we had returned to Mammoth Hot Springs, he made inquiries for the young woman to whom he had been told that Marvin was engaged to be married. He looked her up, and sat a long time with her in her home, offering his sympathy, and speaking words of conso-lation. The act shows the depth and breadth of his humanity.

At the Cañon Hotel the snow was very deep, and had become so soft from the warmth of the earth beneath, as well as from the sun above, that we could only reach the brink of the Cañon on skis. The President and Major Pitcher had used skis before, but I had not, and, starting out without the customary pole, I soon came to grief. The snow gave way beneath me, and I was soon in an awkward predicament. The more I struggled, the lower my head and shoulders went, till only my heels, strapped to those long timbers, protruded above the snow. To reverse my position was impossible till some one came and reached me the end of a pole, and pulled me upright. But I very soon got the hang of the things, and the President and I quickly left the superintendent behind. I think I could have passed the President, but my manners forbade. He was heavier than I was, and broke in more. When one of his feet would go down half a yard or more, I noted with admiration the skilled diplomacy he displayed in extricating it. The tendency of my skis was all the time to diverge, and each to go off at an acute angle to my main course, and I had constantly to be on the alert to check this tendency.

Paths had been shoveled for us along the brink of the Cañon, so that we got the usual views from the different points. The Cañon was nearly free from snow, and was a grand spectacle, by far the grandest to be seen in the Park. The President told us that once, when pressed for meat, while returning through here from one of his hunting trips, he had made his way down to the river that we saw rushing along beneath us, and had caught some trout for dinner. Necessity alone could induce him to fish.

Across the head of the Falls there was a bridge of snow and ice, upon which we were told that the coyotes passed. As the season progressed, there would come a day when the bridge would not be safe. It would be interesting to know if the coyotes knew when this time arrived.

The only live thing we saw in the Cañon was an osprey perched upon a rock opposite us.

Near the falls of the Yellowstone, as at other places we had visited, a squad of soldiers had their winter quarters. The President called on them, as he had called upon the others, looked over the books they had to read, examined their house-keeping arrangements, and conversed freely with them.

In front of the hotel were some low hills separated by gentle valleys. At the President's suggestion, he and I raced on our skis down those inclines. We had only to stand up straight, and let gravity do the rest. As we were going swiftly down the side of one of the hills, I saw out of the corner of my eye the

President taking a header into the snow. The snow had given way beneath him, and nothing could save him from taking the plunge. I don't know whether I called out, or only thought, something about the downfall of the administration. At any rate, the administration was down, and pretty well buried, but it was quickly on its feet again, shaking off the snow with a boy's laughter. I kept straight on, and very soon the laugh was on me, for the treacherous snow sank beneath me, and I took a header, too.

"Who is laughing now, Oom John?" called out the President.

The spirit of the boy was in the air that day about the Cañon of the Yellowstone, and the biggest boy of us all was President Roosevelt.

The snow was getting so soft in the middle of the day that our return to the Mammoth Hot Springs could no longer be delayed. Accordingly, we were up in the morning, and ready to start on the home journey, a distance of twenty miles, by four o'clock. The snow bore up the horses well till mid-forenoon, when it began to give way beneath them. But by very careful management we pulled through without serious delay, and were back again at the house of Major Pitcher in time for luncheon, being the only outsiders who had ever made the tour of the Park so early in the season.

A few days later I bade good-by to the President, who went on his way to California, while I made a loop of travel to Spokane, and around through Idaho and Montana, and had glimpses of the great optimistic, sunshiny West that I shall not soon forget.

A Note on the Readings

Before turning to the sources and notes, a word of warning is in order. Journals and popular articles such as the ones in this book are "accidental history." Their authors probably did not expect them to endure very long, and did not feel an obligation to posterity to make sure every statement was accurate. Compare, for example, Muir's and Owen's descriptions of the Firehole River during an eruption of the Excelsior Geyser. Notice how many different heights were given for the Lower Falls. Less conspicuous, but just as unreliable, are references made to "Colter's Hell," a name which was not, in fact, originally applied to Yellowstone Park at all. These inaccuracies and others do not detract from the selections—this is not a reference book—but they necessitate caution on the readers's part.

The Yellowstone experience has been restricted since the 1880s. Soaping geysers, climbing in the Grand Canyon near the Lower Falls, and swimming in the Hot Springs were terribly destructive pastimes, and dangerous besides. Such activities were so unsuited to the spirit of American national parks that we should not even regret their passing.

Strong feelings were expressed in several articles about Park management, congressional apathy and visitor insensitivity. These are *all* still living issues.

If conflicting information, surprising activities and restless sentiments have aroused your curiousity, then this book has exceeded its own expectations. It has done more than entertain. Perhaps the references in the footnotes and in the bibliography that follow will satisfy your curiosity, but if they don't, that is even better. The urgency and challenge of the closing paragraph in Theodore Roosevelt's article have increased beyond anything he could have dreamed.

A NOTE ON THE READINGS

Sources of the readings I have used in this book are as follows:

1. Mrs. George F. Cowan, "Reminiscences of Pioneer Life: A Trip to the National Park in 1877—An Account of the Nez Perce Raid from a Woman's Standpoint—Incidents and Accidents," from *Wonderland,* 12, March 1904.

2. William O. Owen, "The First Bicycle Tour of Yellowstone National Park," from *Outing,* June 1891.

3. John Muir, "The Yellowstone National Park," from *Our National Parks* (New York: Houghton, Mifflin and Co., 1901).

4. Owen Wister, "Old Yellowstone Days," from *Harper's Monthly Magazine,* March 1936. Reprinted by special permission of the publisher.

5. Rudyard Kipling, extracted from *From Sea to Sea: Letters of Travel* (New York: Charles Scribner's Sons, 1910).

6. Frederic Remington, "Policing the Yellowstone," from *Pony Tracks* (New York: Harper, 1898).

7. Emerson Hough, "Forest and Stream's Yellowstone Park Game Exploration," from *Forest and Stream,* May 5 and June 16, 1894.

8. Charles Dudley Warner, "Editor's Study," from *Harper's,* January 1897.

9. George Anderson, "Work of the Cavalry in Protecting Yellowstone National Park," from *Journal of the United States Cavalry Association,* March 1897.

10. Theodore Roosevelt, "Wilderness Reserves: The Yellowstone National Park," from *Outdoor Pastimes of an American Hunter* (New York: Charles Scribner's Sons, 1923). This article appeared in slightly different form in a Boone and Crockett club book and in *Forestry and Irrigation* as listed in the bibliography.

11. John Burroughs, extracted from *Camping and Tramping with Roosevelt* (Boston: Houghton, Mifflin and Co., 1907).

Notes

1. Mrs. George Cowan

1. Alvin M. Josephy, *Chief Joseph's People and their War* (Yellowstone National Park: Yellowstone Library and Museum Association, 1964).

2. Aubrey L. Haines, *The Yellowstone Story* (Boulder, Colo.: Colorado Associated University Press, 1977), pp. 218-37.

3. Mrs. George F. Cowan, "Reminiscences of Pioneer Life: A Trip to the National Park in 1877—An Account of the Nez Perce Raid from a Woman's Standpoint—Incidents and Accidents," *Wonderland*, 12, March 1904. Mrs. Cowan published her story in several periodicals. The most thorough account of the Cowan party adventure appears in the book by Frank Carpenter, *Adventures in Geyser Land* (Caldwell, Idaho: Caxton Printers, 1935).

2. William O. Owen

1. A brief account of the Owen-Langford controversy can be found in David J. Saylor, *Jackson Hole, Wyoming: In the Shadow of the Tetons* (Norman, Okla.: University of Oklahoma Press, 1970), pp. 103-6. A wealth of original material on this controversy and its results is available in the Yellowstone Park Reference Library in two scrapbooks: *Yellowstone Park Miscellanies,* Part VI (Accession No. 942) and Part VII (Accession No. 943). Nathaniel Langford was a well-known figure himself, having been involved in the establishment of Yellowstone Park and serving five years as its first superintendent.

3. John Muir

1. Linnie Marsh Wolfe, *Son of Wilderness: The Life of John Muir* (New York: A.A. Knopf, 1946), p. 234.

2. John Muir, *Our National Parks* (New York: Houghton, Mifflin and Co., 1901), p. 43. This book was a collection of articles John Muir had written for individual publication in the 1890s. The Yellowstone article appeared in *The Atlantic Monthly* 81 (January 1898; April 1898).

4. Owen Wister

1. G. Edward White, *The Eastern Establishment and the Western Experience* (New Haven: Yale University Press, 1968), p. 70.

2. Owen Wister, *Owen Wister Out West,* ed. Fanny Kemble Wister (Chicago: University of Chicago Press, 1958), p. 59.

231

NOTES

5. Rudyard Kipling

1. Rudyard Kipling, *From Sea to Sea: Letters of Travel* (New York: Charles Scribner's Sons, 1910), pp. 129, 135. In the preface to *From Sea to Sea,* Kipling explained that the book was a gathering of articles he had written for the *Civil and Military Gazette* and the *Pioneer.* These were newspapers in India, the country of his birth and the scene of many of his most famous tales. He was compelled to publish the articles, he claimed, "by the enterprise of various publishers who, not content with disinterring old newspaper work from decent seclusion in office files, have in several instances seen fit to embellish it with additions and interpolations."

6. Frederic Remington

1. See chapter 7 for the story of the most successful of all these early patrols.

2. Owen Wister, *Owen Wister Out West,* ed. Fanny Kemble Wister (Chicago: University of Chicago Press, 1958), p. 182.

3. Ibid., p. 181.

4. The Remington-Wister friendship has been examined in Ben Merchant Vorpahl, *My Dear Wister: The Frederic Remington-Owen Wister Letters* (Palo Alto: American West Publishing Co., 1972). The influence of the west on Remington, Wister, and Roosevelt is the topic of G. Edward White, *The Eastern Establishment and the Western Experience* (New Haven: Yale University Press, 1968).

7. Emerson Hough

1. Two good accounts of the Howell episode are Aubrey L. Haines, *The Yellowstone Story* (Boulder, Colo.: Colorado Associated University Press, 1977), vol. II, pp. 60-67, and Freeman Tilden, *Following the Frontier with F.J. Haynes* (New York: Alfred Knopf, 1964), pp. 357-71. The text of the National Park Protective Act appears in Hiram Martin Chittenden, *The Yellowstone National Park, Historical and Descriptive* (Cincinnati: The Robert Clarke Company, 1895), pp. 348-52. A recent study of the bison protection efforts of the army and their supporters in Yellowstone is Paul Schullery, "'Buffalo' Jones and the Bison Herd in Yellowstone: Another Look," *Montana: The Magazine of Western History,* July 1976, pp. 40-51.

2. Robert Shankland, *Steve Mather of the National Parks* (New York: Alfred Knopf, 1970), pp. 165-66.

9. George Anderson

1. Paul Schullery, *The Yellowstone Archives, Past Present and Future* (M.A. Thesis, Ohio University, Athens, Ohio, 1975), pp. 49-50.

2. Captain George Anderson, *Report of the Superintendent of Yellowstone National Park* (Washington, D.C.: U.S. Government Printing Office, 1894), pp. 9-10.

10. Theodore Roosevelt

1. John Reiger, *American Sportsmen and the Origins of Conservation* (New York: Winchester Press, 1975), p. 113. Reiger does not claim that Yellowstone inspired Roosevelt to become a conservationist—only that his previous experience as a naturalist and hunter had prepared him for conservation work and that the plight of Yellowstone was the catalyst that activated his interest.

2. Paul Schullery, "Theodore Roosevelt in Yellowstone Park," *Montana, The Magazine of Western History*, forthcoming.

11. John Burroughs

1. Theodore Roosevelt, *The Letters of Theodore Roosevelt,* ed. Elting Morrison, vol. III (Cambridge: Harvard University Press, 1951-1954), p. 443.

2. Clara Barrus, *The Life and Letters of John Burroughs* (New York: Houghton, Mifflin and Co., 1925), p. 61.

3. Ibid.

4. John Burroughs, *Camping and Tramping with Roosevelt* (Boston: Houghton, Mifflin and Co., 1907), p. 48.

Suggestions for Further Reading

Any careful study of the history of Yellowstone Park should begin with the magnificent two-volume book *The Yellowstone Story*, by Aubrey L. Haines (Boulder: Colorado Associated University Press, 1977). Among the other useful general histories are Aubrey Haines, *Yellowstone National Park, Its Exploration and Establishment* (Washington: U.S. Government Printing Office, 1974); Hiram Chittenden, *The Yellowstone National Park, Historical and Descriptive* (Cincinnati: Robert Clarke Co., 1895); Louis Cramton, *Early History of Yellowstone National Park and Its Relation to National Park Policies* (Washington: U.S. Government Printing Office, 1932); Merrill Beal, *The Story of Man in Yellowstone* (Caldwell, Idaho: The Caxton Printers, Ltd. 1949); and Duane Hampton, *How the U.S. Cavalry Saved Our National Parks*, (Bloomington: Indiana University Press, 1971).

Some books that deal with the early conservation movement are Roderick Nash, *Wilderness and the American Mind* (New Haven: Yale University Press, 1967); Samuel P. Hays, *Conservation and The Gospel of Efficiency, the Progressive Conservation Movement, 1890-1920* (Cambridge: Harvard University Press, 1959); and John Reiger, *American Sportsmen and the Origins of Conservation* (New York: Winchester Press, 1975).

The development of tourism in the late nineteenth and early twentieth centuries is studied by Earl Pomeroy, *In Search of the Golden West: The Tourist in Western America* (New York: Alfred Knopf, 1957) and Robert Athearn, *Westward the Briton* (New York: Charles Scribner's Sons, 1953).

The bibliography that follows presents a fair portion of the material published about the days of the grand tour. The listing is restricted in several ways.

It includes only material written about the Park before 1916. In 1915 automobiles were allowed to enter the Park, and the following year the National Park Service was created. These two events marked the end of the "Old Yellowstone Days."

With only a few exceptions, the bibliography does not include newspaper accounts. There are too many of these to be presented here. It does not include unpublished materials, such as journals, reminiscences, or interviews. The bibliographies in Haines, *The Yellowstone Story,* offer many of these. The Yellowstone Park Reference Library has a fine collection of such material, as well as hundreds of newspaper clippings.

It does not include routine government reports and correspondence (The Superintendent's Annual Reports are in the Yellowstone Park Reference Library). For more information on this material see the two guides to the Yellowstone Archives, *Introductory Guide and Organization Key to the Yellowstone National Park Archives (pre-1916)* on 49 Reels of 35MM Microfilm (Yellowstone Park: National Park Service, 1976, 41 pp. mimeo) and *Subject Inventory and Organization Key to the Yellowstone National Park Archives (post-1916)* (Yellowstone Park: National Park Service, 1977, 23 pp., mimeo). The Yellowstone Archives, occupying approximately 200 shelf-feet of space, are the collected administrative records of Yellowstone Park. They are an official branch of the National Archives, and are located in Yellowstone Park, Wyoming.

It does not include reports of a purely technical nature, such as scientific studies, except those with unusually colorful narratives or significant authorship.

It does not include articles of a purely editorial or political character, for they tell little or nothing about the tour.

It does include the early guide books. Though these hardly give the feelings or impressions of visitors, they are an essential source of information about the tour. They are listed in their first recognizable edition. Some appeared in many editions, with several title changes.

This list is certainly not complete. The rate at which new material is still being found makes it quite clear that much

236

more is still unidentified. I present here only those which I have come across in my research, and which I find appropriate.

The process of compiling the following bibliography was greatly assisted by several excellent bibliographies already in print, especially Carl P. Russell's *A Concise History of Science and Scientific Investigations in Yellowstone National Park* (Department of the Interior, 1933) and the revision of the Russell bibliography found in *A Bibliography of National Parks and Monuments West of the Mississippi,* Vol. I, (Department of the Interior, 1941). In addition to these, the bibliographies in the books mentioned above, especially the Haines books, were very useful.

To the reader who wishes to share more of the early Yellowstone experience, I recommend these titles. They are no substitute for visiting the Park, but a pleasant ramble through the literature of "Wonderland" is quite a grand tour of its own.

Bibliography

Anderson, A.A. *Experiences and Impressions.* New York: The Macmillan Company, 1933, pp. 89-116.

Anderson, George. "Protection of Yellowstone Park." In *Hunting in Many Lands,* pp. 377-402. Edited by Theodore Roosevelt and George Bird Grinnell. New York: Forest and Stream Publishing Co., 1895.

anon. *A Journey Through the Yellowstone National Park and Northwestern Wyoming, 1883. Photographs of Party and Scenery Along the Route Traveled, and Copies of the Associated Press Dispatches Sent Whilst en Route.* Washington, D.C., U.S. Government Printing Office, 1883.

Atwood, John H. *Yellowstone Park in 1898.* Kansas City, Mo.: Smith-Grieves, 1918.

Ayer, I. Winslow. *Life in the Wilds of America and Wonders of the West.* Grand Rapids: Central Publishing, 1880, pp. 310-20.

Baldwin, Alice Blackwood. *Memoirs of the Late Frank D. Baldwin, Major General, U.S.A.* Los Angeles: Wetzel Publishing Co., 1929.

Ballou, Maturin M. *The New Eldorado.* New York: Houghton Mifflin, 1892, pp. 15-56.

——————. *Footprints of Travel: or Journeyings in Many Lands.* Boston: Ginn and Co., 1901, pp. 362-73.

Batchelder, James. *Notes from the Life and Travels of James Batchelder.* San Francisco: Pacific Press, 1892, pp. 160-84.

Brockett, L.P. *Our Western Empire.* Philadelphia: Bradley, Garretson and Co., 1881, pp. 1227-65.

Bunce, O.B. "Our Great National Park." In *Picturesque America,* pp. 292-316. Edited by William Cullen Bryant. New York: D. Appleton and Co., 1872.

Burton, G.W. *Burton's Book on California and its Sunlit Skies of Glory.* Los Angeles: Times Mirror Publishing Co., 1909, pp. 12-19.

Campbell, Marius R. *Guidebook of the Western United States.* Washington, D.C.: U.S. Geological Survey, Bull. 611, 1915.

Carpenter, Frank D. *The Wonders of Geyser Land. A Trip to the Yellowstone National Park, of Wyoming.* Black Earth, Wis.: Burnett and Son, Printers and Publishers, 1878.

——————. *Adventures in Geyser Land.* Caldwell, Idaho: Caxton Printers, 1935.

Chittenden, Hiram M. *H.M. Chittenden: A Western Epic.* Edited by Bruce LeRoy. Tacoma, Wash.: Washington State Historical Society, 1961, pp. 11-28.

————————. *The Yellowstone National Park, Historical and Descriptive.* Cincinnati: Robert Clarke Co., 1895.

Clampitt, John W. *Echoes from the Rocky Mountains.* Chicago: National Book Concern, 1888, pp. 554-73.

Cleland, A.M. *Through Wonderland.* St. Paul: Northern Pacific Railroad, 1910.

Cole, Cyrenus. *The Two Great Canyons. Excerpts From Letters Written on a Western Journey.* Cedar Rapids, Iowa: The Torch Press, 1908, pp. 7-23.

Dale, Dove (R. Marston). *Franke's Ranche, or My Holiday in the Rockies.* London: Sampson, Low, Marston, Searle and Rivington, 1886, pp. 106-28.

Dana, Edward S. see Grinnell, George Bird.

Dana, John C. et al. *The Far Northwest.* Newark: The Travelers, 1906, pp. 23-26, 39-40.

DeVere, Shele, ed. *Wonders of Science.* New York: Scribner's Sons, 1898, pp. 108-14.

Doane, Gustavus Cheyney. *Battle Drums and Geysers.* Edited by Orrin and Lorraine Bonney. Chicago: The Swallow Press, Inc., 1970, pp. 469-509.

Dudley, W.H. *The National Park from the Hurricane Deck of a Cayuse, or, The Liederkranz Expedition to Geyserland.* Butte City, Mont.: Free Press Publishing Co., 1886.

Dumbell, K.E.M. *California and the West.* New York: J.Pott and Co., 1914, pp. 83-90.

Dunraven, The Earl of. *The Great Divide: Travels in the Upper Yellowstone in the Summer of 1874.* London: Chatto and Windus, 1876, pp. 180-346.

Elliott, L. Louise. *Six Weeks on Horseback through Yellowstone Park.* Rapid City, S.D.: Rapid City Journal, 1913.

Ellsworth, Spencer. *A Pilgrimage to Geyser Land, or Montana on Mule Back.* Lacon, Ill., 1883.

Enock, C. Reginald. *Farthest West.* New York: Appleton, 1910, pp. 66, 96, 100.

Field, Eugene. *Sharps and Flats.* Edited by Slason Thompson. New York: Charles Scribner's Sons, 1900, I: 60-62, 68-70, 74-75.

Field, Henry M. *Our Western Archipelago.* New York: Scribner's Sons, 1895, pp. 212-44.

Finck, Henry T. *Pacific Coast Scenic Tours.* New York: Scribner's Sons, 1907, pp. 279-93.

Fletcher, C.G. *A Cowboy Camp Through the Yellowstone.* Published by the Author, 1896.

Fountain, Paul. *The Eleven Eaglets of the West.* New York: Dutton, 1906, pp. 173-95.

Francis, Francis. *Saddle and Moccasin.* London: Chapman and Hall, 1887, pp. 1-40.

Gannett, Henry. *North America.* London: Edward Stoddard, 1898, pp. 40-53.

Gay, F.D.B. *Salt Lake City to Yellowstone Park.* Salt Lake City: R.D. Grow Printing Co., 1915.

Gerrish, Rev. Theodore. *Life in the World's Wonderland.* Biddeford, Maine: Theodore Gerrish, 1887, pp. 180-242.

Gibson, John. *Great Waterfalls, Cataracts and Geysers.* London: T. Nelson and Sons, 1887, pp. 73-87, 230-57.

Gillis, Charles J. *The Yellowstone National Park and Alaska.* New York: J.J. Little and Co., 1893, pp. 11-28.

Grinnell, George Bird. "Zoological Report." In William Ludlow, *Report of a Reconnaisance from Carroll, Montana Territory, on the Upper Missouri, to the Yellowstone National Park, and Return, made in the Summer of 1875.* Washington, D.C.: U.S. Government Printing Office, 1876, pp. 59-89.

Grinnell, George Bird, and Dana, Edward S. "Geological Report." In William Ludlow, *Report of a Reconnaisance,* etc., 1876, pp. 130-32.

Grinnell, George Bird. *Beyond the Old Frontier.* New York: Scribner's Sons, 1913, pp. 90, 281, 306-21.

Gunnison, Almon. *Rambles Overland.* Boston: Universalist Publishing House, 1884, pp. 27-82.

Guptill, Albert B. *Practical Guide to Yellowstone National Park.* St. Paul: F.J. Haynes and Bro., 1890.

Hallahan, D.F. *Tourists in the Northwest.* Philadelphia: F. McManus Jr. and Co., 1914, pp. 42-86.

Hamilton, William. *My Sixty Years on the Plains.* New York: Forest and Stream Publishing Co., 1905, pp. 51-69, 158-73.

Harrison, Carter. *A Summer's Outing and the Old Man's Story.* Chicago: Donohue, Henneberry and Co., 1891, pp. 15-81.

Hatfield, W.F. *Geyserland and Wonderland.* San Francisco: Hicks-Judd Co., 1902.

Haupt, Herman, Jr. *The Yellowstone National Park.* New York: J.M. Stoddard, 1883.

Hayden, Ferdinand Vandiveer. *Sixth Annual Report of the U.S. Geological Survey . . . for the year 1872.* Washington, D.C.: U.S. Government Printing Office, 1873, pp. 11-85.

——————— . "Le Parc National des Etats-Unis." In *Le Tour du Monde Nouveau; Journal des Voyages,* pp. 289-352. Edited by Edward Charton. Paris: Hachette, 1874.

——————— . *The Yellowstone National Park and Mountain Regions of Portions of Idaho, Nevada, Colorado and Utah.* Boston: L. Prang and Company, 1876.

240

_____. "Yellowstone." In *The Pacific Tourist; Williams'*
Illustrated Transcontinental Guide of Travel from the Atlantic to the
Pacific Ocean, pp. 292-309. Edited by Henry T. Williams. New York:
H.T. Williams Publishing Co., 1877.

_____. *Twelfth Annual Report of the U.S. Geological and*
Geographical Survey of the Territories . . . for the Year 1878. Washington, D.C.: U.S. Government Printing Office, 1883.

_____. *The Great West: Its Attractions and Resources.* Bloomington, Ill.: Charles R. Brodix, 1880, pp. 29-38.

Haynes, F.J. *Haynes Souvenir Album; Yellowstone Park.* St. Paul: F.J. Haynes, 1909.

_____. Haynes New Guide; *The Complete Handbook of*
Yellowstone National Park. St. Paul: Haynes Picture Shops, Inc., 1910.

Heasley, J.A. *A Summer Vacation in the Yellowstone National Park.* Grand Rapids: Central Publishing, 1910.

Heath, Charles A. *A Trial of a Trail.* Chicago: The Franklin Press, 1905.

Henderson, G.L. *Yellowstone Park Manual and Guide.* Mammoth Hot Springs, Wyo.: Privately printed, 1885.

Hendrickson, T.H., *Grand Excursion to Yellowstone Park and Pacific Coast.* Brooklyn, 1896, pp. 1-28.

Henely, Louise Miller. *Letters From the Yellowstone, 1914.* Grinnell, Iowa: Ray and Frisbie, 1914.

Hewitt, Edward R. *A Trout and Salmon Fisherman for Seventy-Five Years.* New York: Charles Scribner's Sons, 1948, pp. 15-17.

Hirshberg, Julius. *Von New York nach San Francisco: Tagebuchblatter.* Leipzig; Verlag von Veit, 1888, pp. 74-111.

Holmes, Burton. *Travelogues, Volume Six: The Yellowstone National Park; The Grand Canyon of the Arizona; Moki Land.* New York: McClure, 1908, pp. 5-112.

Howard, Oliver O. "Supplementary Report; Non-Treaty Nez Perce Campaign." In *The Report of the Secretary of War, 1877-1878.* I:585-660. Washington, D.C.: U.S. Government Printing Office, 1878.

_____. *Nez Perce Joseph.* Boston: Lee and Shepard Publishers, 1881, pp. 239-52.

Hubbard, Alice and Elbert. *A Little Journey to the Yellowstone Park.* East Aurora, N.Y.: The Roycrofters, 1915.

Hyde, John. *Official Guide to the Yellowstone National Park.* St. Paul: Riley Brothers, 1886.

James, George Wharton. *Our American Wonderlands.* Chicago: McClurg, 1915, pp. 203-13.

Johnson, Clifton. *Highways and Byways of the Rocky Mountains.* New York: Macmillan, 1910, pp. 215-32.

Jones, W.A. *Report Upon the Reconnaisance of Northwestern Wyoming, Including The Yellowstone National Park . . . 1873.* Washington, D.C. U.S. Government Printing Office, 1875.

Keane, A.H., ed. *The Earth and Its Inhabitants.* New York: Appleton, III: 217-21, 353-59.

Kenny, R.D. *From Geyserdom to Show-Me-Land. A Covered Wagon Excursion in 1896.* Clyde Park, Mont.: Published by the Author, 1926.

Kipling, Rudyard. *From Sea to Sea; Letters of Travel.* New York: Charles Scribner's Sons, 1906, II:136-89.

Ludlow, William. *Report of a Reconnaisance from Carrol, Montana Territory, on the Upper Missouri, to the Yellowstone National Park, and return, made in the Summer of 1875.* Washington, D.C.: U.S. Government Printing Office, 1876.

McCutcheon, John T. *Drawn From Memory.* New York: The Bobbs-Merrill Company, Inc., 1950, pp. 76-77.

Marston, E. see Dale, Dove.

Mershon, William B. *Recollections of My Fifty Years Hunting and Fishing.* Boston: The Stratford Co., 1923, p. 113.

Miles, Nelson A. *Personal Recollections.* Chicago: Werner, 1896, pp. 294-95, 302-5.

Miller, Joaquin. "Yellowstone Park." In *Picturesque California and the Region West of the Rocky Mountains, from Alaska to Mexico,* II: 421-32. Edited by John Muir. New York: J. Dewing Co., 1888.

Morris, Mrs. James E. *A Pacific Coast Vacation.* New York: Abbey Press, 1901, pp. 236-55.

Murphy, John. *Rambles in Northwestern America.* London: Chapman and Hall, 1879, pp. 209-22.

Murphy, Thomas D. *Three Wonderlands of the American West.* Boston: The Page Co., 1912, pp. 1-59.

Norris, Philetus W. *The Calumet of the Choteau and other Poetical Legends of the Border.* Philadelphia: J.B. Lippincott and Co., 1883.

Oszkar, Vojnich. *From Budapest to Sitka; Travel Notes.* Budapest, Hungary: Published by the Author, 1894, pp. 55-131.

Parkinson, Edward S. *Wonderland; or Twelve Weeks in and out of the United States.* Trenton, N.J.: MacCrellish and Quigley, Printers, 1894, pp. 223-55.

Peattie, Elia W. *A Journey Through Wonderland.* St. Paul: Northern Pacific Railroad, 1890.

Pierrepont, Edward. *Fifth Avenue to Alaska.* New York: G.P. Putnam's Sons, 1884.

Porter, T.C. *Impressions of America.* London: C.A. Pearson, Ltd., 1899, pp. 24-93.

Price, Sir Rose Lambert. *A Summer On the Rockies.* London: Sampson, Low, Marston and Co., 1898.

Raymond, Rossiter W. *Camp and Cabin.* New York: Fords, Howard, and Hulbert, 1880, pp. 153-207.

Reclus, Elisee. *The Earth and Its Inhabitants.* New York: Appleton, 1898, XVII: 353-59.

Remington, Frederic. *Pony Tracks.* New York: Harper, 1898, pp. 174-92.

Richardson, James. *Wonders of the Yellowstone.* New York: Scribner, Armstrong, and Co., 1873.

Riley, W.C. *Yellowstone National Park.* Portland, Maine: Chisolm Brothers, 1889.

Roberts, Edwards. *Shoshone and Other Western Wonders.* New York: Harper and Brothers, 1888, pp. 174-275.

Roosevelt, Theodore. *The Wilderness Hunter: An Account of the Big Game of the United States and its Chase with Horse, Hound, and Rifle.* New York: G.P. Putnam's Sons, 1893, pp. 175-77, 434-35.

Rutgers, Lispenard. *On and Off the Saddle, Characteristic Sights and Scenes from the Great Northwest to the Antilles.* New York: G.P. Putnam's Sons, 1894, pp. 11-20.

Saltus, Sanford J. *A Week in the Yellowstone.* New York: Knickerbocker Press, 1895.

Schauffler, Robert H. *Romantic America.* New York: Century, 1913, 134-60.

Schmide, Carl. *A Western Trip.* Detroit: The Herald Press, 1910.

Schwatka, Frederick, and Hyde, John. *Through Wonderland with Lieutenant Schwatka.* St. Paul: Northern Pacific Railroad, 1886.

Senn, Nicholas. *Our National Recreation Parks.* Chicago: W.B. Conkey, 1904, pp. 17-92.

Sessions, F.C. *From Yellowstone Park to Alaska.* New York: Welch, Fracker and Co., 1890, pp. 12-39.

Seton, Ernest Thompson. *Wild Animals At Home.* New York: Grosset and Dunlap, 1913.

Sheridan, Philip H., and Sherman, William T. *Inspection Made in the Summer of 1877 by Generals P.H. Sheridan and W.T. Sherman.* Washington, D.C.: U.S. Government Printing Office, 1878, pp. 70-83.

Sheridan, Philip H. *Report of Lieutenant General P.H. Sheridan, dated September 20, 1881, on his expedition through the Big Horn Mountains, Yellowstone Park, etc.* Washington, D.C.: U.S. Government Printing Office, 1882, pp. 1-39.

Shields, C.O. *Hunting in the Great West.* Chicago: Donohue, 1883, pp. 50-65.

Skinner, Milton P. *The Yellowstone Nature Book.* Chicago: A.C. McClurg and Co., 1924.

——————. *The Birds of Yellowstone National Park.* Roosevelt Wildlife Bulletin, Vol. II, No. 1, February 1925.

——————. *Bears in the Yellowstone.* Chicago: A.C. McClurg and Co., 1925.

Smith, F. Dumont. *Summit of the World.* Chicago: Rand McNally and Co., 1909.

——————. *The Book of 100 Bears.* Chicago: Rand McNally and Co., 1909.

Stanley, Edwin J. *Rambles in Wonderland.* New York: D. Appleton and Co., 1878.

243

Steele, David M. *Going Abroad Overland.* New York: G.P. Putnam's Sons, 1917, pp. 102-11.

Stennett, W.H., *The North and West.* Chicago: Chicago and North-Western Railway Co., 1876.

Stoddard, John L. *John L. Stoddard's Lectures.* Chicago: Shuman, 1911. Vol. X: 207-304.

Strahorn, Carrie A. *Fifteen Thousand Miles by Stage.* New York: G.P. Putnam's Sons, 1911, pp. 254-86.

Strahorn, Robert. *Handbook of Wyoming.* Chicago: Knight and Leonard, 1877, pp. 110-26.

_____. *To the Rockies and Beyond.* Omaha: Omaha Republican, 1878, pp. 133-41.

_____. *Montana and Yellowstone Park.* Kansas City: Ramsey, Millet and Hudson, 1881.

Strong, W.E. *A Trip to Yellowstone National Park in July, August and September, 1875.* Washington, D.C.: privately printed, 1876.

Synge, Georgina M. *A Ride Through Wonderland.* London: Sampson, Low, Marston and Co., 1892.

Taylor, Charles M., Jr. *Touring Alaska and the Yellowstone.* Philadelphia: George W. Jacobs and Co., 1901, pp. 285-388.

Thayer, William M. *Marvels of the New West.* Norwich, Conn.: Henry Bill, 1888, pp. 59-81.

Timmons, William. *Twilight on the Range.* Austin: University of Texas Press, 1962, pp. 66-70.

Turrill, Gardner S. *A Tale of the Yellowstone; or, In a Wagon Through Western Wyoming and Wonderland.* Jefferson, Iowa: G.S. Turrill Publishing Co., 1901.

Van Tassell, Charles. *Truthful Lies.* Bozeman, Mont.: Van Tassell, 1913.

Vaughn, Robert. *Then and Now; or Thirty-Six Years in the Rockies.* Minneapolis: Tribune, 1900, pp. 345-67.

Wallace, Dillon. *Saddle and Camp in the Rockies.* New York: Outing Publishing Co., 1911, pp. 288-91.

Wallace, R.C. *A Few Memories of a Long Life.* Published by the Author, 1900, pp. 57-61.

Warren, F.K. *California Illustrated, Including a Trip Through Yellowstone Park.* Boston: DeWolfe, 1892.

Wendt, Edmund C. *Random Notes of a Trip, including a few words about the Yellowstone National Park.* New York: Trows Printing and Binding Co., 1883.

Wheeler, Olin D. *6,000 Miles Through Wonderland.* St. Paul: Northern Pacific Railroad, 1893.

_____. *Indian Land and Wonderland.* Chicago: Northern Pacific Railroad, 1894.

_____. *Yellowstone National Park.* St. Paul: W.C. Riley, 1901.

Wiley, William H. and Sarah K. *The Yosemite, Alaska and the Yellowstone.* London: John Wiley and Sons, 1893, pp. 171-230.

Wingate, George W. *Through the Yellowstone Park on Horseback.* New York: O. Judd Co., 1886.

Winser, Henry J. *The Yellowstone National Park: A Manual For Tourists.* New York: C.P. Putnam's Sons, 1883.

Wood, Stanley. *Over the Range to the Golden Gate.* Chicago: Donnelley, 1908, pp. 307-8.

Wright, William H. *Ben, The Black Bear.* New York: Charles Scribner's Sons, 1910, pp. 102-107, 120.

——————. *The Grizzly Bear.* New York: Charles Scribner's Sons, 1909, pp. 142-82.

Articles

Allen, Margaret A. "A Family Camp in Yellowstone." *Outing,* November 1885, pp. 157-59.

Anderson, George. "Camping in the Yellowstone National Park." *Youth's Companion,* October 17, 1895, p. 488.

Anderson, George. "Work of the Cavalry in Protecting the Yellowstone National Park," *Journal of the United States Cavalry Association,* March 1897, pp. 3-10.

Andrews, M.E. "Yellowstone Park." *Out West,* April 1903, pp. 545-46, and November 1903, 455-72.

anon. "American Exploring Expeditions in the Great West." *Nature* (London), August 21, 1873, pp. 331-32.

anon. "Seeing the Yellowstone Park." *Forest and Stream,* July 26, 1883, p. 501.

anon. "Notes on the Yellowstone Park." *Forest and Stream,* April 25, 1889, p. 275.

anon. "Lenz's World Tour Awheel." *Outing,* February 1893, pp. 378-83.

anon. "Autos in the Yellowstone." *American Forestry* 21 , August 1915, p. 880.

Baker, Ray Stannard. "A Place of Marvels." *The Century Magazine,* August 1903, pp. 481-91.

Beard, Dan. "In a Wild Animal Republic." *Recreation,* December 1901, pp. 417-23.

Cape, Henry F. "A Nation's Playground." *The World Today,* June 1905, pp. 631-39.

Chapman, Arthur. "Vacation Jaunts to Uncle Sam's Playgrounds." *Outdoor World and Recreation,* July 1913, pp. 22-26.

Clark, Addison Neil. "Bear Studies in the Yellowstone." *Outdoor Life,* August 1909, pp. 145-52.

Clark, Ralph E. "Wyoming Summer Fishing and the Yellowstone Park." *Outing,* July 1908, pp. 508-11.

——————. "Over the Old Cooke City Trail." *Recreation,* August 1909, pp. 76-77, 95.

Comstock, Theodore B. "The Yellowstone National Park." *The American Naturalist* 8 (February 1874): 65-79.

Cope, E.D. "Present Condition of the Park." *The American Naturalist* 19 (November 1885): 1037-40.

Cope, H.F. "A Nation's Playground." *World Today*, June 1905, pp. 631-39.

Corthell, Mrs. N.E. "A Family Trek to the Yellowstone." *Independent*, June 29, 1905, pp. 1460-67.

Cowan, Mrs. George F. "Reminiscences of Pioneer Life." *Contributions to the Historical Society of Montana* IV (1903): 156-87.

————. "Reminiscences of Pioneer Life: A Trip to the National Park in 1877—An Account of the Nez Perce Raid from a Woman's Standpoint—Incidents and Accidents." *Wonderland*, March 12, 1904.

Dale, Stephen M. "Through the Yellowstone in a Coach." *Ladies Home Journal*, August 1904, pp. 5-6.

Davis, Chester C. "Motoring Through Wonderland." *American Motorist*, October 1915, pp. 593-96.

De Vallibus, "The Wonders of the Yellowstone." *The Contributor*, October 1884, pp. 5-9, 47-49, 86-88.

Drake, O.S.T. "A Lady's Trip to the Yellowstone Park." *Every Girl's Annual* (London), 1887, p. 348.

Durland, V. "Yellowstone National Park; the Wonderland of America." *Travel*, July 1908, pp. 454-56.

Eccles, James. "The Rocky Mountain Region of Wyoming and Idaho." *Alpine Journal* 19 (August 1879): 241-53.

Eldridge, M.O. "Touring Yellowstone Park on Government Highways." *World Today*, November 1910, pp. 1263-72.

Ellworth, F.W. "Yellowstone Park, Bankers Trip." *Moody*, November 1912, pp. 367-75.

Elmendorf, Dwight L. "Yellowstone National Park." *Mentor*, May 13, 1915, pp. 1-11.

Emmons, Myra. "From New York to Heaven." *Recreation*, December 1901, pp. 431-34.

Fennel, James Carson. "In the Yellowstone Park." *Californian Illustrated Magazine*, August 1892, pp. 348-63.

Fenneman, N.M. "The Yellowstone National Park." *Journal of Geography* 11 (June 1913): 314-20.

F.F.F. "A Modern Pilgrimage to the Mecca of the Sportsman and Tourist." *American Field*, October 10, 1885, p. 348.

Finck, Henry T. "A Week in Yellowstone Park." *The Nation* 45 September 1887, pp. 166-69.

————. "Yellowstone Park in 1897." *The Nation* 65 (October 7, 1897): 276-77.

————. "Yellowstone Park as a Summer Resort." *The Nation* 71 (September 27, 1900): 248-50.

Fisher, S.G. "Journal during Campaign against the Nez Perce Indians, 1877." *Contributions to the Historical Society of Montana* II (1896): 269-82.

Fordyce, C.P. "A Walking Trip through Yellowstone Park." *Recreation*, December 1911, pp. 262-63.

Foster, Harriet D. "Sagebrushing in Yellowstone Park." *Recreation*, July 1910, pp. 53-55.

Francis, Francis. "The Yellowstone Geysers." *Nineteenth Century*, March 1882, pp. 369-77.

Frankland, Edward. "A Great Winter Sanitarium for the American Continent." *Popular Science Monthly*, July 1885, pp. 289-95.

Freeman, L.R. "Ski-Runners of the Yellowstone." *National Magazine*, February 1904, pp. 611-14.

Geikie, Archibald. "The Geysers of Yellowstone." *MacMillan's Magazine*, October 1881, pp. 421-35.

Gibbon, John. "The Wonders of the Yellowstone." *Journal of the American Geographical Society* 5 (1874): 112-37.

Griffen, Robert A. "Fred Munn, Veteran of Frontier Experiences, Remembered the Days he Rode with Miles, Howard and Terry." *Montana* 16 (Spring 1966): 50-64.

Gordon-Cumming, Constance F. "The World's Wonderlands in Wyoming and New Zealand." *Overland Monthly*, January 1885, pp. 1-13.

Gordy, Wilbur. "A Trip to Yellowstone Park." *Perry Magazine*, November 1901, pp. 85-90.

Grosvenor, Gilbert H. "The Land of the Best." *National Geographic Magazine*, April 1916, pp. 327-430.

Guptill, Albert B. "Yellowstone Park." *Outing*, July 1890, pp. 256-63.

Hague, Arnold. "The Yellowstone Park as a Forest Reservation." *Nation*, January 5, 1888, pp. 9-10.

——————. "The Yellowstone National Park." *Scribner's Magazine*, May 1904, pp. 513-27.

——————. "Yellowstone National Park." *American Forestry* 19 (May 1913): 300-17.

Hallock, Charles. "Sketches of the Yellowstone Country." *American Field* 17 (1882): No. 5, pp. 73-74; No. 6, pp. 89-90; No. 7, p. 105; No. 8, p. 121; No. 9, p. 137.

Hamp, Sidford. "Exploring the Yellowstone with Hayden, 1872. Diary of Sidford Hamp." Edited by Herbert Brayer. *Annals of Wyoming*, October 1942, pp. 253-98.

Hayden, Ferdinand Vandiveer. "Our Great West and the Scenery of Our National Parks." *American Geographical Society Journal* 6 (1876): 196-211.

Henderson, C.H. "Through the Yellowstone on Foot." *Outing*, May 1899, pp. 161-67.

Hofer, Elwood. "Winter in Wonderland." *Forest and Stream* 38 (1887): No. 1, pp. 222-23; No. 2, pp. 246-47; No. 3, 270-71; No. 4, pp. 294-95; No. 5, pp. 318-19.

——————. "Hunting with a Camera." *Forest and Stream*, May 31, 1888, pp. 370-71.

——————. "The President's Park Trip." *Forest and Stream*, June 13, 1903, p. 464.

Hough, Emerson. "Forest and Stream's Yellowstone Park Game Exploration." *Forest and Stream*, May-June 1894.

Jack. "With Forsyth up the Yellowstone." *American Field*, March 20, 1886, pp. 277-78.

Jordan, David Starr. "The Story of a Strange Land." *Popular Science Monthly*, February 1892, pp. 457-58.

——————. "The Yellowstone Park." *Around the World*, July-August, 1894, pp. 148-51.

King, F.B. "In Nature's Laboratory: Driving and Fishing in Yellowstone Park." *Overland Monthly*, June 1897, pp. 594-603.

Langdon, Palmer H. "Through the Yellowstone in the Saddle." *Forest and Stream*, July 1915, pp. 408-10.

Leckler, Barnard H. "A Camping Trip to the Yellowstone National Park." *American Field*, January 12, 1888, pp. 41-42.

Lenz, Frank G. "Yellowstone Park." *Outing*, February 1893, pp. 378-83.

Lindsley, Elmer. "A Winter Trip Through the Yellowstone National Park." *Harper's Weekly*, January 29, 1898, pp. 106-7.

McGuire, J.A. "Camping in the Yellowstone." *Outdoor Life*, May 1911, pp. 479-86.

McNeil, Martha. "Wagon Trip to Yellowstone—1894." *The Wi-iyohi* (Bulletin of the South Dakota Historical Society) 17 (August 1, 1963): 1-7.

Maguire, H.N. "Wonders of the Yellowstone Region." *Chambers Journal* 51 (1882): 315.

——————. "The Black Hills and American Wonderland." *The Lakeside Library* 4 (1882): 298-301.

Marshall, William I. "An Evening in Wonderland." *Proceedings of the National Education Association* (1881), 132-43.

Martonne, Emmanuel de. "Le Parc National du Yellowstone." *Annales de Geographie* 22 (1913): 134-48.

Mills, Enos A. "The Rocky Mountain Region." *Country Life in America*, 1912, pp. 25-30, 46.

Mitchell, S. Weir. "Through Yellowstone Park to Fort Custer." *Lippincotts Magazine*, 1880: 25, pp. 688-704; 26, pp. 29-41.

Muir, John. "The Yellowstone National Park." *Atlantic Monthly*, April 1898, pp. 509-22.

——————. "The Yellowstone Park." *San Francisco Bulletin*, October 27, 1885.

North, A.W. "Alone in the Yellowstone; Riding in the Path of the Pioneers before the Season Opens in the Park." *Sunset*, August 1911, pp. 131-40.

Owen, W.O. "The First Bicycle Tour of the Yellowstone National Park." *Outing*, June 1891, pp. 191-95.

Pickett, William D. "The Yellowstone Park in Early Days." *Forest and Stream*, 1908: February 1, 168-70; February 8, 208-10.

Rainsford, W.S. "Camping and Hunting in the Shoshone." *Scribner's*, September 1887, pp. 292-311.

248

Raymond, R.W. "The Heart of the Continent: The Hot Springs and Geysers of the Yellowstone Region." *Harper's Weekly,* April 5, 1873, pp. 272-74.

Roberts, Edwards. "The American Wonderland." *Art Journal* 50 (July 1888): 193-98; (November): 325-28.

Robertson, P.D. "Vacationing in the Land of Geysers and Friendly Bears." *Countryside Magazine,* June 1915, pp. 331-34.

Rollins, Alice. "The Three Tetons." *Harper's New Monthly Magazine,* May 1887, pp. 869-90.

Roosevelt, Theodore. "An Elk-Hunt at Two-Ocean Pass." *Century Illustrated Monthly Magazine,* September 1892, pp. 713-19.

——————. "Wilderness Reserves." *Forest and Irrigation* 10 (June 1904): 250-59; (July): 300-09.

Savage, Joseph. "The Wonders of the Yellowstone." *Western Home Journal,* September 19, 1872.

Sedgwick, Henry D., Jr. "On Horseback through the Yellowstone." *World's Work,* June 1903, pp. 3569-76.

Sheridan, Philip H. "The National Park and Northern Yellowstone Region." *American Field,* December 9, 1882, p. 398.

Sherman, Thomas Ewing. "Across the Continent, II-The National Park." *Woodstock Letters* II (1882): 27-28.

Shiras, George, III. "Silver-tip Surprises." *Forest and Stream,* 1909: July 10, 48-50; July 17, 88-91.

Smith, N.D. "Yellowstone, The Summit of America." *Travel,* February 1915, pp. 9-13.

Stoddard, Charles Warren. "In Wonderland." *The Ave Maria,* 47 (1898): No. 7,200-203;No. 8, 237-41; No. 9, 257-61; No. 10, 295-99; No. 11, 326-30.

Story, H.L. "Six Weeks on the Headwaters of the Yellowstone." *Forest and Stream,* January 26, 1882, p. 505.

Sweet, Elnathan. "Horseback in Yellowstone Park." *Country Life,* June 1, 1912, pp. 88-90.

Thatcher, Moses. "The Falls of the Yellowstone." *The Contributor,* January 1884, pp. 140-43.

Thayer, Wade Warren. "Camp and Cycle in Yellowstone Park." *Outing,* April 1898, pp. 17-24.

Thomas, T.H. "Pencil and Pen among the Geysers and Gorges of the Yellowstone National Park." *The Graphic,* August 11, 1888, pp. 157-64; August 18, pp. 189-96.

Thwaites, F.T. "Through Yellowstone and the Tetons—1903." *National Parks Magazine,* March 1962, pp. 8-11.

Townsend, M.T. "A Woman's Trout Fishing in Yellowstone Park." *Outing,* May 1897, pp. 163-64.

Van Blarcom, W.D. "The Yellowstone National Park." *National Magazine,* September 1897, pp. 541-50.

Vest, George Graham. "Notes of the Yellowstone Trip." *Forest and Stream,* November 8, 1883, p. 282.

249

Walker, I.W. "Glories of the Yellowstone." *Recreation,* August 1899, pp. 103-4.

Warner, Charles Dudley. "Editor's Study." *Harper's,* January 1897, pp. 320-25.

Weikert, A.J. "Journal of a Tour through the Yellowstone National Park in August and September, 1877." *Contributions to the Historical Society of Montana* 6 (1904): 153-74.

Wheeler, Olin D. "Game in the Yellowstone National Park." *Recreation,* May 1896, pp. 221-25.

Whitmell, Charles. "The American Wonderland, The Yellowstone National Park." *Reports and Transactions of the Cardiff Naturalists Society* 17 (1885): 93.

Wilcox, E.V. "To Improve the Service in Yellowstone Park." *Recreation,* July 1902, pp. 36-37.

Worswick, F.H. "The Yellowstone Park." *Manchester Geographical Society Journal* 15 (January-March 1899): 38-55.